THE FUTURE OF HIGHER EDUCATION IN THE AGE OF GLOBALIZATION

Edited by Noel V. Lateef

The future has many names. For the weak, it's unattainable. For the fearful, it's unknown. For the bold, it's ideal.

– VICTOR HUGO

Education is the mainspring of our economic and social progress—it is the highest expression of achievement in our society, ennobling and enriching human life.

– JOHN F. KENNEDY

FPA Global Vision Books

Foreign Policy Association
470 Park Avenue
New York, New York 10016
212-481-8100
FAX: 212-481-9275
www.fpa.org

The Foreign Policy Association, founded in 1918, is a private, nonprofit, nonpartisan educational organization that stimulates wider interest and more effective participation in, and greater understanding of, world affairs among American citizens. It is the nation's oldest organization devoted to citizen education in international affairs.

The views expressed in this book are the authors' and do not represent those of the Foreign Policy Association.

Cover Design: Tonya Leigh

Interior Design: Shane Kroutil

Library of Congress Catalog Card Number: 2015952338
ISBN: 9780871242532

Printed in the United States of America

DEDICATED
TO MY FATHER,
VICTOR LATEEF,
U.S. FOREIGN SERVICE OFFICER AND WWII VETERAN
FEBRUARY 16, 1921 – AUGUST 18, 2015

Contents

INTRODUCTION

Noel V. Lateef
President, Foreign Policy Association

Higher education is at a crossroads. The value proposition made by American colleges and universities is being openly questioned. In the words of Hunter R. Rawlings III, president of the Association of American Universities: "Most of the barrage of criticism stems from looking at universities as businesses: bloated, expensive, out of date, ripe for disruption like the music and newspaper industries." If public disquiet were not bad enough, government is revisiting its compact with higher education and, for the first time, the U.S. Department of Education is devising a comprehensive system for rating colleges and universities on value and access.

Even as they are put on the defensive, making the case for their relevance as humanistic institutions, many colleges and universities are shedding their domestic husks and pursuing strategic forays abroad. In expanding their global footprint, experimenting with offshore models ranging from outreach offices to international branch campuses to quasi-independent, comprehensive campuses, institutions of higher learning are giving new meaning to Winston Churchill's observation that the "empires of the future will be the empires of the mind."

As incubators of new information transfer and communications technologies, institutions of higher learning have accelerated integration of the world economy. Indeed, research universities are key players in the phenomena known as globalization, characterized by unprecedented movement of people, goods, capital and, of course, ideas.

Ironically, the prodigious pace of globalization has called into question whether universities themselves have adapted to this bold new world. Are universities preparing graduates for future challenges by exposing them to diverse cultures and enabling them to be globally competent? Opportunities to plunge into international life abound at some institutions, while others have yet to make credible global offerings to their students and faculty.

With the blurring of international and domestic issues, we can foresee that so-called "intermestic" developments will loom large in the future. Today, we face challenges, ranging from climate change to nuclear proliferation, that are among the most ominous in all of human history. Fully engaging higher education communities will be critical to addressing these challenges. In this regard, at the direction of Secretary-General Ban Ki-moon, the United Nations has rolled out its Academic Impact Program:

i) To bring into association with the United Nations, and with each other, institutions of higher learning throughout the world.

ii) To provide a mechanism for such institutions to commit themselves to the fundamental precepts driving the United Nations mandate, in particular the realization of the universally determined Millennium Development Goals.

iii) To serve as a viable point of contact for ideas and proposals relevant to the United Nations mandate.

iv) To promote the direct engagement of institutions of higher education in programs, projects and initiatives relevant to this mandate.

In addition to helping achieve sustainable goals for development, institutions of higher learning can contribute to the renewal of the international system, with emphasis on preventing violence, through education, mediation and early warning. These "pillars of prevention," as set out by David A. Hamburg, former president of the Carnegie Corporation of New York, need to be institutionalized if the international community is to resolve conflicts constructively and peacefully.

Universities set standards for our global society. In one of the most impactful speeches ever delivered in the Foreign Policy Association forum, Richard Levin, then-president of Yale University, highlighted this role of universities in addressing global issues. In leading by example, he observed, universities can contribute to the effort to curtail global warming. Yale's early commitment to reduce carbon emissions would be emulated by scores of universities in the United States and around the world, with wide-ranging influence on global thought leaders.

While we must be prepared, as it has been said, for challenges we cannot yet foresee, with knowledge not yet developed, using tools not yet invented, few institutions are better situated to anticipate the future than universities. For, as Harvard University's president, Drew Faust, has observed, the task of institutions of higher learning "is to illuminate the past and to shape the future."

What is clear is that a growing number of American institutions of higher learning are wary of sloughing over the international dimension to their mission. Increasingly, internationalization is seen as a compelling way to respond to globalization, with institutions customizing their definitions of internationalization to their unique circumstances.

At Princeton, for example, internationalization is defined by the university's leadership as "more fluid interactions among global academic communities and increased cultural literacy for students." The overarching goal at Princeton is to be "an American university with a broad international vision." Central to this vision is the international exchange of students and faculty. In the words of Dean of the College Nancy Malkiel, Princeton has a "responsibility to produce globally competent citizens, i.e., students that have substantive knowledge about international affairs, and empathy with and appreciation for other cultures, foreign language proficiency and the practical ability to function in other cultures." Rather than going the route of satellite campuses, Princeton insists its students not be shielded from "the full-blast experience of being embedded within a foreign culture."

The Massachusetts Institute of Technology also eschews the satellite campus strategy. "We cannot replicate MIT anywhere else," says President Rafael Reif. MIT seeks to tackle the great global challenges of our times through a global network of universities that share its mission of research and innovation. Few institutions can match MIT's ambitious efforts with online education via its edX platform, which has engaged more than 2.2 million individuals from 196 countries in its first two years.

And then there is the global network strategy of New York University championed by its eloquent president, John Sexton. This is academia on a grand scale: sixteen sites on six continents, from a 55-acre estate in Florence, Italy, to comprehensive campuses in Abu Dhabi and Shanghai, all taught by NYU professors. According to Sexton, "If you had said to Leonardo or to Michelangelo, 'You can only do your art if you do it only here,'" then "you would not have gotten them to come to you." Universities have always been circulating systems, he says, and "universities have always operated beyond sovereignty."

Sexton's bold vision cannot be dismissed as quixotic or futuristic. NYU is the archetype of a university that can produce critical, empathetic thinkers who are self-aware and cross-culturally competent. Its model, however, is just one of many that universities consider when adapting to globalization. The various prototypes provided by Princeton, MIT, NYU and other universities all have the same goal: to ensure that universities are able to develop graduates who are at home in the world and who are capable of contributing to solutions for problems on a global scale. As Columbia University's president, Lee Bollinger, posits: to combat global challenges like climate change, poverty, and censorship, "universities—not nongovernmental organizations, not the government, not private enterprises, but universities—are the one institution that we have to depend on."

The stereotype of the university as detached from the "real world" is increasingly out of date. In a beleaguered world, the university as *deus ex machina* offers a beacon of innovation, aspiration and hope. The need for a proactive role by these institutions is not without urgency. H.G. Wells observed: "Life is a race between education and disaster." This observation seems particularly apt today. In some quarters, shaping minds under the guise of education is compounding global challenges. Learning to think critically, in the best tradition of the liberal arts, has never counted for more. In the words of Clinton Lee Scott: "Freedom of the mind is the beginning of all freedoms." In the Age of Globalization, the prospects for peace and prosperity are greatly enhanced by institutions of higher learning that prepare open-minded world citizens.

THE LION IN THE PATH OF
HIGHER EDUCATION TODAY

Hunter R. Rawlings III
President, Association of American Universities

I want to begin by saying how deeply honored I am by this opportunity to receive the Madison Medal for two reasons above all. First, because I have such a high respect and genuine affection for Princeton, its faculty, students and leaders, including Chris Eisgruber, Shirley Tilghman, Harold Shapiro and Bill Bowen, and my fellow classicists Bob Goheen, whom I worked with for many years, and Bob Connor, who was my dissertation advisor and mentor and remains my close friend. Second, because I am a devotee of my fellow Virginian James Madison. I have a home four miles from his house, Montpelier, and I have been much engaged in its restoration and in founding a Center for the Constitution there. I also teach a bit about Madison, and when I do, I generally start with his education here at the College of New Jersey, which shaped his scholarly temperament and critical skills. With Justice Sotomayor here—and I must say it is a great honor to join her in these festivities—I think I shall not say too much about Madison this morning.

Now a word about my title, "The Lion in the Path." When I was studying Latin at Haverford College with Howard Comfort, an old-fashioned Quaker educator, he interrupted the class one day to give us an unexpected and seemingly irrelevant piece of advice. "Young men," he said, "at several points in your life you are going to be asked to present public lectures. On some of those occasions, you will receive this request many months before your lecture, and your host will demand a title from you, at a time when you have no idea what title to use and, in fact, no idea of what you are going to say. Occasionally, your host will insist on extracting a title from you. For these occasions, I have the perfect title: 'The Lion in the Path.' It is perfect because: a) it sounds challenging and dramatic; and b) it is meaningless and commits you to nothing in advance. Remember this title and use it."

Now, I have to admit that until two years ago, I never had the nerve to follow Professor Comfort's advice. But then I got old enough to stop worrying about how this title might appear to audiences, and I have started using it, putting it to the test first at a lecture at Harvard. It worked just fine. When the Princeton authorities demanded a title from me a few months ago, I followed suit, and here we are today. I offer it to you for your use—just please be good enough to cite Professor Howard Comfort when you do so.

So, let's talk about the lion in the path of higher education today. As you all know, higher education bashing has become a popular blood sport in the U.S. It is hard to pick up a newspaper or magazine or read an online periodical without being confronted by an article attacking our universities. The most common complaint, of course, concerns the high price of tuition and the mountain of student debt. But there are many others: stultification of the curriculum, the failure of students to graduate on time, the proliferation of administrators and staff, the leftward tilt of the faculty, the poor teaching of the faculty, the impenetrable diction of the faculty, even the "irrelevance" of the faculty (a recent charge in the friendly editorial page of *The New York Times*).

Most of this barrage of criticism stems from looking at universities as businesses: bloated, expensive, out of date, ripe for disruption like the music and newspaper industries. After years of recession, falling middle class salaries, and rising tuition (much of it caused by withdrawal of state support), college is viewed by many Americans as a purely instrumental means of preparing for a job, any job. Credentialing is dominant now and fits well with American pragmatism, love of business, and desire for efficiency. This is one of the principal reasons for the (overhyped) reaction to online education in the last fifteen months: MOOCs [massive open online courses] and other online instruments seemed to offer a quick, cheap fix for the notoriously inefficient nature of academia. Never mind that the quality of these courses is still suspect, completion rates are ridiculously low, and they violate almost every principle research has taught us about the best ways for students to learn.

Adding fuel to the fire, politicians from the President to members of Congress, governors and state legislators are piling on, calling for change in the form of greater accountability, cheaper "delivery systems," learning outcomes measures, usually reductionist, and rating systems, always reductionist. Universities are on the defensive, hard-pressed to make their value proposition in the face of so much criticism.

At the same time, U.S. colleges and universities have never been so much in demand by American families and by the rest of the world, have never been ranked more highly in every conceivable international rating system, and have never contributed so much to the production of critical knowledge, to national security, and to national economic growth. And they have never before exercised such positive influence on their local economies, indeed, on the quality of life, even on the viability, of their neighborhoods. Think what West Philadelphia would be without Penn, or New Haven without Yale, or Pittsburgh without Carnegie Mellon and Pitt. Not to mention the spawning of entire high-tech powerhouses in Silicon Valley by Stanford, in Massachusetts by MIT and Harvard, in North Carolina by UNC Chapel Hill and by Duke and North Carolina State Universities.

Other countries are now doing whatever they possibly can to emulate American universities and even our liberal arts colleges. Look at Singapore, where Yale is collaborating with the National University of Singapore to start a high-end, traditional American liberal arts college with a new East/West core curriculum; China, which is creating partnerships with multiple American universities; even India, where a group of entrepreneurs is founding an American-style liberal arts college. It is ironic that what these countries especially envy is our liberal arts colleges, at a time when much American opinion regards them as expensive relics.

So, how do we make sense of this peculiar state of affairs, this paradox at the heart of the critique of American higher education?

First, a very brief history lesson. Our colleges and universities became the best in the world for four essential reasons: 1) They have consistently been uncompromising bastions of academic freedom and autonomy; 2) They are a crazily unplanned mix of public and private, religious and secular, small and large, low-cost and expensive institutions, all competing with each other for students and faculty and for philanthropic and research support; 3) Our major universities combined research and teaching to produce superior graduate programs and, with the substantial help of the federal government, built great research programs, particularly in science; and 4) Our good liberal arts colleges patiently pursued great education the old-fashioned way: individual instruction, careful attention to reading and writing and mentoring, passion for intellectual inquiry, premium on original thought—in other words, we have remained true to the idea of enabling students to develop their own knowledge and talents and personalities, the 19th-century German Humboldtian ideal of Bildung, or education of the whole person for citizenship in a culture.

Today, we take these four facts for granted. That is myopic and threatens to become dangerous. Other countries as small as Singapore and as large as China now recognize why our higher education model is so strong and are trying desperately to emulate our success, but they can succeed only to a limited degree. Freedom is the *sine qua non* for great universities, and diversity and competition have driven our performance. Authoritarian countries with top-down, government-sponsored universities cannot reproduce our "system": primarily because it is not a "system." This explains why Asian universities now want to partner with American universities: Without us, educators there know they cannot have open universities whose purpose is to educate the whole person rather than train thousands of technocrats. They know that without full academic freedom, they have a hard time teaching real history, real social science, and even real literature. And by the way, their students know the difference: That is why they are pouring into our universities at unprecedented rates for undergraduate education and even into prep schools here. They want the kind of open, critical education we offer here.

In spite of their obvious success and the huge demand for their "product," American universities suffer criticism here at home for several quite unsurprising reasons.

First, with the recession and the declining income of the middle class and the massive withdrawal of state support for public universities, college has indeed become less affordable for many American families.

Second, Americans have bought the message that their children must go to college to have a chance for a decent job. The result is that while in 1970, one-third of high school graduates went to college, in 2012, one-half did. The pressure is on families to send children to college at precisely the time when it has become more difficult to afford.

This is a familiar scenario in this country: Just as Americans want the services offered by the federal government but do not want to pay for them with their tax dollars, Americans want a college education for their kids, but states do not want to pay for it with state funds. So enrollments in college burgeon, state support goes down, tuition goes up, classes get bigger because faculty get cut, students fail to graduate on time because they can't get the classes they need and they have to work long hours and borrow a lot of money. Is it any surprise people don't like this scenario and blame universities for it? I think not. We are trying to educate an all-time high percentage of citizens in a democracy where income inequality has reached dangerous proportions and where a college education has become a private interest, not a public responsibility.

Third, universities, public and private alike, are now very big players. When I was growing up, colleges and universities were bucolic oases of learning removed from the major rhythms of American life. They were, for the most part, quiet and sedate outposts of the privileged few, almost all white, who could pursue higher education, while the vast majority of Americans were content with the high school degree that afforded them access to steady jobs. And higher education then had little to do with the American economy, much less with the needs and interests of other countries.

Today, research universities are multi-billion dollar enterprises that comprise vast businesses as disparate as complex medical centers, entertainment industries in the form of intercollegiate athletic franchises, high-tech companies spawned in university laboratories, government-sponsored institutes doing most of the nation's basic, and a fair amount of its applied, research and development, public service centers reaching farmers and small-business owners across whole states, real estate magnates buying up neighborhoods and whole segments of major cities, entire campuses abroad and, now, online-education companies pursuing profit here and around the world. The teaching of undergraduate students on campus has become a quaint, tiny fraction of these universities' purpose and function.

This is why universities find themselves today constantly on the front page of newspapers, engaged in urban development fights, mired in the health care debate, confronting athletic scandals that affect not just their reputation but their very identity, and turning over their exhausted presidents every few years as boards of regents and governors intrude into what has become the biggest and most public business in many states. When I started my Ph.D. program in Classics here at Princeton almost fifty years ago, I thought I was entering something akin to the priesthood. Today, as president of the Association of American Universities (AAU) visiting certain states, I feel as though I am Citizen Kane!

My point is this: Anything as big and public and consequential as a research university is going to garner its share of news, and that frequently means, given the news business, bad news. We should get used to the fact that we will have to endure a lot of criticism, much of it unwarranted and unfair. It comes with the territory.

The fact is, however, that some of the criticism of our universities is justified: We have, many of us, relegated undergraduate education to a low place in academia by devaluing undergraduate teaching, and we have broadened and loosened the curriculum to the point where at many universities it is a flabby smorgasbord of courses bearing no relationship to each other, utterly lacking in coherence. It is also true that as enrollments have risen, academic rigor has declined and grades have inflated.

In addition, until recently, we have not paid enough attention to limiting our costs and to running efficient operations through sensible policies and practices. And we have probably taken the high-tuition, high-financial aid strategy as far as it can reasonably go. We need simplicity and more transparency in tuition. We need to do a better job of finding and helping indigent students. And we need to be more responsive to the problems confronting the middle class.

This is not to mention the monster called intercollegiate athletics. Probably the most disheartening facet of our universities today is that many of the best of them are running gigantic entertainment businesses with billions of dollars in revenue, multi-million-dollar coaches, TV networks, and the like, in which the entertainers, namely the so-called student athletes, are not paid for their work, and everyone else is. This is a business ripe for disruption, and signs are that disruption is coming in the forms of judges' opinions on "pay for play," student athletes' attempts to unionize, and public reaction to fraudulent academic programs for athletes.

But the real threat to higher education today is, in my opinion, not internal; it is ideological: the expectation that universities will become instruments of society's will, legislators' wills, governors' wills, that they will be required to produce specific quantifiable results, particularly economic, and to cease researching and teaching certain subjects that do not fit the utilitarian model. Last year Senator Coburn got an amendment to the Senate budget bill essentially requiring the National Science Foundation (NSF) to stop funding research in political science. Texas has instituted a system to quantify professors' work and evaluate them according to the number of students they teach and the grant dollars they bring in. Florida came close last year to charging extra tuition to students studying humanities at state colleges in order to discourage the practice. President Obama wants the

Education Department to rate universities on a numerical scale, and many states are now already evaluating universities on the basis of the average earnings of their alumni eighteen months after graduation. We are in the age of data, we measure anything that can be measured, and we treat what we measure as dispositive: We take the part for the whole.

Albert Einstein apparently kept a sign in his office that read, "Not everything that counts can be counted, and not everything that can be counted counts." This aphorism applies all too well to our current rage for "accountability." As Derek Bok points out in his recent book, *Higher Education in America*, "Some of the essential aspects of academic institutions—in particular the quality of the education they provide—are largely intangible and their results are difficult to measure." Frankly, this is an obvious point to make, but all of us have to make it, often, in today's commodifying world. Quantity is much easier to measure than quality, so entire disciplines and entire academic pursuits are devalued under the current ideology, which puts its premium on productivity and efficiency and, above all else, on money as the measure.

Maria Popova, who writes a blog called "Brain Pickings," wrote this: "In an age obsessed with practicality, productivity, and efficiency, I frequently worry that we are leaving little room for abstract knowledge and for the kind of curiosity that invites just enough serendipity to allow for the discovery of ideas we didn't know we were interested in until we are, ideas that we may later transform into new combinations with applications both practical and metaphysical."

I am seriously concerned about the tendency of some members of Congress to stop funding the apparently impractical. Here's why: See this iPhone? It depends upon seven or eight fundamental scientific and technological breakthroughs, such as GPS, multi-touch screens, LCD displays, lithium-ion batteries, and cellular networks. How many of those discoveries were made by Apple? None. They all came from research supported by the federal government and conducted in university and government laboratories. Apple makes a great product, but it depends upon government-sponsored science, much of it curiosity-driven, not economically-driven.

The most succinct encapsulation of the value of curiosity to practical pursuits came from Michael Faraday. When asked by William Gladstone, chancellor of the Exchequer, about the utility of electricity, Faraday is purported to have replied, "One day, sir, you may tax it."

My friend, Francis Collins, Nobel Prize winner and director of the National Institutes of Health, talks about "the last frontier of medical research"—neuroscience. "There are 86 billion neurons in here," he says, tapping his forehead with an index finger. "Each of those has maybe a thousand connections. So the complexity of this structure exceeds anything else in the known universe, and some have even worried that our brains are not complicated enough to understand our brains." President Obama has called on the country to focus even more scientific attention upon the study of the brain for these very reasons. I am certain that, with funding and attention, many breakthroughs in understanding the brain will come forth in the next few years.

But let me tell you something: Whatever neuroscientists discover, they will have a hard time matching what emerged from Emily Dickinson's brain well over a century ago:

> *The Brain—is wider than the Sky—*
> *For—put them side by side—*
> *The one the other will contain*
> *With ease—and You—beside—*
> *The Brain is deeper than the sea—*
> *For—hold them—Blue to Blue—*
> *The one the other will absorb—*
> *As Sponges—Buckets—do—*
> *The Brain is just the weight of God—*
> *For—Heft them—Pound for Pound—*
> *And they will differ—if they do—*
> *As Syllable from Sound—*

There are scientific and there are poetic renderings of the brain. I am drawn to both, but Dickinson's poem rises above the material realm into the pure ether of aesthetics, philosophy, and religion. For reasons unknown to scientists, and to the rest of us, we human beings aspire to understanding and joining with higher things, universal things, things we cannot see or touch. I don't know how to measure the value of Emily Dickinson's poem, but clearly she knew how to measure the brain, the sky, the sea, and even God.

Whatever we do, let's not let the bean counters diminish the creation and teaching of qualitative things.

Now, given what I have been saying about trends in Americans' views of higher education, you might conclude that I think we are going downhill. After all, when I was a kid, Berkeley and UCLA and the University of Texas were essentially free: Their states thought it was a public responsibility to educate citizens through college. For my part, when I was a Ph.D. student here at Princeton, I was fortunate enough to have a federal fellowship, the NDEA: that's a National Defense Education Act fellowship to pursue advanced work in ancient Greek and Latin! Can you imagine Congress passing such a bill today? I love the idea that my study of the Classics counted as part of the national defense.

But even though in some ways the 60s was a golden age for public confidence in, and support of, higher education in all its dimensions, I am no pessimist about the future of our universities.

Let me describe three very concrete reasons why I am optimistic: They are here in the auditorium this morning. I want to introduce you to three students who were generous enough to come to this event today and watch their old professor receive the Madison Medal. Their stories are far more persuasive than any arguments I can make.

First, Bill Clausen, Cornell B.A. in Classics, Oxford M.A., first-class honors. Please stand up, Bill. Bill now teaches Latin and Classics and Philosophy at Washington Latin Public Charter School in the northern reaches of the District of Columbia, traditionally the home of many of the worst urban schools in America.

Thanks to Bill's invitation, Elizabeth and I spent a day there a month ago, visiting classes, talking with students and administrators. The overwhelming impression we received is of a school that works—a serious learning community emphasizing the need for all its members to be thoughtful people in the broadest and deepest senses. It is incredibly diverse, mirroring the diversity of DC. It is not selective: Students get in through a lottery, and many of them get there every morning after traveling on the subway an hour or more.

The principal of Washington Latin School, Diana Smith, is also here today. Diana graduated from Princeton with a major in Classics *summa cum laude* and Phi Beta Kappa. Diana knows what it takes to make a good school, and with the help of Bill and the rest of her dedicated faculty, she has made one in the nation's capital.

Bill and Diana are on the front line of the battle in America to solve two of our biggest problems: corrosive inequality and the hopeless prospects confronted by many of our children. Most of us in this room have important jobs, but I feel that Bill Clausen and Diana Smith have the hardest, the most important, and the best jobs: mentoring the kids who most need a good school and a good education.

The next person I want to introduce to you is Heng Du, the most astonishing student I have ever had. Heng came to this country from China with her mother at the age of 14, when she could barely speak English. She attended public schools on Long Island, worked hard, excelled, and entered Cornell as an architecture major. In her first year there, she transferred to the College of Arts and Sciences and became a Classics major. I had the pleasure of teaching her second-semester Greek. Heng worked hard, excelled, mastered Greek and Latin and, in her senior year, began the study of classical Chinese.

She then made her only mistake: She decided to go to graduate school in classical Chinese, rather than in Greek and Latin. She earned a Master's degree at the University of Colorado in order to enhance her knowledge of ancient Chinese, then entered the doctoral program at Harvard, where she is now embarked on her dissertation on the very earliest, recently discovered Chinese texts. Oh, and by the way, Heng is fluent in German and Japanese as well as English and Chinese.

When I consider Heng's commitment to education and her life trajectory, I stand in awe. I cannot conceive of this level of dedication, and when I consider what it would be like for me to try to do, in Asia, what she has done in America, I just laugh at myself. What Heng can accomplish in comparing ancient languages and cultures, and in taking the principles developed in classical philology of the West and applying them to classical texts in the East, would have been unthinkable when I was studying Classics fifty years ago. This is the new world of American higher education—it is global, and it is incredibly exciting!

Finally, let me introduce you to Lillian Aoki. Lillian appeared three years ago in my lecture course on Greek intellectual and political history, and when someone named Aoki kept getting the highest grades in the class on papers, I had to find out who she was. So I asked her to come to office hours, where I learned she was a chemistry major! That was striking enough, but she added that she would probably also major in history because she was fascinated by epistemological questions: How, with our limited capacities, do we try to know the world scientifically? And how do we try to know it through the humanities and social sciences? This is not what your ordinary college junior aspires to! Lillian next took my seminar on the influence of the Classics upon America's Founders (particularly Madison, of course), where she contributed wisely to discussions and wrote an incredibly mature paper on how the Founders used scientific reasoning and Greek and Roman history in fashioning their arguments at the Constitutional Convention and in the ratification debates. She also did a nice job of finding the holes in their reasoning which, it must be said, were not rare.

Lillian has a striking capacity to work in both science and humanities with a deeply inquiring mind. When she graduated in 2012 and I learned that Lillian wanted to take a year off before grad school, I importuned her to come work on science policy at the AAU office in Washington, where she quickly became, at the age of 21, the go-to person on everything from the principles of academic freedom to energy research, and from enhancing STEM [science, technology, engineering, and mathematics] education to a study of the return on federal investment in research.

One wants to consult Lillian because of a simple, but increasingly rare quality: She thinks. Lillian actually thinks about things, and now she is doing her thinking in the graduate program in environmental sciences at the University of Virginia. My only advice to you this morning is: Hire Lillian Aoki as soon as you can. If you don't, I will try to do it again.

Bill and Heng and Lillian inspire me: They are devoted to their work. They make their classes vibrant and enjoyable, whether they are teaching them or taking them. And they make our research universities fantastic places to be. The next time you read another article maligning our universities or saying the humanities are dead, think of Bill and Heng and Lillian, and stop worrying.

FOR WHAT IT'S WORTH:
THE VALUE OF A UNIVERSITY
EDUCATION

Amy Gutmann
President, University of Pennsylvania

In 2010 PayPal co-founder and Facebook "angel" investor Peter Thiel announced he would annually award $100,000 each to twenty young people for them to drop out of college and spend two years starting a tech-based business. "You know, we've looked at the math on this, and I estimate that 70 to 80 percent of the colleges in the U.S. are not generating a positive return on investment," Thiel told an interviewer, explaining his view that we are in the midst of a higher education bubble not dissimilar to the housing and dotcom bubbles of previous decades. "Education is a bubble in a classic sense. To call something a bubble, it must be overpriced and there must be an intense belief in it…. There's this sort of psycho-social component to people taking on these enormous debts when they go to college simply because that's what everybody's doing."

Since his announcement, more than sixty Thiel Fellows have decamped from university—a significant number of them from Stanford, MIT, and Ivy League schools—to follow their dreams of entrepreneurial glory. Thiel says he hopes his program will prod more people to question if a college education is really worthwhile: "Education may be the only thing people still believe in in the United States. To question education is really dangerous. It is the absolute taboo. It's like telling the world there's no Santa Claus."

Far from being dangerous, the exercise of questioning the value of a college education has never been more important. For many Americans, the grim employment realities since the start of the Great Recession of 2008 have called the value of higher education into question. So we all would do well to ask: Do universities provide private and public benefits commensurate with their private and public costs?

This is a complex, but not impossible, question to answer. The simplest response is to tally the added income benefits a university education accrues to its graduates, subtract its added costs, and determine if, in fact, benefits exceed costs. Some economists have done this quite well. The overwhelming answer is that a college education has paid off for most graduates to date, has increased rather than decreased its wage premium as time has gone on, and can be expected to continue to do so moving forward. If well-paid equates to worthwhile, then the worth of a college education can be settled by the net wage premium of the average college graduate over the average high school graduate—there would be little more to discuss in the matter.

But it would be a serious mistake to equate the value of a university education to the wage premium earned by its graduates. If higher education is to be understood as something more—something much more—than a trade school in robes, before answering the question of whether a university education is worthwhile, we must first address the more fundamental—and more fundamentally complex—question of mission: What should universities aim to achieve for individuals and society?

It is reassuring to those who believe in the worth of a university education—and all the more so in a high-unemployment, low-growth economy—to show that the average person with a college education earns a lot more over her lifetime than the average high school graduate, even after subtracting the cost of college. But even if we are reassured, we should not allow ourselves to be entirely satisfied with that metric, because economic payback to university graduates is neither the only aim, nor even the primary aim, of a university education. Rather, it is best to consider the value-added proposition of higher education in light of the three fundamental aims of colleges and universities in the 21st century:

- The first aim speaks to who is to receive an education and calls for broader access to higher education based on talent and hard work, rather than family income and inherited wealth: Opportunity, for short.

- The second aim speaks to the core intellectual aim of a university education, which calls for advanced learning fostered by a greater integration of knowledge not only within the liberal arts and sciences, but also between the liberal arts and professional education: Creative Understanding, for short.

- The third aim is an important consequence to the successful integration of knowledge, not only by enabling and encouraging university graduates to meaningfully contribute to society, but also in the creation of new knowledge through research and the application of creative understanding: Contribution, for short.

Although the challenges of increasing opportunity, advancing creative understanding, and promoting useful social contribution are not new, they take on a renewed urgency in today's climate. Jobs are scarce. The United States is perceived to be declining in global competitiveness. Gridlock besets our political discourse and increasingly seems to define our national sense of purpose as well. In this environment, it behooves us to remind those who would propose to reform higher education by simply removing some or all of it of the apt observation of the "Sage of Baltimore," H.L. Mencken: "There is an easy solution to every human problem—neat, plausible, and wrong."

Many external obstacles to educational and economic opportunity exist in the United States—including poverty, broken families, and cutbacks in public support—which warrant our national attention and, in some instances, urgent action. No one credibly claims that greater access to college education will solve all or even most of these issues. But there is good reason to believe that greater access to high-quality higher education is a vitally important tool in building a more just, prosperous, and successful society. We can, and we must, do a better job in meeting the three fundamental goals of opportunity, creative understanding, and contribution to afford the utmost benefits of higher education for both personal and societal progress. Taking to heart the ethical injunction "Physician, heal thyself," I focus here on what universities themselves can do to better realize their primary aims.

Starting with the first: What can universities do to help increase educational opportunity? For low- and middle-income students, gainful employment itself is likely to be the most basic economic advantage of a college degree. A recent Brookings Institution study found college is "expensive, but a smart choice," noting that almost 90 percent of young college graduates were employed in 2010, compared with only 64 percent of their peers who did not attend college. Moreover, college graduates are making on average almost double the annual earnings of those with only a high school diploma. And this advantage is likely to stick with them over a lifetime of work. Perhaps most relevant is that even in the depths of the Great Recession, the unemployment rate of college graduates was less than half that of high school graduates, and never exceeded 5.1 percent. Clearly, the more affordable universities make their education to qualified young people from low- and middle-income families, the more we will contribute to both educational and economic opportunity. Other things being equal, universities provide even greater value-added opportunity to low- and middle-income students than to their wealthier peers.

It is especially important to note that opening the door to higher education can have profound effects on both an individual's lifetime earnings and lifelong satisfaction, regardless of whether or not that door is framed by ivy. Less selective two-year, four-year, and community colleges have an especially important role to play here, as selective universities cannot do everything: Their focus on cutting-edge study and discovery limits their ability to engage in compensatory education. (The ability to work with a broad range of student readiness is one of the great advantages of community colleges and some less selective institutions, an advantage we risk forfeiting as an ever-higher percentage of the cost of an education is shifted from state and government support to individual responsibility.) Nonetheless, the available data show that selective universities can provide greater access to qualified students from low- and middle-income families than they have in the past.

My concern for increasing access began with a focus on recruiting qualified students from the lowest income groups. Learning more led to the conclusion that increasing access for middle-income students should also be a high priority. At Penn, we began by asking: What proportion of students on a set of selective university campuses (that included Penn) comes from the top 20 percent of American families as measured by income? The answer (as of 2003) was 57 percent.

Since all colleges and universities should admit only students who can succeed once admitted, selective colleges and universities also need to ask: What percent of all students who are well qualified come from the wealthiest 20 percent? Thirty-six percent of all highly qualified seniors (with high grades and combined SATs over 1,200) come from the top 20 percent, while 57 percent of selective university students come from this group. Thus, the wealthiest 20 percent of American families are overrepresented on our campuses by a margin of 21 percent. All of the other income groups are underrepresented. Students from the lowest 40 percent of income distribution, whose families earn under about $41,000, are underrepresented by 4.3 percent. The middle 20 percent, who come from families earning $41,000 to $61,000, are underrepresented by 8.4 percent. Students from the second highest income group, whose families earn between $62,000 and $94,000, are also underrepresented by 8.4 percent.

Increasing access to our universities for middle- and low-income students is both an especially worthy, and an increasingly daunting, challenge in the wake of the Great Recession. Before the Recession, taking financial aid into account, middle- and low-income families were spending between 25 percent and 55 percent of their annual income to cover the expense of a public four-year college education. That burden has skyrocketed in the past five years, especially for middle-income students who are ineligible for Pell grants and who attend public universities whose public funding (in many cases) has been decimated. This has led to a situation where a student from a typical middle-income family today may pay less to attend Penn than many flagship public universities!

Yet private universities too have experienced a painful financial squeeze. Only by making student aid one of their highest priorities and successfully raising many millions of dollars from generous donors can most private institutions afford to admit students on a need-blind basis and provide financial aid that meets full need. This may be the reason why only about one percent of America's 4,000 colleges and universities are committed to need-blind admissions and to meeting the full financial need of their undergraduate students. An even smaller group—just a tiny fraction—of universities are committed not only to meeting the full financial need of all students who are admitted on a need-blind basis, but also to providing financial aid exclusively on the basis of need. Those of us in this group thereby maximize the use of scarce aid dollars for students with demonstrated financial need.

At Penn, a focus on need-only aid has enabled us to actually lower our costs to all students from families with demonstrated financial need. Since I became president, we have increased Penn's financial aid budget by more than 125 percent. And the net annual cost to all aided undergraduates is actually 10 percent lower today than it was a decade ago when controlled for inflation. Penn also instituted an all-grant/no-loan policy, substituting cash grants for loans for all undergraduates eligible for financial aid. This policy enables middle- and low-income students to graduate debt-free, and opens up a world of career possibilities to graduates who otherwise would feel far greater pressure to pick the highest paying rather than the most satisfying and promising careers.

Although much more work remains, Penn has significantly increased the proportion of first-generation, middle- and low-income, and underrepresented minority students on our campus. In 2013, one out of eight members of Penn's freshman class will be—like I was—the first in their family to graduate from college. The percentage of underrepresented minorities at Penn has increased from 15 percent to 22 percent over the past eight years. All minorities account for almost half of Penn's student body. After they arrive, many campus-wide initiatives enable these students to feel more at home and to succeed. Graduation rates for all groups are above 90 percent.

It is also important to note that the benefit of increasing opportunity extends far beyond the economic advancement of middle- and low-income students who are admitted. Increased socio-economic and racial diversity enriches the educational experience for everyone on a campus. By promoting greater understanding of different life experiences and introducing perspectives that differ profoundly from the prevailing attitudes among the most privileged, a truly diverse educational environment prods all of us to think harder, more deeply, and oftentimes more daringly.

This observation speaks to the second aim of a university education: cultivating creative understanding. Our universities face a daunting challenge: We must immerse students in the unprecedented torrent of new knowledge our contemporary society has unleashed, while at the same time somehow providing them with the intellectual tools to make cogent sense of it all. They must be facile with facts and figures, quick in apprehension, and yet slow to jump to easy and ready conclusions. This is the essence of training them to think creatively, as they will be called to do in addressing the most challenging problems facing the world of today and tomorrow. We must optimize their global comprehension, a term used here in the broadest possible sense: global not just as in transnational, but more pointedly as in all-encompassing, as in integrating multiple and oftentimes contradictory perspectives. It will be their global understanding that makes our highly educated students economically competitive, intellectually innovative, and primed for continued lifelong learning.

So what does this need to cultivate global understanding in the 21st century require of our universities? Among other things, I suggest it demands that we foster intensive learning across academic disciplines within the liberal arts and integrate that knowledge with a much stronger understanding of the role and responsibilities of the professions. Whether the issue is health care or human rights, unemployment or immigration, educational attainment or economic inequality, the big questions cannot be comprehended—let alone effectively addressed—by the tools of only one academic discipline, no matter how masterful its methods or powerful its paradigms.

Consider, for example, the issue of climate change in a world that is both more interconnected and more populous than ever before. To be prepared to make a positive difference in this world, students must understand not only the science of sustainable design and development, but also the economic, political, and other issues in play. In this immensely complex challenge, a good foundation in chemical engineering—which is not a traditional liberal arts discipline nor even conventionally considered part of the liberal arts (engineering is typically classified as "professional or pre-professional education")—is just as important as an understanding of economics or political science. The key to solving every complex problem—climate change being one among many—will require connecting knowledge across multiple areas of expertise to both broaden and deepen global comprehension and, in so doing, unleash truly creative and innovative responses.

A liberal arts education is the broadest kind of undergraduate education the modern world has known, and its breadth is an integral part of its power to foster creative understanding. But it is a mistake to accept the conventional boundaries of a liberal arts education as fixed, rather than as a humanly alterable product of particular historical conditions.

In my own field of political philosophy, for example, a scholarly approach centered on intellectual history ceded significant ground in the 1970s to critical analysis of contemporary public affairs, which was a paradigm common to many earlier generations of political philosophers. Were the liberal arts motivated solely by the pursuit of knowledge for its own sake, and not by any concern for worldly relevance, then it would be hard to make sense of such shifts. In the case of this important shift in political philosophy, scholars thought it valuable, in the face of ongoing injustice, to revive a tradition of ethical understanding and criticism of society.

A liberal arts degree is a prerequisite to professional education, and most liberal arts universities and their faculties stand firmly on the proposition that the liberal arts should inform the professions. Why then are liberal arts curricula not replete with courses that teach students to think carefully, critically, and creatively about the roles and responsibilities of professionals and the professions? Perhaps we are assuming that students will make these connections for themselves or that it will suffice if professional schools do so later. Neither of these assumptions can be sustained.

For example, we must not assume that students themselves will translate ethics as typically taught in a philosophy curriculum into the roles and responsibilities of the medical, business, and legal professions. The ethical considerations are too complex and profoundly affected by the institutional roles and responsibilities of professionals. Many lawyers, for example, are part of an adversarial system of justice; many doctors are part of a system where they financially benefit from procedures the costs of which are not paid directly by their patients; and many businesspeople operate in what is commonly called a free market, where external interferences are (rightly or wrongly) presumed, *prima facie,* to be suspect. These and many other contextual considerations profoundly complicate the practical ethics of law, medicine, and business.

My primary point is this: Although the separation of the liberal arts from the subject of professional roles and responsibilities may be taken for granted because it is so conventional, it really should strike us as strange, on both intellectual and educational grounds, that so few courses in the undergraduate curriculum explicitly relate the liberal arts to professional life. This is a puzzle worthy of both intellectual and practical solution.

I propose that we proudly proclaim a liberal arts education, including its focus on basic research, as broadly pre-professional and optimally instrumental in pursuit of real-world goals.

This stark separation of the practical and theoretical was not an inevitable outgrowth of earlier educational efforts, nor has it ever been universally accepted. In fact, it flew in the face of at least one early American effort to integrate the liberal arts and professional education. In his educational blueprint ("Proposals Relating to the Education of Youth in Pennsylvania"), which later led to the founding of the University of Pennsylvania, Benjamin Franklin called for students to be taught "every Thing that is useful, and every Thing that is ornamental." Being a principled pragmatist, Franklin immediately addressed an obvious rejoinder that no educational institution can teach everything. And so he continued: "But Art is long, and their Time is short. It is therefore propos'd that they learn those Things that are likely to be most useful and most ornamental."

As Franklin's intellectual heirs, we recognize that something educationally significant is lost if students choose their majors for either purely scholastic or purely professional reasons, rather than because they want to be both well educated and well prepared for a likely future career.

The introduction of distribution requirements for all majors is one way of responding to this potential problem. The glory and strength of American liberal arts education is its enabling undergraduates to keep their intellectual sights and their career options open, while cultivating intellectual curiosity and creativity that will enhance any of the career paths they later choose to follow. These are among the most eminently defensible aims of a liberal arts education: to broaden rather than narrow the sights of undergraduates and to strengthen rather than stifle their creative potential.

I propose that we proudly proclaim a liberal arts education, including its focus on basic research, as broadly pre-professional and optimally instrumental in pursuit of real-world goals. At its best, a liberal arts education prepares undergraduates for success in whatever profession they choose to pursue, and it does so by virtue of teaching them to think creatively and critically about themselves, their society (including the roles and responsibilities of the professions in their society), and the world. So what can we do to bolster this optimal educational system as envisioned by Franklin? As 21st-century colleges and universities, we can build more productive intellectual bridges between liberal arts and professional education. We can show how insights of history, philosophy, literature, politics, economics, sociology, and science enrich understandings of law, business, medicine, nursing, engineering, architecture, and education—and how professional understandings in turn can enrich the insights of liberal arts disciplines. We can demonstrate that understanding the roles and responsibilities of professionals in society is an important part of the higher education of democratic citizens.

This leads to the third aim of a university education: maximizing social contribution. Here in particular is where the university's age-old focus on training scholars and advancing scholarship bumps up against its relatively recent focus (first brought to the fore by German and American research universities of the mid- and late-19th century) on discovery and creation of new knowledge. The sweep of the university's place in society is long, going back more than a thousand years; in that context, the role of the modern research university in America, dating back just to the 1870s, is a comparatively recent innovation. It is nevertheless a development that has had far-reaching and profound consequences in areas ranging from health and medicine to physics and material sciences, the social sciences, and the humanities. Basic research now plays an integral role in our understanding of the liberal arts, and we have come to understand our colleges and universities not just as training grounds for the next generation of fully prepared democratic citizens, but no less as vital economic engines of discoveries that drive future waves of innovation and human progress.

These are discoveries such as those made by Dr. Carl June and his team at Penn's Abramson Cancer Center, with contributions from colleagues at the Children's Hospital of Philadelphia. Their pioneering research with individualized cancer treatments produced a reengineered T-cell therapy. Just in time, too, for young Emma Whitehead, who was stricken with advanced leukemia when she was just five years old. Under Dr. June's care, Emma, now seven, has beaten her cancer into remission. She's back at school, laughing and learning and playing with her friends. Her miraculous recovery not only means a renewed chance at a long, fulfilling life for her and her parents—it promises renewed hope for so many who are ravaged by cancer.

In university classrooms and laboratories across the country, the brightest minds are leveraging research and discovery to contribute to the social good. Most of these stories are not as dramatic as Emma's, but each in its own way has changed and will continue to change how we live and work and understand our world. The full tale of the benefits that universities bring extends far beyond technological and medical advances. We help governments build good public policy based on robust empirical data garnered from university research. We build better international cooperation through the study of languages and cultures, economic markets, and political relations. We strengthen economies by fostering scores of newly discovered products, markets, and industries. We safeguard our collective health and well-being with insight into global phenomena and systems such as climate change, shifting sea levels, and food supply and agricultural production. All the vital basic and applied research being conducted by universities cannot be accounted for in any one list—the sum is too vast. What I can sum up here is this: If we do not do this research, no one will.

Colleges and universities also contribute to society at the local level by modeling ethical responsibility and social service in their institutional practices and initiatives. Their capital investments in educational facilities contribute to the economic progress of their local communities. Colleges and universities at every level can be institutional models of environmental sustainability in the way they build and maintain their campuses.

While the core social contribution of universities lies in both increasing opportunity for students and cultivating their creative understanding, the analogous core social contributions of universities in the realms of faculty research and clinical service are similarly crucial. And both are only strengthened by better integrating insights across the liberal arts and the professions. An education that cultivates creative understanding enables diverse, talented, hardworking graduates to pursue productive careers, to enjoy the pleasures of lifelong learning, and to reap the satisfactions of creatively contributing to society. The corresponding institutional mission of colleges and universities at all levels is to increase opportunity, to cultivate creative understanding, and—by these and other important means such as innovative research and clinical service—to contribute to society.

At their best, universities recruit hardworking, talented, and diverse student bodies and help them develop the understandings—including the roles and responsibilities of the professions in society—that are needed to address complex social challenges in the 21st century. To the extent that universities do this and do it well, we can confidently say to our students and our society that a university education is a wise investment indeed.

THE LIBERAL ARTS AND PRESIDENTIAL LEADERSHIP

Nannerl O. Keohane
former President of Wellesley College and of Duke University

I am indeed honored to address this gathering of leaders of colleges historically committed to a strong liberal arts education and glad that my husband, Robert Keohane, who is chairing the presidential search committee of his alma mater, Shimer College, is also attending the conference. All of us are here in part to celebrate the impressive record of our campuses and reaffirm our commitment for the future. But there are also challenges that we need to face together. We should pool our ideas and energies and think strategically about how we can most effectively champion liberal arts education today and in the future. My task is to set the stage for these discussions.

Here is how I will proceed: First, I will say a few words about the liberal arts as a historic phenomenon with much resonance in our world today. Then I will present four arguments that may be useful to you as you confront the skeptics. Finally, I will talk briefly about leadership and how you can make a difference.

THE LIBERAL ARTS THROUGH HISTORY

Any one of you here today could give a persuasive definition of the liberal arts and doubtless have done so many times. I am especially fond of Thomas Cronin's definition of the liberal arts as "the liberating arts—freeing us from prejudice, dogmatism and parochialism, from complacency, sentimentality, and hypocrisy, from sloppy reasoning and careless writing." A liberal arts education doesn't always accomplish all those things, but it surely gives us a good beginning. Cronin has presided over two liberal arts colleges, and his definition appears in a recent book, entitled *Leadership and the Liberal Arts*, edited by J. Thomas Wren. Here's another pungent definition of a liberal education by Louis Menand, in *The Marketplace of Ideas*, as "a background mentality, a way of thinking, a kind of intellectual DNA that informs work in every specialized area of inquiry."

Ironically, of course, this very broad, capacious form of education we call the liberal arts is rooted in a specific curriculum from classical and medieval times, including rhetoric, arithmetic, geometry, the trivium, and the quadrivium. But it would be wrong to assume that because it has such ancient roots, this kind of education is outdated, stale, fusty, or irrelevant. The liberal arts lend themselves particularly well to contemporary high-tech methods of imparting knowledge.

We all wrestle with the challenges of educating students who are used to multitasking, doing their homework while listening to music on their iPods and texting on their iPhones. For such students, the web-based facilities of exciting liberal arts courses are particularly salient. What would Aristotle or Erasmus or Robert Maynard Hutchins not have given for a technique that allows one to tour the world's greatest museums, looking closely at the details of countless masterpieces, explore the ruins of ancient castles and pyramids and forums, join archeological digs at your desk, turning objects around to see all sides of them, visualize problems in geometry or astronomy or mathematics in several dimensions and work out their solutions?

An excellent example of the power of multimedia coupled with the liberal arts is a general education course sometimes taught at Harvard University by Stephen Greenblatt as English 126, "Imaginary Journeys." The course is described as being "about global mobility, encounter, and exchange at the time that Harvard College was founded in 1636. Using the interactive resources of computer technology, we follow imaginary voyages of three ships that leave England in 1633. [Each student is assigned to one of the ships, which are separated by a storm and therefore visit different destinations and experience different fates.] Sites include London's Globe Theatre, Benin, Barbados, Brazil, and Mexico." The course was inspired by

Yo Yo Ma's Silk Road project, and the website provides an incredible wealth of material from many different sources—music, art, literature, architecture, history, geography. With this kind of course in mind, it seems that the liberal arts could almost have been designed for sophisticated online learning, so far from being stale or fusty are these ways of knowing.

And this kind of education is more and more appealing to students and teachers at universities around the world. Donald Markwell, the warden of Rhodes House, recently gave a series of lectures in Canada entitled "The Need for Breadth." He refers to a "surge of interest" in liberal education in "many other countries." He mentions new programs at the Universities of Melbourne and Western Australia, the Universities of Manchester and Warwick in the UK. He cites a major address in London by Yale's Richard Levin, in which Levin noted that "Asian leaders are increasingly attracted to the American model of undergraduate curriculum," specifically because of the two years of breadth and depth in different disciplines provided before a student chooses an area of concentration or embarks on professional training. Levin described liberal arts honors programs at Peking University, Yonsei University in South Korea, and the National University of Singapore; he also referred to liberal arts curricula at Fudan University, Nanjin University, and the University of Hong Kong.

In her recent book, entitled *Not for Profit: Why Democracy Needs the Humanities*, Martha Nussbaum notes that she has been recently involved in discussions about creating a liberal arts curriculum in The Netherlands, Sweden, India, Germany, Italy, and Bangladesh.

Yet, as we know, the trends in the U.S. are in the opposite direction. And this is not just a recent problem. Louis Menand cites evidence that in the U.S., the "proportion of undergraduate degrees awarded annually in the liberal arts and sciences has been declining for a hundred years, apart from a brief rise between 1955 and 1970, which was a period of rapidly increasing enrollments and national economic growth." Thus, paradoxically, as a liberal arts education becomes more appealing to leaders and families in Asia and elsewhere in the world, it is losing ground in our own country.

At least three factors are at work in this decline: a) the creation of increasingly specialized disciplines and the rewards for faculty members of advancing knowledge in those areas; b) the economic premium that is thought to reside in a highly technical form of preparation for careers; and c) a growing focus on graduate education from the early 20th century to the present day. These developments have clearly not been beneficial for American undergraduate education. "Liberal education in crisis" is a tiresomely familiar theme, and countless commissions, reports, and study groups have attempted to address it. I am under no illusions that I have the magic key to resolve a problem that has stumped so many brilliant educators. But these questions are not just theoretical quandaries for you. They are the issues you confront almost every day: How do we defend liberal education against the skeptics—parents, potential students, the media, the marketplace, even some trustees and students?

Arguments for the Liberal Arts Today

I will offer four arguments designed to defend the liberal arts (as distinct from vocational or narrowly pre-professional training) as the best education for undergraduates. I will discuss these arguments in order from the narrowest to the most capacious, so you can take your pick depending on your audience or your personal preference.

The first, most practical defense: I would argue that the liberal arts (and sciences) are the best possible preparation for success in the learned professions—law, medicine, teaching—as well as in the less traditionally learned but increasingly arcane professions of business, finance, and high-tech innovation.

There are many ways to study any discipline; the subjects that make up the liberal arts curriculum are not themselves inherently liberal. As our colleague, President Lynn Pasquarella of Mt. Holyoke, has recently reminded us, one can study the humanities in a technical rather than a liberal fashion—narrow, esoteric, with no attempt to broaden or challenge the mind to consider critically what one has learned. And one can also study biology or physics, political science or anthropology, even economics in a more or less liberal fashion. So my first claim is that a liberal arts education, including a liberally oriented study of the natural and social sciences, presents material in a context that will be much more useful to budding lawyers or physicians or venture capitalists than a narrowly construed preparation in their "own field."

For example, if you study neuroscience with a sense of awe about the complexities of the human brain, and some attention to questions about what it means to be human, not just a technical focus on the darting neurons, or study biology with an awareness of the bewildering diversity and richness of our natural world rather than attending only to the way the molecules fit together, you will have a better background as a physician when you go to medical school or a scientist when you get your Ph.D. Surely your bedside manner or your classroom techniques will also be much improved! And if you study some history and philosophy, you will be much better prepared as a lawyer or financier than if you study only law or a narrowly construed pre-business program. Our eldest granddaughter, Charlotte (a very happy although slightly chilly first-year student at Bowdoin College this year and a prospective MD), is going to major in neuroscience, which is taught at Bowdoin in a way that surely engages critical thinking and liberal learning.

So my first defense of liberal learning is what you are taught and the way you learn it: the materials a doctor or financial analyst or physicist or humanist needs to know, but taught in a liberally construed fashion, so that you look at the subject from many different dimensions and incorporate the material into your own thinking in ways that will be much more likely to stay with you and help you later on. There are several distinct advantages of this way of learning: It's insurance against obsolescence. In any rapidly changing field (and every field is changing rapidly these days), if you only focus on learning specific materials that are pertinent today, rather than learning about them in a broader context, you will soon find that you have no use for these bits of knowledge, and your training will have become valueless. Most important, with a liberal education you will have learned how to learn, so that you will be able to do research to answer questions in your field that will come up years from now, questions that nobody could even have envisioned today, much less taught you how to answer. That's all part of the first defense!

The second, slightly less utilitarian defense of a liberal arts education is that it hones the mind, teaching focus, critical thinking, and the ability to express oneself clearly both in writing and speaking—skills which are of great value no matter what profession you may choose. It's not just that you are taught specific materials in a liberally designed context, but more generally, it's the way your mind is shaped, the habits of thought that you develop.

When I discussed this talk with Nancy Malkiel, a Smith graduate who was dean of the college at Princeton for 24 years, she told me a story that makes this point exactly. As dean, Nancy worked hard to create appealing incentives for students to major in some of the less frequented fields, to take the pressure off econ or poli sci. At Princeton's commencement last year, the mother of a student Nancy had advised, who had chosen quite happily to major in religion, accosted her and said: "Dean Malkiel, you told my daughter to major in religion, and she still doesn't have a job!" Nancy gently pointed out that the young woman had graduated only a few minutes earlier and assured the mother that things would almost certainly work out. And sure enough, a few weeks ago the mother was riding a bike across the Princeton campus and stopped to say hello to Nancy and said: "Guess what? My daughter did get a job! She was volunteering at a non-profit global organization, and they were really impressed that she could write so clearly and elegantly, do research on any topic she was assigned to cover, assemble the evidence to make persuasive arguments, and analyze complex problems, so they offered her a job."

These are the skills a liberal arts education instills in us. They were well described by no less an authority than a former dean of Harvard Law School, Erwin Griswold, cited in a recent speech by Dean Martha Minow. Griswold was discussing an ideal vision of the Law School, but his arguments fit a liberal education wherever it is provided: "You go to a great school not so much for knowledge as for arts or habits; for the art of expression, for the art of entering quickly into another person's thoughts, for the art of assuming at a moment's notice a new intellectual position, for the habit of submitting to censure and refutation, for the art of indicating assent or dissent in graduated terms, for the habit of regarding minute points of accuracy, for the art of working out what is possible in a given time; for taste, for discrimination, for mental courage, and mental soberness." That's the second argument.

My third argument for a liberal arts education is that a liberal arts education is the best education for citizenship in a democracy like our own. In the book I cited earlier, *Not for Profit*, Martha Nussbaum points out that from the early years of our republic, educators and leaders have "connected the liberal arts to the preparation of informed, independent, and sympathetic…citizens." Nussbaum argues that democracies need "complete citizens who can think for themselves, criticize tradition, and understand the significance of another person's sufferings and achievements." She lists the skills democratic citizens need: to "think well about political issues affecting the nation; to recognize fellow citizens as people with equal rights; to have concern for the lives of others; to grasp what policies of many types mean for the opportunities and experiences of one's fellow citizens; to imagine well a variety of complex issues affecting the story of a human life; to judge political leaders critically, but with an informed and realistic sense of the possibilities available to them; to think about the good of the nation as a whole, not just that of one's local group," and "to see one's own nation, in turn, as part of a complicated world order." These are the kinds of skills a liberal arts education fosters.

At a time when democracy is struggling to be born in countries around the world, and countries that have long enjoyed democracy are struggling to sustain it against pressures of multiple varieties, this may be the best of all the arguments for a liberal arts education. We need citizens who can think for themselves, who can assess arguments made by people who have a stake in a particular outcome, attend to nuances in difficult policy situations, and respect the interests and the dignity of others who are not like them.

The fourth argument for a liberal education, in addition to the way materials are presented, the habits of mind that are instilled, and the preparation for democratic citizenship, is even broader; it is in many ways my favorite of the four.

When I was at Wellesley and Duke, I occasionally used a memorable image at convocation as the new academic year began. With due credit, I borrowed it from Michel de Montaigne's 16th-century essay, "Of Solitude." Montaigne lived an active life in many ways, with family, friends, political positions, much travel; but he was exceptionally well aware of the importance of occasional solitude. Montaigne's favorite place for writing and reflection was the tower library on his estate in southwestern France, to which he climbed by a series of narrow staircases reaching to the very top of his domain, with a view of the vineyards and grain fields, a ceiling carved with some of his favorite quotations, and lines of books and manuscripts around the shelves. If you visit his estate, you can still see that library and understand directly what his life was like.

Inspired by that beloved space, Montaigne used the arresting image of the "back room of the mind." He thought of his own mind as a kind of tower library to which he could retreat even when he was far from home, filled with quotations from wise people and experimental thoughts and jokes and anecdotes, where he could keep company with himself. He suggested that we all have such back rooms in our minds and that the most valuable and attractive people we know are those who have rich and fascinating intellectual furniture in those spaces rather than a void between their ears. When I used this image, I would counsel students to think of their college education as above all a way of furnishing the "back rooms of their minds." In this way, they would be much better conversationalists, so that their company would be sought out by others, rather than being regarded as a simpleton or a bore, and they would also be better prepared to relish solitude, whether they chose it or it was imposed on them.

Countless students and their parents have told me that they recalled that image of the "back room of the mind" many years afterwards and had found it helpful through many periods in their lives. Virginia Woolf used a different spatial image to make a similar point in her book *Three Guineas,* when she talked about the importance of cultivating taste and the knowledge of the arts and literature and music. She argues that people who are so caught up in their profession or business that they never have time to listen to music or look at pictures lose the sense of sight, the sense of sound, the sense of proportion. And she concludes: "What then remains of a human being who has lost sight, sound and a sense of proportion? Only a cripple in a cave."

One more spatial image in support of this fourth argument, from a recent speech by my successor as president of Duke University, Richard Brodhead: Dick Brodhead is an eminent scholar of American literature and strong proponent of the liberal arts. He spoke of the human capacity to "make things that outlive their makers," and he asserted that as we make or enjoy such things, "We go out in spirit toward the works of others." Humans have the distinctive ability, he continued, "to exit the confines of our own experience and take up mental residence in spaces created by others." And when we do so "with sufficient intensity of feeling, we in turn have a chance to be changed. This is the way we annex understandings that have been struggled toward by others that we would never have reached on our own. This is how we get to see the world differently from the way our own minds or cultures habitually present it." One example here: In addition to neuroscience, my Bowdoin granddaughter Charlotte is planning to concentrate in art history, a passion that she never knew she had until she got to Bowdoin and discovered the excellent museum, fine arts department, and engaging colleagues. Although there are good art works in her home, no one in her family is an artist, so this is not something she cared much about as she was growing up; instead, it's a newly discovered personal dimension that will enrich her life immeasurably going forward. And that's my fourth argument for a liberal arts education: furnishing the back room of your mind, preparing yourself for both society and solitude.

My final argument for the liberal arts will resonate with many of you in this gathering, although it is unlikely to convince the skeptics. This is the argument that a liberal arts education admits you to a community of scholars, both professional and amateur, spanning the ages. Here, I would quote one of my predecessors as president of Wellesley, Alice Freeman (later Alice Freeman Palmer). When she presided over Wellesley in the last part of the 19th century, it was quite unusual for girls to go to college (as indeed it still is today in some parts of the world). She gave a well-known speech to answer the repeated question she got from girls and their families, "Why go to college?" Alice Freeman said: "We go to college to know, assured that knowledge is sweet and powerful, that a good education emancipates the mind and makes us citizens of the world." The sweet and powerful knowledge imparted by a liberal arts education is specifically designed to fulfill this promise, as no other kind of education can be: It emancipates the mind and makes us citizens of the world.

Alice Freeman Palmer's phrase "citizen of the world" has impeccable liberal arts credentials. It was first coined by Plutarch to describe Socrates.

Martha Nussbaum published a book with that title in 1997. And it nicely loops back to my third and fourth arguments: Liberal knowledge, sweet and powerful, broadens our perspective beyond the narrow confines of our own experience and makes us good citizens not just of our countries, but of the whole world. As the time-honored phrase used by the presidents of several colleges and universities in conferring the baccalaureate degree would have it, "I welcome you to the company of educated men and women."

So five nested arguments for the liberal arts: a) providing the "deep background" materials people need for their professions and business occupations, in a long-term, capacious fashion rather than a narrowly technical immediacy that will quickly become obsolete; b) honing the mind with skills that are useful in any profession and any life; c) preparing us well for citizenship in a democracy; d) furnishing the back room of the mind; and e) admitting us to a community of learned and curious men and women, making us better citizens not only for our communities and our country, but the world.

Presidential Leadership

Armed with these arguments and others you will devise or read about, how do you, as a college president, go about making the case for the liberal arts? What tactics should you use? Here's an especially delicious quote from President *emeritus* of Whitman College Tom Cronin, who notes that "effective leadership remains in many ways the most baffling of the performing arts. Intuition, flare, risk-taking, and sometimes even theatrical ability come into play." This point really resonates for me, as I'm sure it does for some of you as well. Leadership is itself an art, and to make the case for the liberal arts, you should be quite ready to use your personal flare, intuition, theatrical ability, and even take some risks. Don't feel you have to confine your arguments to sober and conventional arenas. However, you also have to be savvy and cagey or your theatricality can backfire; as Cronin says, this is a particularly baffling kind of art.

In my book, *Thinking about Leadership*, I define a leader as follows: "Leaders determine or clarify goals for a group of individuals and bring together the energies of members of that group to accomplish those goals." Leaders do this in all kinds of groups, from the most informal committee to the largest nation state. The responsibilities of the president of a college or university are among the weightiest of the forms of leadership. If you take my definition as one guide to action, you can think of your role as a presidential leader in this way: You are clarifying what a liberal arts education means for your college (and the world) and galvanizing the energies of the faculty and trustees and student leaders to pursue that goal. In fact, one of the primary responsibilities for you as president of a liberal arts college is to support the liberal arts, which are basic to the historic mission and self-understanding of your institutions. There are a number of ways to do this; I'll briefly suggest four of them.

First and most obvious, you should use the bully pulpit of the college presidency deliberately and effectively to make the case for the liberal arts. You should consider how you can use the occasions of convocation, commencement, ground-breakings for new buildings, speeches to the local Rotary Club or the state 4-H club convention, addresses to alumni clubs, all the kinds of events where you are called upon to speak. This is a truly precious opportunity that few other leaders have: to address your community in situations where there is likely to be respectful attention to your message, at least for a while! Use the opportunity with zest!

A few minutes ago I referred to my having cited Montaigne on the "back room of the mind" at several convocations and mentioned how many students and their parents had later recalled this phrase and how it had helped shape their lives. I remember also the speech I gave to the faculty of Duke soon after 9/11. I was scheduled to present the annual report of the president to the Academic Council, and I used that opportunity to speak from the heart about the crucial importance of the liberal arts to help us deal thoughtfully with the horrors of that day. I paid homage, of course, to the scientists and engineers who would help us understand how buildings can be built to withstand shocks and how to construct exit ways, but I noted that nothing the engineers could teach us would keep crazed men from smashing large jets into tall buildings to make a point about their political views. I talked about the importance of the social sciences in helping us understand that human, social dimension of 9/11 and do our best to prevent a repetition of the day, and also understand and appreciate the motives and sacrifices of the people who gave their own lives to save others. But I reserved my deepest praise for the humanities, which provided the context and frameworks for sharing and dealing with our grief and shock. So many people spoke of how poetry or music had provided for them the best, indeed the only, way to grapple with what had happened.

As part of my speech I told a personal story, as one can sometimes do very effectively on such occasions. Shortly after 9/11, when all our Duke obligations and events had been cancelled to allow everyone to focus on understanding what had happened and honoring the dead, Bob and I decided spontaneously to drive to Wilmington, to walk along the ocean at Wrightsville Beach. I was driving at one point, Bob was napping, and the local classical music station played the Fauré Requiem somewhere along a stretch of Interstate 40 in eastern North Carolina. I listened with intense emotion to the movement entitled "Dona Eis Requiem," Give to Them Peace. I was overcome with emotion and had to pull over to the side of the road. And as I told the Duke faculty, that was the first time I fully acknowledged the sorrow and shock of the events and found solace.

This is the kind of use you can make of the bully pulpit: In your speeches you can draw on the particular credibility and dignity of the president to make the case for the education your college provides.

The second way you can use your presidential leadership in supporting the liberal arts is to "put your money where your mouth is." That means using your fund-raising skill and obligations to raise money for exciting programs like Greenblatt's "Imaginary Journeys." You can make this case effectively to foundations and generous alumni who remember their own liberal arts education fondly, and thus enhance the resources available for this purpose.

I remember with particular delight a fund-raising conversation with Kathryn Wasserman Davis, a dedicated Wellesley alumna and close friend. Kathryn wanted to make a major gift to the college to advance international understanding, which had been her own Ph.D. field many decades earlier. Together, we worked to an outcome that gave joy to both of us and many other people: Kathryn's gift would be the naming, foundational gift for a new art museum at Wellesley, a badly needed enhancement of our liberal arts mission. We had one of the earliest and best art history departments in the country and a fine collection mostly donated by alumnae and their families, but only paltry and badly designed space to show and study these works of art. Kathryn and I agreed that art is a truly international language and that Wellesley's museum would include works that would speak directly to that purpose, works from many countries and eras. And, after our partnership in building the museum, Kathryn herself took up painting in her 80s and has become a highly respected artist on Mt. Desert Island, Maine.

In addition to using your bully pulpit wisely and putting your fund-raising acumen where your mouth is, the third example of presidential leadership in support of the liberal arts could be the way you honor faculty members. With the teaching awards and other distinctions your college offers, make sure to single out for praise and support those who have been most effective in advancing the liberal arts mission of your institution through their teaching. You can cite their innovative course work and impact on the lives of their students, linking this specifically to the power of the liberal arts. You can ensure that these awards and recognitions are appropriately highlighted in college publications and in messages to parents and prospective students.

One more way in which you can use your leadership as president, perhaps the most effective of all: You can be a model for emulation, by others on campus and by the outside world, in the ways you use and embody liberal arts learning in your own discourse, both formal and informal. If you cite examples of fine literature, draw on instances from history, refer to the arts and describe learning in the sciences in liberal terms, you will set an example for others and have an influence greater than you may expect. Rhetoric was one of the original *artes liberales*, and it can still be one of the most transformative.

CONCLUSION

Taking my own advice about larding your language with liberal learning, I will conclude by quoting from three poems I discovered in a brochure on a recent visit to the Georgetown University School of Foreign Service in Doha, Qatar. Each poem is about journeying. I was myself on a fascinating journey, visiting universities in the Gulf States, where I had never been, and I was impressed to find ten poems in different languages featured in the admissions brochure for a school of foreign service in the Middle East. Because journeying is an apt metaphor for a liberal arts education, one that I and many of you often use, these three fragments provide an especially appropriate conclusion to this speech.

The first lines were written in Greek by Constantine Cavafy, a late-19th/ early-20th century poet who lived in Alexandria, from one of his best-known works, *Ithaka*. In translation: "When you start on your journey to Ithaka/ pray that the road is a long one/full of adventure, full of knowledge." This captures for me the lifelong learning aspect of a strong liberal arts education, full of adventure, full of knowledge, and we hope that the road is a long one.

The second citation is a few lines from Emily Dickinson, 19th-century American, written to a grieving friend: "Intimacy with Mystery, after great Space, will usurp its place/Moving on in the Dark like Loaded Boats at Night/though there is no Course, there is Boundlessness." A good liberal arts education makes us intimate with mystery, and also helps us move in the dark by providing a sense of byways through the boundlessness.

And the final poem, written in Arabic, is by Al-Sha'afi:

> *According to the measure of hardship are heights achieved,*
> *And he who seeks loftiness must keep vigil by night;*

As for he who wants heights without toil,
He wastes his life seeking the impossible—
So seek nobility now, then sleep once more (finally),
He who seeks pearls must dive into the sea.

As this final poem reminds us, a liberal arts education is not always easy; it involves close attention, taking risks, exploring uncharted territory, diving into the sea. But despite these challenges, the deep rewards of a liberal education are surely worth it, for all the reasons I've mentioned and many others that you will each devise to make your case vigorously as presidents committed to this cause. Good luck with your task, and happy journeys!

Finding Our Place and Making Connections: Liberal Arts Education in Today's World

Sunder Ramaswamy
President, Middlebury Institute of International Studies at Monterey

I feel a particular kinship and attachment to this esteemed university, without even quite realizing it, because of your founder, Cyrus Hamlin. As history notes, after his time here in Istanbul, where he helped in the founding of Robert College, which became Boğaziçi University, he returned to his native New England and became the president of Middlebury College in 1880, a place I have called my "professional home" since 1990. Cyrus Hamlin is particularly known for his tenure at Middlebury because he took the important and courageous decision to open up the previously all-male liberal arts college to women. The first woman, May Belle Chellis, was admitted in 1883: Today's graduating class from Middlebury College is 50 percent female (Bain, 1999).

Hamlin had the courage and conviction of his principles, upbringing and life experience to follow through with decisions at a time when they were unpopular or discouraged in the conservative academe. When we think that the world around us is particularly tough, and that taking a stand or making a decision is next to impossible, it might help to think back to educators like Hamlin and the decisions that he took—whether in helping found this august university in a far away land or admitting women in a prestigious New England liberal arts college.

Like the many educators before me this evening, I often wonder about the world around me and what we are doing at our own institutions to prepare our students to face the challenges of the 21st century. I am a development economist by profession but also the president of the Monterey Institute of International Studies (MIIS), with the emphasis on *international*.

Some time back, I finished reading Fareed Zakaria's book—*The Post-American World*. He starts off with a set of premises that we can all relate to. Over the last five to six hundred years, there have been three mega- shifts in power across the global landscape—shifts of such magnitude that they basically altered the distribution of power that shaped "international life—its politics, economics, society and culture."

The first was the rise of the Western world. This was a process, as we all know, that began in the late 14th/early 15th century and accelerated into the late 18th/early 19th century. This period produced "modernity" as we define it, and with it, a rapid rise and expansion of science and technology; markets, trade and capitalism; and the twin agricultural and industrial revolutions. This period also coincided with the gradual recession of the Asian civilizations and the rise of the nations of the West.

The second tectonic shift took place in the waning years of the 19th century and had to do with the rise of the United States. The U.S. became one of the most powerful nations in the world (and, some would argue, for a few decades the sole superpower). Since the end of World War II, the U.S. has dominated the global discourse in the areas of military strength, support for freedom and democracy, push for free markets, international organizations, science and technology, and popularity of "soft power."

Zakaria posits that we are now living through the third great power shift of our era—"the rise of the rest." As the phrase connotes, in the last decades of the 20th century and the start of the 21st, countries from the "non-western" part of the world have been experiencing and sustaining growth rates that were once unthinkable. Sure, there have been booms and busts, but the secular trend is clearly upward. The unleashing of economic dynamism has been most visible in Asia but is not just confined to that continent; in fact, parts of the Middle East, Africa and regions of Latin

America are experiencing this economic burst. Indeed, perhaps for the first time ever, and certainly when you reflect on the number of people who are being impacted by this economic transformation, we are witnessing genuine global growth and development. These changes are creating an international system in which countries in all parts of the world are no longer objects or observers, but players in their own right. It is the birth of a truly different sort of a global order. It is what many commentators call "Globalization 2.0." Relations have moved from interrelations between nation-states to relations between corporations, to relations between individuals—all across space and time—actively aided by travel, communications and technology.

As power has diffused from nation-states to other actors, groups and individuals have been empowered, and hierarchy, centralization and control are being undermined. NGOs, corporations, and other networks are mushrooming every day, operating as if the "world is their stage," to borrow from William Shakespeare.

In the words of David S. Grewal (2008), "We also live in a world in which our relations of sociability—our commerce, culture, ideas, manners —are increasingly shared, coordinated by newly global conversations in these domains, but in which our politics remains inescapably national or local, centered in the nation-states or sub-national states that are the only loci of sovereign decision making." Of course, this translates to the existence of a perennial tension between preparing students (and tomorrow's citizens/ workers) for a globalized world, but one in which they will also find themselves rooted and participating in a localized community.

I recall on a recent transatlantic British Airways flight from India, the opening lines of the in-flight magazine went something along the lines: "Many decades back, British Overseas Airways Corporation, the precursor of the modern British Airways, was a British company, headquartered in Britain and operating throughout the world; now British Airways is a global corporation that just happens to be located in Britain!" If you reflect on this sentiment, it is an interesting inversion of "corporate identity and operations" that is true not just of British Airways but of many other players today.

The kinds of opportunities and challenges posed by these seismic changes is precisely what interests educators like us. Our students are living through an experience in which time and consciousness take on new dimensions. Such shifts require what American Civil War historian James McPherson calls, albeit for a different era, "adaptive versatility" (2003).

From my experience of teaching students from all around the world at Middlebury College for over eighteen years, we were keen on educating young people in the tradition of the "liberal arts" in that it "embodied a method of discourse as well as a group of disciplines." The college location in Vermont offered an inspirational setting for learning and reflection, reinforcing our commitment to integrating environmental stewardship into both our curriculum and our practices on campus. Yet, the college also reached far beyond the Green Mountains, offering a rich array of undergraduate and graduate programs that connected our community to other places, countries and cultures. We tried to engage students' capacities for rigorous analysis and independent thought within a wide range of disciplines and endeavors and to cultivate the intellectual, creative, physical, ethical, and social qualities essential for leadership in a rapidly changing global community. Through the pursuit of knowledge, unconstrained by national or disciplinary boundaries, students who came to Middlebury learned to engage the world (Middlebury College, 2006).

I have had the privilege of heading MIIS for the past seven years, which is now a graduate school of Middlebury. It was an institute founded in 1955 by three language teachers who believed that the most important contribution they could make to society was to train professionals to work across cultural and linguistic boundaries. They sought to shrink the differences among people around the world by building bridges of linguistic, cultural and historical understanding. They knew that viewing issues in single dimensions, whether political or economic or geographic, could not deliver a complete picture of the problems or lead to lasting, meaningful solutions.

Today, nearly sixty years later, the focus of the Institute remains the same: solutions. We provide an international professional graduate education to students seeking to make a difference in the world—people whose goal is to quite literally be the solution to the world's most pressing problems.

"Be the solution" is much more than a slogan, though. It is a statement of purpose for every MIIS student and, I think it's safe to say, every member of the Institute community. We are all here because we recognize the difference that overcoming intercultural barriers can make in solving so many of the problems we see in the world today.

The phrase "be the solution" grew out of a concept that is central to both our mission and the way we approach teaching and learning at MIIS, a concept we call *pragmatic idealism.*

Some might consider that phrase an odd juxtaposition of words. In fact, the word idealism has often been used disparagingly to imply people's views or beliefs or goals are unworkable or not grounded in reality. That might be true at times when you're speaking of idealism in its purest form and in isolation. But *pragmatic idealism* is, by definition, grounded in the real, in a practical approach to problems that involves systematic analysis, planning and implementation of solutions.

Pragmatic idealism takes right-brain intuition and creativity and balances it with left-brain sequencing and logic. It takes big, bold concepts and initiatives and breaks them down into a series of practical steps designed to make a tangible difference in the world.

Pragmatic idealism lies at the very core of the Institute's academic philosophy and can be seen clearly in our focus on experiential, immersive learning and the real-world issues that we ask our students to analyze, strategize and attempt to solve.

Many of the pressing problems of our times—global poverty, climate change, rise of terrorism, access to potable water, to name a few—require so much more than simply being "good at one subject" or the other. Real-world problems are rarely one-dimensional; they aren't simply policy or business or engineering or language or environmental problems. They grow out of a complex, multifaceted and unique set of circumstances that both describes the problem and must inform responses to it. To tackle such seemingly intractable problems, it seems to me, the liberal arts provides a foundation upon which edifices of professional and specialized knowledge can be built.

As T. S. Eliot so wisely noted a long time ago, "Where is the wisdom we have lost in knowledge? Where is the knowledge we have lost in information?" To which I would like to add, "Where is all the information we have lost in the data?"

We are constantly faced with a tsunami of information—this often starts in school, building up through much of our educational system. "What information consumes is rather obvious—it consumes the attention of its recipients. Hence a wealth of information often creates a poverty of attention" (Middlebury College Strategic Plan, 2006).

We live in a world characterized by what can be called "continuous partial attention"—this is when you are on the Internet or cell phone or iPad, while also watching TV, typing on your computer and answering a question from your child. That is, you are multitasking your way through the day, continuously devoting only partial attention to each act or person you encounter.

It might be the malady of our times. As Thomas Friedman observed, "We have gone from the Iron Age to the Industrial Age to the Information Age to the Age of Interruption" (2006). All we do now is interrupt each other or ourselves with instant messages, emails and cell phone rings. Who can think, write or innovate under such conditions? Educators need to educate students about "filters" and how to separate good information from garbage, to see patterns in data and in the myriad interactions around us.

As Martha Nussbaum (2007) so persuasively writes, "Cultivation of the imagination during the critical years at school and college is essential to fostering creativity and innovation. It has also been found that teaching critical thinking and argumentation is essential in order to foster healthy debate inside a business world that might too easily become complacent or corrupt....Too often, knowledge is not a guarantee of good political behavior, but ignorance is a virtual guarantee of bad behavior."

So, to me, a keen understanding of this messy and complex world is the crux of an education process. If we can deliver to our students an ability to "really understand" the world around them, "see patterns and make connections," and make it possible for them to have "hope"—that they can indeed continue to go out and change the world, as Gandhi exhorted—then we have done well with our mission as educators.

I would like to conclude by reciting a well-known passage from Rabindranath Tagore, the Indian Nobel laureate. It is a passage I have thought about a lot over the years, and it remains as relevant for educators and citizens today as it was at the time of India's independence in 1947.

> *Where the Mind is without fear*
> *And the head is held high*
> *Where knowledge is free*
> *Where the world has not been*
> *Broken up into fragments by*
> *Narrow domestic walls*
> *Where words come out from the*
> *Depths of truth*
> *Where tireless striving*
> *Stretches its arms towards perfection*
> *Where the clear stream of reason*
> *Has not lost its way*
> *Into the dreary desert sand of dead habit*
> *Where the mind is led forward*
> *By thee, into ever widening thought and action*
> *Into that land of freedom*
> *My father, let my people awake.*

ENDNOTES

Bain, David. *The College on the Hill: A Browser's History for the Bicentennial* (Middlebury, Vermont: Middlebury College Press, 1999).

Friedman, Thomas. "The Age of Interruption." *The New York Times*. 5 July 2006.

Grewal, David S. *Network Power* (New Haven: Yale University Press, 2008).

"Knowledge Without Boundaries: Middlebury College Strategic Plan." http://www.middlebury.edu/media/view/143121/original/MiddleburyStrategicPlan2006.pdf. 2006.

McPherson, James M. *Battle Cry of Freedom: The Civil War Era* (New York: Oxford University Press, 2003).

Nussbaum, Martha. "Cultivating the Imagination." *The New York Times*. 17 October 2010.

Tagore, Rabindranath (1910). *Rabindranath Tagore* (Gitanjali Publisher: Digireads.com, 2005).

Zakaria, Fareed. *The Post-American World* (New York: W.W. Norton Publishers, 2009).

Can We Meet
the Challenge?

Mary Sue Coleman
President, University of Michigan

How will it feel to become a second-class nation? Inferior in technological innovation, second-class in artistic creativity, a follower rather than a leader? This is possible—not certain—but a very real danger if the United States continues on its present course.

The United States can claim 35 of the world's top fifty research universities, but we face intense competition from other nations that see the economic advantage of strong research universities.

The U.S. share of global research spending declined from 39 percent in 1999 to 34 percent in 2010 and is expected to keep falling, according to a 2012 report from the National Academy of Sciences. While the growth in U.S. spending on R&D is increasing by 3.2 percent per year, China is escalating its investment at six times that rate (20 percent), and other nations are expanding advanced education on a scale mirroring that of the United States in the last century.

Moreover, we now see a reverse of the "brain drain" that brought so much talent to our shores. Four in ten students pursuing science and engineering doctorates at U.S. universities are from other countries. Many of them who once would have chosen to live in America now plan on returning home because they see a bright future for their scientific work there, and U.S. immigration standards impose barriers to retaining this trained talent.

This might not be so worrisome if U.S. undergraduate enrollment in math and science fields could meet our long-term need for research scientists. We know it cannot. Only a small fraction of our undergraduates study the natural sciences or engineering compared with near majorities in Singapore, China, and France.

While in earlier times our country rallied around science, education, and advanced learning, today these are not national priorities. We confuse the prevalence of modern technology with national strength in science. But the core of technology, as well as other advances, is science. Nations on the rise see support of research universities as an investment in the future; unfortunately, many Americans speak of it only as a cost.

Vigorous concerted action to support basic research is paramount in contemporary America. Putting a man on the moon was extraordinary but relatively simple compared with tackling global climate change, for example. Recognizing the complexity of the problems we face augurs the capacity to solve them—as a nation and as global citizens.

No other American institution rivals higher education's commitment to discovering and sharing knowledge at its most basic level. At the research university I lead, we have developed powerful partnerships regionally and internationally to benefit our state and the larger world.

The University of Michigan, Michigan State University, and Wayne State University, all public universities, began collaborating in 2006 by forming the University Research Corridor (URC) to leverage the tremendous strengths of our scientists. Today the URC ranks among the country's top university research regions.

The University of Michigan is also working with Qatar University to conduct social science research in the Gulf States; with the University of Ghana to train OB/GYNs to be experts in family planning; and with the University of São Paulo to better understand adrenal cancer's prevalence in Brazil.

For U.S. universities to maximize their strengths, we must be decisive, creative, agile, and inclusive. That means:

- Supporting a culture of risk-taking. Faculty seeking grant funding often must demonstrate how a project might be directly applicable to a practical advance. But the most creative and novel studies—the ones that often do lead to breakthroughs—can sometimes be stymied. We must ensure that our best minds have the support to follow innovation wherever it leads. At Michigan, for example, we are committing $100 million for medical researchers to conduct novel science in a "fast forward" manner.

- Intensifying interdisciplinary research. Advances in medicine, for instance, will depend on combinations of biology, nanotechnology, information sciences and engineering. When Michigan pledged $30 million to hire 100 junior faculty members—during the depths of the recession—the qualification was that scholars work in teams, across boundaries, to tackle society's thorniest problems. Emerging combinations will yield unimaginable discoveries that will improve lives.

- Expanding our reach by offering a high-quality, affordable education, not only for low-income students but also for students from middle-class families who face hardship owing to the recent recession. Widening our doors develops the talents of all of our citizens, including bringing more exceptional students into STEM [science, technology, engineering, and mathemathics] fields.

- Spending public money efficiently, encouraging greater philanthropic support, and ensuring that students complete degrees in a timely manner can motivate taxpayers, corporations, foundations, and state and federal governments to strengthen their support for our endeavors.

- Ensuring that strong undergraduate teaching is part of the larger research continuum. At Michigan, we emphasize that research and teaching are not antithetical; we are proud of the fact that we are one of the great universities of the country, distinguished in both teaching and research, and that we help create the next generation of leaders and scientists and an educated citizenry. Now more than ever, the research university must provide a thriving culture for entrepreneurs and risk-takers whose discoveries will help us meet today's challenges and position us to meet tomorrow's.

Fault Lines in the Compact: Higher Education and the Public Interest in the United States

Ronald J. Daniels
President, Johns Hopkins University

Phillip M. Spector
Vice President of Strategic Initiatives, Johns Hopkins University

Rebecca Goetz
Research Assistant, Johns Hopkins University

The research university stands as one of the most admired and emulated of American institutions. Year after year, American universities dominate the international rankings of institutions of higher education. The demand for places in American programs continues to grow, and the quality of matriculating students continues to improve. The prospects for students graduating from American universities continue to strengthen, as measured along dimensions as varied as enhanced lifetime earnings, life expectancy, and quality of civic participation. And the research contributions of American universities continue to command scientific recognition and fuel economic innovation and life-saving discoveries.

And yet, in spite of these achievements, the relationship between government and the university in the United States is, in the minds of many commentators, fraught. The points of conflict are many: federal governmental failure to protect the real value of research investment; marked reductions in state support for public universities; non-trivial university tuition increases that have raised vexing issues of access and affordability (and triggered threats of governmental intervention); and highly publicized and acrimonious governance conflicts that have pitted publicly appointed state governing boards against university leaders (on subjects ranging from program priorities to the use of technology to cost control and pricing).

There is no gainsaying that throughout American history the role of the university has commanded the attention and intervention of government. This is to be expected. Under the neoclassical framework, government has a central role to play in addressing a host of market failures involving higher education and in ensuring the Jeffersonian promise of equality of opportunity.

And, indeed, over the years, governments and universities had forged a robust and dynamic compact in the United States. Public institutions and instruments have shaped the growth of the modern American university: The federal government has invested over $500 billion in academic research and $1.7 trillion in student aid since 1970, has created and financed a range of grant and loan programs aimed at subsidizing student participation, and oversees a vast system of regional accreditation that seek to address quality and related concerns. State governments—in many cases, aided by federal legislation and support—have founded state public universities and actively supported their activities, providing direct appropriations to institutions as well as grant aid to students. At the same time, our universities have returned countless benefits to the communities in which they reside, anchoring and accelerating the economies in the surrounding areas, serving as engines for upward mobility and economic advancement, and birthing countless world-altering discoveries for the betterment of humanity.

It is against this backdrop of decades of constructive collaboration, one that has conferred staggering benefits on American society, that the current malaise between university and government is so disturbing.

In this paper, we explore the state of the compact between the government and the university in the United States and the prospects for constructive reengagement. In the first part of the paper, we discuss the rationales for government intervention in the higher education sector. In Part II, we briefly sketch the history of the compact between the government and universities and the ways in which government has shaped and supported the flourishing of the sector. In Part III, we canvass the sources of the contemporary conflict between the government and higher education, which we argue has been exacerbated by the economic and social impact of the Great Recession. In Part IV, we identify several ideas for institutional and policy reform, while also locating these questions in a broader debate about intergenerational equity and the capacity of government to invest in our future. We argue that, although there is scope for more creative use of policy instruments to redress some of the current tensions between the state and research universities, ultimately a broader and more systematic set of interventions aimed at redressing rising inequality in the United States is necessary.

PART I: THE ROLE OF GOVERNMENT

The market for higher education is beset by several frailties—public goods, human capital market failures, information asymmetries, and equity concerns—that demand government intervention.

To be sure, the state has not always produced efficacious regulation in this domain. And yet, this should not be seen as an argument for an end to government's role altogether. One must instead ask how it can intervene in a targeted manner that responds to the risks posed by institutional actors, so the public can obtain the benefits of private initiative, investment, and ingenuity in this area without distortion of incentives or danger of abuse.

PUBLIC GOODS AND POSITIVE EXTERNALITIES

Some share of the benefits of post-secondary education—promotion of research and discovery, inculcation of civic values, and economic growth—accrue to the public good and not to individual students alone. This means that without government support, the education and research activities associated with higher education will be under-supplied from a social welfare perspective. Take, for example, basic research activity. Without supplementary funding, it is unlikely that private parties will dedicate a significant amount of their resources to such research, which has grounded much of the industrial innovation and other achievements whose benefits extend far beyond the university itself. Columbia University Provost *emeritus* Jonathan Cole estimated that "perhaps as many as 80 percent of new industries are derived from discoveries at American universities." The widespread social benefits of these research activities provide a clear rationale for government investment.

Wholly apart from their contributions to basic research, universities are among the most powerful engines for economic growth and development.

Higher educational attainment has been connected to reduced crime rates, lower unemployment rates, and reductions in public spending on assistance and social support programs. One recent study shows that an additional year of average university level education in a country raises national output by a remarkable 19 percent. The university is also a powerful source for upward social economic mobility for its students and their families (this rationale overlaps with the equity rationale below). For all of these reasons, the state has a prevailing interest in nurturing the sector.

A range of intangible benefits can also be traced to higher education. For example, volunteerism and voting rates are higher among those with Bachelor's degrees than high school graduates. Universities also play a central role in advancing civic culture and community cohesion. These non-pecuniary benefits to society provide yet another powerful set of rationales for government involvement.

Imperfections in Human Capital Markets

The state also has a strong interest in intervening in higher education to right failures in human capital markets that constrain the ability of students to finance their education.

Banks are often reluctant to provide private loans to students, due to their inability to secure collateral in students' prospective human capital and their difficulty of anticipating students' likelihood of academic success and future economic prospects. In the best of circumstances, banks will charge a risk premium that will often price students—who are reluctant to accumulate substantial amounts of debt at such an early age—out of higher education. This is a particular challenge for students of lower socioeconomic backgrounds, leading to distributional effects. All of these problems lead to suboptimal private lending in higher education and a need for government intervention to compensate for these failures by reducing the amount students need to borrow.

Information Asymmetries

Since post-secondary education is inherently optional, and potential post-secondary students are of an age where they should be regarded as being capable of making rational and informed decisions regarding the future course of their education, the government should perhaps be wary of exercising a paternalistic role in shaping those decisions. However, there may be some modest scope for government intervention to resolve information asymmetries between students and post-secondary institutions. Accordingly, the state has a role in requiring those institutions that receive public funds to publish information respecting the quality of the entering class, the quality and character of the academic program, student completion rates, faculty research activity, and career placement patterns for graduates.

Equity

Given the considerable role that institutions of higher education play as gatekeepers to economic opportunity and professional advancement, the representation of various communities in these institutions and the social consequences of admissions policies must be taken seriously. Most universities are committed to recruiting the strongest possible student body, and the admissions decision is typically merit driven. Even so, universities present a unique capability to remedy persistent and self-perpetuating ethnic or socioeconomic imbalances in higher education and society at large. States have an interest in supporting and preserving the unique role of universities as a force for equal opportunity for its citizens and making sure that all citizens are given a chance to obtain the skills and training that are essential to upward mobility in our knowledge-based society.

Part II: The Forging of the Compact

For each of these reasons, and in each of these ways, the state has played a fundamental role in shaping higher education in the United States. The compact we know today was forged over time across the sweep of American history: The university did not always act in response to the needs of the state, and the state did not always act in the interest of the university. However, over time, history reflected a dawning recognition of the two institutions' indispensable relationship.

Even before the American Revolution, colonial governments dedicated transportation taxes, sales taxes, and other sources of revenue to the founding and maintaining of a college in each colony. The methods and types of institutions varied from state to state, but there was, even then, a commitment to supporting the provision of higher education and a belief that education was a fundamental state interest.

The relationship only grew stronger during the first century of the republic. One key moment in this relationship occurred in 1862, when Congress enacted the Morrill Land Grant Act, through which the federal government would provide land grants to certain eligible states to support collegiate programs in "useful arts" such as agriculture, mechanics, and military instruction. Over the next thirty years, Congress would expand the sweep of the Morrill Act to the entire nation. These statutes set a powerful precedent: They expanded undergraduate colleges into the university model across the United States with multiple programs beyond the liberal arts, and they enlisted the states in an effort to make higher education accessible to groups outside of the privileged elites, making them available to the working classes of the period.

The first half of the 20th century saw the emergence of state legislatures as major players in their own right in the funding of higher education: States in the Midwest and the West, in particular, used tax revenues to fund and grow universities into the tens of thousands of students. The levels and types of support varied considerably from state to state. California, for example, made access to education a priority and charged no tuition, while other states saw higher education as a privilege and kept tuition at public institutions higher. Nonetheless, this area saw the expansion of state support that would eventually lead to the creation of renowned public research universities that operate at the level of private institutions, while working to serve a larger segment of the state's population.

The federal government would stake out an even more influential and striking role in expanding access to higher education with the GI Bill in 1944, which guaranteed up to four years of tuition, fees, and a stipend at a U.S. institution of higher education in exchange for service in the U.S. military. By 1947, veterans accounted for 49 percent of college admissions. The increases in enrollments spurred by the GI Bill and continuing through the 50s and 60s led to the acceptance of enrollment-based funding at the state level, allowing public universities to absorb the new students without dramatically increasing tuition levels. The federal government, concerned about the growth of diploma mills and looking to protect veterans and taxpayer dollars, also began making eligibility for funds contingent on accreditation. This program laid the foundation for increasing access and affordability through portable student grants, which would become one of the most important forms of federal support for higher education in the next half of the century.

Soon after the GI Bill, two documents set the modern trajectory for the federal government's involvement in U.S. higher education for the next fifty years, one on the issue of research support, the other on funding: Vannevar Bush's *Science: The Endless Frontier* (1945) argued for the essential role of federal support for basic research, using competitive grants to universities. Over the next several decades, a host of federal agencies would harness the research talent at universities to create what Clark Kerr would later call the "Federal Grant University"—about twenty institutions received almost 80 percent of federal research funds. Support for university research is still one of the federal government's most important avenues of support for higher education.

At the same time, the "Truman Commission Report on Higher Education" chronicled fundamental concerns with equity and access in higher education. Among its influences, the Truman Report would lay the groundwork for future financial aid policies. One of the most historic steps along this path at the federal level was the passage of the Higher Education Act of 1965, and then the amendments to it in 1972, which established direct grants and loans to students. The Basic Educational Opportunity Grant, later renamed the Pell Grant, remains a major source of aid for low-income students. These grants are portable, allowing students to become consumers of education and forcing institutions to compete for their aid dollars. The federal government has continued to raise the maximum grant amount, and spending on the program more than doubled between 2000 and 2010. Many state governments also took steps in this period to make higher education more affordable and accessible to a significant portion of the population through appropriations to institutions and low tuition.

PART III: FAULT LINES AND THE GREAT RECESSION

And yet, despite these energetic state interventions in higher education, fault lines have emerged in the relationship in recent years.

One area of very real tension concerns the level of government financial support for higher education. The many reasons for the state to invest in higher education remain as true today as they did in earlier times (perhaps even more so given the rise of the human capital economy), and yet the willingness and/or capacity of government to invest in higher education has waned. On average, state-level support for higher education has declined 25 percent in the last decade, while in many states the cuts have been steeper still (National Research Council, 2012). What is more, the level of state support for higher education is significantly lower than it was a few decades ago: In 1990, states spent an average of $9,100 per student on higher education, while in 2011, the number dropped to $6,700 per student, both in 2011 dollars.

A similar (although softer) trajectory can be seen in federal research investment: After the dramatic doubling of government investment in NIH research during the Clinton administration, the real value of support has declined almost 20 percent in the last decade. As a consequence, the average age of a first NIH Transformative Research Award (R01) has risen steadily, while the success rate for applications has steadily declined. The consequences of this government withdrawal have been profound for our universities and their research mission, as well as the status of the United

States as the world's leader in research (and industrial competitiveness): As other countries continue to increase their research expenditures, the U.S. share of world R&D expenditures has declined significantly. All of this has occurred at the precise moment when universities with academic health centers in the United States are also wrestling with significant changes to health care models and declining clinical revenues, making it even more difficult for them to weather these financial shocks.

Another fault line has surfaced around issues of cost and affordability. Universities have raised tuition significantly in recent years: While median family income rose 147 percent from 1982 to 2007, tuition and fees rose 439 percent over the same period. The share of income families spend on higher education has risen for decades, and the rise has been sharpest for low-income families, who need to spend about half of their income to send a child to college. Despite efforts by several of the leading American research universities to augment financial aid, and the expansions to Pell Grants and other federal aid programs instituted by the Obama administration, there has been a declining level of participation by low- and moderate-income students in four-year university programs. In 2010, the Advisory Committee on Student Financial Assistance presented a report to Congress on increasing inequality in college access: While total college enrollment had increased over the past few decades, the study found that between 1992 and 2004 enrollment rates of academically qualified low-income high school graduates in four-year colleges decreased from 54 percent to 40 percent (Advisory Committee on Student Financial Assistance, 2010).

Still another area of tension has concerned value and innovation. Empirically, the benefits of higher education have clearly been shown (particularly in relation to lifetime earnings and risks of unemployment). However, many have begun to question the objective and mission of a university, questioned the pedagogical approach of universities, and inserted themselves into academic decision-making. Universities are increasingly viewed as engines of job creation and wealth. More than ever, their essential role as wellsprings of citizenship and social welfare is overlooked. Governors have sought to scale back low-enrollment programs or fields with less perceived utility post-graduation, such as the humanities, and have sought to tie funding to job placement and similar metrics. Critics have also pointed to declining completion rates as evidence that universities may not be accomplishing their fundamental education mission, as well as to recent studies that reach a similar conclusion. One recent analysis by sociologists Richard Arum and Josipa Roksa (2011) maintains that 45 percent of students had effectively made no progress in critical thinking, complex reasoning, and writing in their first two years at U.S. colleges and universities. (Notably, two recent studies by the Council for Aid to Education contradict that finding, arguing that there is a significant improvement in students' performance between their freshman and senior years.)

Each of these concerns might have continued to vex the relationship between the state and higher education, but would not have commanded the policy salience they do today, if not for the devastating impact of the Great Recession. In 2008 and 2009, the U.S. labor market lost 8.8 million jobs, and total wealth declined by $15 trillion. The median household income fell to its lowest level since 1996, meaning that the recession effectively wiped out the middle class income gains for the last fifteen years. The effects of the contraction on the higher education sector have been profound and varied. At one level, the Great Recession placed enormous financial stress on the states' fiscal capacities and constricted their abilities to maintain their investments in higher education. At another level, the Great Recession impaired the ability of many families who suffered wealth and income reductions to provide the level of anticipated support for their children's enrollment in universities. Finally, universities themselves were directly buffeted by the effects of the Great Recession in the form of significant decreases in private donations, endowment reductions, and increased demands for financial aid support.

Although the country has started to recover from the Great Recession, the challenges surrounding the federal government's fiscal pressures continue to impact the sector. For instance, federally mandated sequestration will reduce NIH funding by another 7.8 percent, the largest cut in its history. The price of attending a four-year public university in the United States will have increased 27 percent above the rate of inflation across the last five years, even though average family incomes will have actually declined during that period, even when adjusted for inflation (Oliff, Palacios, Johnson, & Leachman, 2013). Colleges are downsizing: Some have cut as many as 200 academic programs, while also slashing funds for instructional staff, libraries, and student services. More and more students are choosing to enroll first in community colleges instead of four-year schools, but community colleges also face significant budget cuts. Sixty-nine percent of Americans now feel that college is unaffordable and that there are highly qualified students who cannot gain access to a university education (Immerwahr & Johnson, 2010).

We must explore new approaches to financial assistance that do a more effective job of addressing market failures and aligning resources to areas of need. All of this in turn has fueled mounting concern and heightened rhetoric on the part of government officials regarding questions of rising costs, declining completion rates, and the value of a college education. Officials in Wisconsin, Virginia, Montana, and other states have attacked universities for rising costs and have imposed tuition freezes, even as state spending declines. Florida Governor Rick Scott has proposed charging different rates of tuition for different majors in an effort to drive students toward STEM [science, technology, engineering, and mathmatics] fields, saying, "If I'm going to take money from a citizen to put into education, then I'm going to take that money to create jobs." North Carolina Governor Patrick McCrory has argued that there is no value to the humanities and said, "If you want to take gender studies, that's fine. Go to a private school and take it…. But I don't want to subsidize that if that's not going to get someone a job." And President Obama has made college affordability one of the centerpieces of his second-term agenda, emphasizing that government "can't just keep on subsidizing skyrocketing tuition" and even suggesting that universities would need to keep costs down or lose federal funding.

PART IV: NEW APPROACHES AND ENDURING QUESTIONS

It may be tempting to dismiss many of these tensions as cyclical and believe that when the economy rebounds, states will reinvest, tensions will cool, and the earlier equilibrium of constructive collaboration will return. However, there are reasons to believe that these recent tensions reflect deeper structural issues, and the Great Recession has raised fundamental and vexing questions surrounding the strength, durability, and content of the compact between state and university that command attention and resolution.

At one level, addressing the conflict will require renewed federal and state efforts in devising innovative and thoughtful regulatory approaches. For instance, we must explore new approaches to financial assistance that do a more effective job of addressing market failures and aligning resources to areas of need. One promising set of options that has won favor in recent years involves income-contingent loan repayment programs, through which students pay what they can up front and contract with the government to defer any remaining payments until they graduate and are working. At that time, they pay any deferred fees as a fixed percentage of their income, an obligation enforced through the tax code. The loans address concerns of liquidity, enforceability, and complexity in the current system and the daunting fear of students that they will not be able to pay back loans. This approach to student debt has been popular in Britain and Australia for years; although the United States has offered an income contingent plan for federal loans, it is not widely used by students, many of whom are not aware of their repayment options or are put off by the program's complexity. The Obama administration has taken steps to simplify the process and make information more available to borrowers, and the administration's proposed 2014 budget included an expansion of the option to all borrowers, eliminating the income caps and other barriers that currently make some students ineligible.

We can also do a better job of addressing the scope of states to undermine the U.S. government's expenditure of funds through the opportunistic substitution of federal for state funds. As one example, the 2009 federal stimulus created a $48.6 billion State Fiscal Stabilization Fund that provided direct formula-based grant aid to states to advance essential education reforms. However, 23 states cut spending on higher education in the first year that they received the federal funds. And six of those states slashed spending on higher education while increasing their total state spending, suggesting that rather than using stimulus funds to offset necessary cuts, the grant allowed them to divert education spending elsewhere (Cohen, 2010). We need to explore methods of federal funding that limit the opportunities for this substitution, including rewards to states that increase their spending, directives to states to maintain certain levels of investment to receive federal funds, or the provision of funds to states through competitions that are keyed to appropriate criteria rather than formulas.

And we should seek policy tools to redress the widening gap between the magnitude of state investment in, and state regulation of, higher education. Often a state will provide relatively little in the way of investment in its higher education system, but involve itself extensively in the internal affairs of its universities. For example, the University of Colorado receives only 4 percent of its budget from the state (the average public university receives about 20 percent) and finds itself the target of significant and obtrusive regulations and intervention. The state approves and reviews all academic programs, establishes admissions standards, and prescribes standards for construction and capital improvement. It is time to start a conversation about the importance of parity in the scope of funding and intervention. This could include incentives for states to withdraw from governance in situations where they have a de minimis stake in operational support or even a national conversation to develop norms and expectations for state regulation in a sector under strain.

And yet, universities also must shoulder their share of the burden for addressing the tensions in higher education. The call has gone out for universities to reduce tuition and control costs, and they must respond with purpose. Of course, the precise cause of rising costs in higher education is a matter of some debate. One theory blames rising costs on stagnating productivity and says it is difficult for a labor-intensive industry such as education to substitute capital for labor, and so as wages rise, so inevitably do costs. Another theory, proposed by Howard Bowen (1980), argues that universities' principal goals are excellence, influence, and prestige, and they are prepared to spend whatever is necessary to achieve these goals—in particular, as revenues increase from tuition, endowments, and donations, so unavoidably will expenditures and costs. William Bowen (2012) argues that there are inefficiencies too fundamental to how universities are structured to be easily resolved, including fixed costs such as specialized laboratories and faculty with highly specialized talents.

Whatever the cause, universities cannot remain unstirred much longer to the changes roiling the industry around them. These changes include not only the enormous financial strain in the U.S. economy, with the accompanying calls for higher education to reduce tuition and control costs, but also involve the manifold changes occasioned by the information age: Higher education is famously one of the few industries that until now have managed largely to hold at bay the disruptive and potentially transformative effects of technological development in the information age. Universities still have largely failed to explore the opportunities of this age, opportunities with the capacity not only to reshape and reduce administrative costs and improve services to students, but also expand mission and reach, augment revenue and reshape pedagogy in ways we have never seen before. And yet, in truth, all of the above approaches can only take us so far. The problems we face are broader than higher education and cannot be solved by higher education policy standing alone.

The Great Recession exposed in a profound way the weakening of the middle class in America. Middle- and low-income families were hit the hardest by the downturn, and they have been the slowest to recover. Families in high-poverty areas lost the highest percentage of their wealth and were the most likely to be unemployed during the recession. A middle class upbringing is no longer a guarantee of lifetime success, with a third of Americans raised in the middle class falling below the middle class as adults.

For most of U.S. history, higher education was one of the most powerful mechanisms for social mobility in the nation and served as a powerful counterforce to rising stratification. However, caught in a spiral of rising tuition and declining state investment, compounded by the fiscal effects of the Great Recession, the capacity of higher education to play this role is itself in jeopardy. The historic rate of growth in educational attainment has slowed—the percentage of those under 34 with a Bachelor's degree has remained virtually unchanged for decades—and the gap in enrollment rates between students from low- and high-income families has risen steadily over the last forty years. Only 11 percent of students from the bottom quintile ever graduate, compared to 53 percent from the top. Our education system is not helping low-income students reach the same attainment as their higher income peers.

As economists Claudia Goldin and Lawrence Katz (2008) argue, these trends in educational attainment deeply compound the problems of income equality across the American economy. The Great Recession has only widened this gap, with the college educated recovering more quickly and bearing less of the brunt of the crisis. Those with a college degree actually gained 187,000 jobs from December 2007 to January 2010, while those with high school diplomas or less lost 5.6 million jobs in this period, and another 230,000 during the recovery (Carnevale, Javasundera, & Cheah, 2012). More than half of the jobs created during the recent recovery from the recession have gone to workers with a college degree or higher, even though they make up only a third of the labor force.

Since the founding of the republic, universities have been a powerful force for upward social mobility and forward economic progress, just as the state has been a powerful force in building and shaping the modern university.

One of the principal ways to narrow this divide is to invest in pre-K, K-12 education, higher education, training, and technology—in short, invest in tomorrow. And yet, the government is ill-equipped to take these steps. There is perhaps no greater impediment to addressing the endemic problems plaguing society than the crushing growth in entitlement spending (particularly health care). This fiscal burden is subverting the scope for federal and state investment in education and starving the country of the investments that—at each stage in U.S. history—have nourished a cycle of innovation and growth that has accrued to the benefit of all. The current approach to retirement funding is nothing less than a dramatic intergenerational transfer. To take only one example, the Medicare funding formulas mean that male recipients only paid a dollar for every three received. Because they live longer, the discrepancy is even greater for women.

Without meaningful reform of these sorts of spending patterns, we are tilting our priorities toward consumption at the expense of investment. We are, simply put, forfeiting our capacity to invest in the next generation, in the capacity to create and converse and experiment and innovate. Ironically, universities are better positioned than most institutions to drive the innovations that will bend the health care cost curve, at the very moment when health care costs are leading to disinvestment. Unless and until the core issue of intergenerational equity and, more specifically, entitlement reform is addressed squarely by government, the likelihood that either the federal or state governments will be able to resume their vanguard role in ensuring the next stage of the great American experiment with higher education is dim indeed.

PART V: CONCLUSION

Since the founding of the republic, universities have been a powerful force for upward social mobility and forward economic progress, just as the state has been a powerful force in building and shaping the modern university. For much of our history, this cooperative arrangement has been at the heart of the American experiment and the American dream.

Nevertheless, it is the thesis of this paper that several forces are conspiring to test the stability and durability of this compact and pose significant risks to the strength of American higher education and to the country as a whole. To some degree, we believe that the preservation of the compact requires a willingness of government and university to adopt more innovative instruments to ensure alignment of universities with well-established public goals. It also requires energetic public leadership that is aimed at preserving (and, indeed, enhancing) the level of state investment in higher education, given the sundry public benefits associated with this sector. But most significantly, we believe that the durability of this compact cannot be isolated from the broader debates and concerns over growing inequality in the country (which were given particular salience by the wrenching economic losses associated with the Great Recession). Simply put, in the absence of a vigorous and systematic approach to the challenge of income equality in a human capital society, the more likely it is that universities will be saddled with the symbolic burdens associated with the failure to live up to the Jeffersonian ideals of equal opportunity. This is a lesson that stakeholders in modern research universities ignore at their peril.

Internationalization: Its Central Role in Higher Education

Foreign Policy Association Medal Acceptance Remarks

Ruth J. Simmons
President, Brown University

Thank you, Noel Lateef, members of the Board of the Foreign Policy Association, distinguished guests. I want to extend to all of you the warmest greetings from the Brown University faculty, staff, students, and trustees.

Let me say that since I was a young girl, I've been entranced with how individuals of good will influence the way that others across the world see their countries. Growing up in the South in the 1950s, under a public policy at odds with what I knew to be fair and just, I marveled at the fact that from outside our country, there were voices of comfort and reason questioning our nation's social policies. It was the actions of such people, at home and abroad, that encouraged me to imagine a time when our nation's domestic practices would change.

So rather than accept limitations on where my abilities could take me, I worked to improve my mind and to learn about the mysterious world outside of my segregated neighborhood. I also began to believe that the world would be considerably improved if concern for others were broader than our immediate neighborhood.

At age 17, I set off to Mexico to learn Spanish and live with a Mexican family. That was a difficult but stimulating experience, and it instilled in me a lifelong interest in continuing this wonderful journey around the world to deepen my understanding of how to positively affect human relations.

I subsequently added French to my course of study and traveled to France the following year with the Experiment in International Living. Such organizations make it possible. Think about it: Here's a kid from Houston's inner city who, with no resources whatsoever, stumbles upon organizations like the Experiment and, magically, is transformed outside of this environment.

I decided there could be nothing better than this, so I chose to major in languages. My decision to focus on languages made a good deal of intellectual sense to me. But at the same time, choosing language study was an act of defiance and a fitting response to the narrowness and insularity that segregation bred.

To choose international study was to break the color line, to overturn career restrictions, and to learn without the weight of cultural stigma. Because of that choice, it has been my great fortune to have a career in which, at every turn, involvement in world cultures and affairs has been not only possible, but central to my daily work.

Universities have gone a long way in improving their approach to internationalization, and I'm delighted. When I first started my career, all of us internationalists were sort of shoved off to the side.

Today, internationalization occupies a central role in our universities. I think that's a very good thing. Even with our increasingly ambitious international goals, there's still an enormous amount we must all do to ensure our interest in and commitment to world affairs results in the kind of global equilibrium that increases the potential for stability, peace and prosperity.

In university life, I'm proud to say, where the sharing of knowledge across borders is widely acknowledged and accepted, and where modern tools greatly facilitate shared learning, scholarship and research, there is great hope and growing evidence that we can make a major contribution to that equilibrium through access to learning.

Mindful of the time, I'm going to skip to the end of my comments. There's so much I could tell you about Brown. It is a wonderful place because our students are so involved in international life and because they believe passionately that it is their duty to be involved and to be knowledgeable about world affairs. I'm very proud of that.

I think universities will continue their important work in crossing borders. But I hope we can also increasingly extend this work to inner cities and remote areas, to minorities and working-class men and women because they too will help to elect and shape leaders. They too will prepare their children to embrace or forsake global understanding. They too hold the key to advancing our cause.

The participation of all citizens in world affairs could not be more urgent than in these troubled and volatile times. I'm especially pleased to stand in this endeavor with you who are here this evening.

THE AMERICAN
UNIVERSITY TODAY

Vartan Gregorian
President, Carnegie Corporation of New York
and former President, Brown University

L et me begin by noting that the American university is incomparably the most democratic in the world. It's popular in the best sense of the term, admitting and educating unprecedented numbers of men and women of every race and socioeconomic background. Students from every corner of the world—and here I speak for myself, as well—have found a place in the nation's incredible variety of colleges and universities, public or private, large or small, secular or sectarian, urban or rural, residential or commuter. Today there are more than 3,600 colleges and universities in the United States, including some 1,400 public and private two-year institutions.

U.S. colleges and universities enroll more than 19 million students and annually grant nearly 3 million degrees. Higher education employs more than 3.6 million people, including 2.6 million faculty, in what amounts to a more than $380 billion business.

The diversity of our education system gives it strength, great strength. Individual institutions have traditionally emphasized different functions that have complemented each other by addressing different local, regional, national, and international needs. They also provide educational opportunities to diverse populations by expanding scientific and technical knowledge, providing opportunities for continuing education, and also opening their doors to the world. Until several years ago, two-thirds of all students from foreign countries studying abroad were in the United States; two-thirds of the entire international student body that went abroad studied in the United States.

In the last century, enrollment in American higher education grew from 4 percent of the college-age population in 1900 to almost 70 percent by the year 2000. Our student body, moreover, is incredibly diverse. Following a long period of little or no growth in total enrollment, the nation's institutions of higher education are now seeing the biggest growth spurt since the baby boom generation arrived on campus in 1960.

Between 1995 and 2015, enrollments are expected to increase 16 percent, and one-third of the increase will be members of minority groups. By 2015, minority enrollment is anticipated to rise by almost 30 percent to 2 million in absolute numbers, representing almost 38 percent of undergraduate education.

Clearly there is a strong case to be made for the fact that American higher education is a vital and successful endeavor. But let me take a few moments here to review its history and highlight several aspects of higher education in the United States in order to understand the underpinnings of its success.

The first major opportunity for the expansion of American higher education came in 1862. Even in the middle of the Civil War, and despite the fact that 500,000 people died in the greatest tragedy of American history, President Abraham Lincoln enacted the Morrill Act, which established land-grant universities throughout the United States. The Morrill Act coincided with the Industrial Revolution, and it helped to establish universities just about everywhere the people of the United States were, and where they needed institutions of higher education that addressed their particular needs. Some of our current universities grew from these roots, such as the University of California, Irvine, which deals with agriculture; in Wisconsin, the state university includes a focus on the fact that the dairy industry is important; in Minnesota, the mining industry, and on and on. Because of the needs of the state, the resources of states were tapped at the time and folded into the educational curriculum.

The second most important revolution that happened, in addition to land-grant universities—which, by the way, have produced, since their inception, some 20 million degrees—was the establishment of the National Academy of Sciences. Again, it is remarkable to note that President Lincoln had such faith in the strength and continuity of the U.S. that, in 1863, while the Civil War raged on, he signed another piece of landmark legislation—a law that created the National Academy of Sciences. The Academy, which was established to advise Congress on "any subject of science or art," has done that job well and expanded to include the National Research Council, the National Academy of Engineering, and the Institute of Medicine.

It was not until World War II, though, that the federal government began supporting university research in a significant way. Prior to that, research was done in Europe and in corporate laboratories. To strengthen U.S. growth in science, President Franklin Roosevelt established a commission headed by Vannevar Bush, a former professor at the Massachusetts Institute of Technology. The landmark report was published in 1945 and adopted by President Truman. In this piece, a beautiful report entitled *Science: The Endless Frontier*, Bush noted that the business of industry naturally took the lead in applied research but was deterred by marketplace considerations from conducting pure research. Bush argued that it was the federal government's responsibility to provide adequate funds for basic research, which pioneers the frontiers of human knowledge for the benefit of society. He also wrote that the nation's universities were, by their very nature, best suited to take the lead in conducting basic research. Public funding, he said, would promote competition among researchers, and projects could be selected on the merits through a peer review process. Bush suggested a federal agency should oversee the program, and Congress created the National Science Foundation to do the job in 1950.

The agency got off to a slow start, but after October 1957, when Sputnik was launched, support for science, science education, and basic research rose rapidly. From 1960 to 1966, federal spending on research not associated with defense leapt from $6 billion a year to almost $35-$40 billion. Until recent years, federal investment in research rarely fell below $20 billion a year, and much of this money went to universities. Giving the universities—that's the difference—giving the universities the lead in basic research turned out to be a brilliant policy. Instead of being centralized in government laboratories, as science tended to be in other parts of the world, scientific research became decentralized in American universities. This policy spurred a tremendous diversity of investment. It also gave graduate students significant research opportunities and helped spread scientific discoveries far and wide for the benefit of industry, medicine, and society as a whole.

Another revolutionary phase in American higher education came about in 1944 and was known as the GI Bill of Rights. This legislation ranks up there in importance with the Morrill Act because the law, enacted at the height of World War II, opened the doors of America's best colleges and universities to tens of thousands of veterans returning from the battlefields, ordinary Americans who had never dreamt of going to college and who were now actually being encouraged to do so by their government. The G.I. Bill made an already democratic system of higher education even more democratic in ways that were simply inconceivable in Europe and other parts of the world. In the following decades, the GI Bill—and its legislative offspring enacted during the wars in Korea and Vietnam, and now Iraq and Afghanistan—has resulted in the public investment of more than $60 billion in education and training for about 18 million veterans, including 8.5 million in higher education. Currently, the United States offers an education benefit as an incentive for people to join its all-voluntary military forces.

Shortly after World War II, in 1946, Congress also created the prestigious Fulbright scholarships, which all of you are familiar with and which have been enormously successful. All in all, there have been some 235,000 American and foreign Fulbright scholars—146,000 alone from countries other than the U.S. The program was created, by the way, as one of the best ways of investing in international education.

In 1947, the democratization of higher education was advanced when the President's Commission on Higher Education recommended that public education be made available up to the 14th grade, thus opening the door to the development of community colleges, or two-year colleges, which are now playing a major role in American higher education but also pointing to some of the problems I will discuss later.

In a more recent effort to promote international cooperation and security, Congress enacted the National Security Act of 1991, which provides scholarships for undergraduates and graduate students to study many of the less well-known languages and cultures in key regions of the world, including East Asia, Central Asia, and the Middle East, not to mention Eastern Europe, the former Soviet Union, and Africa.

Another major landmark was the creation of federal loan grant guarantees and subsidy programs, as well as outright grants for college students. In the decades since its founding in 1965, the Federal Family Education Loan Program has funded more than 74 million student loans worth more than $180 billion. And in the years since the 1973 Pell Grant program—named after Senator Claiborne Pell—was created, more than $100 billion in grants has been awarded to an estimated 30 million postsecondary students.

Last but not least, let me add something important about Pell grants:

When they were proposed, there was a big debate about whether to give the money to university presidents or to give it directly to students so the funds would be portable. It was decided—in fact, Clark Kerr of the University of California, who led the Carnegie Commission on Higher Education, recommended—that the money be designated as portable by students, because this would create competition among universities. Many of Clark Kerr's friends stopped talking to him after that recommendation, including his president. Thus, we can see that land-grant universities, the National Academy of Sciences, the GI Bill, Pell grants, and a host of other innovative strategies for advancing American higher education and increasing access to colleges and universities played a major role in enriching and expanding American education at the college and university level.

Naturally, the civil rights movement in the United States and the end of formal, legal discrimination also contributed to advancing higher education and educational access. In this connection, I should mention that my late friend, the noted sociologist David Riesman, said that the greatest contribution to the American economy in the post-war period was the liberation of women. He was right, because today almost 54-58 percent of students enrolled in American higher education are women, and that, along with the advancement of minorities—especially Asians and African Americans—is truly revolutionary.

Now let me turn to the problems facing American higher education. There are many things I can talk about. Problem number one is that when there was no competition, America could afford duplication in its higher education. The nation could afford to have thousands of colleges and universities because they provided educated leaders and skilled labor, but at the same time, unskilled workers—those who could not afford higher education or even dropped out of school—could still find jobs in manufacturing and so on. But today that's not the case. So duplication in education is no longer affordable, and quality has become very important and a key to competition among educational institutions.

Perhaps the second most important problem is the state of public universities, which, as I indicated earlier, were created to be funded by public sources. Private institutions had to rely on private sources, on philanthropy. And parenthetically, ladies and gentlemen, as you know, philanthropy is a big deal in the United States. Annually, some $350 billion in philanthropic giving is disbursed by Americans, and not only by the rich; 70 percent of this sum comes from families with incomes of less than $100,000 a year. Giving has become an American phenomenon. Even during presidential campaigns and debates, candidates now have to reveal the amounts of their philanthropic giving, because otherwise they will be known as being stingy, being cheapskates.

But now the barriers between public and private funding of universities have all but disappeared. Both private and public universities seek support from private sources as well as from the public, with one major difference: When I came as a freshman to Stanford University, in 1956, tuition and fees were $750 at Stanford and $50 at the University of California, Berkeley. Now all the costs have gone astronomically high. Colleges and universities have to keep up with inflation and support the costs of laboratories, technology, stocking their libraries, building and maintaining dormitories and other facilities, paying for athletics, paying for health and other types of insurance, providing health, food, counseling and other services, paying for legal and government affairs and public affairs departments, etc. In short, universities nowadays are like city-states. But what has changed over the years is that individual states can no longer afford, by themselves, to pay for public higher education. For example, I am told that today only 8 or 9 percent of the funding needed for the University of Michigan comes from the state of Michigan; in Missouri, it is 9-10 percent; Maryland, 9-10 percent, etc. The rest has to come from tuition, fees, federal research grants, federal loans and grants, as well as philanthropy, which was not how the system of supporting public higher education was supposed to work.

In addition, when Pell grants were inaugurated, there were two components: loans and outright grants. As time has passed, the proportion of loans and grants has changed so that today, more loans are given than grants. Hence, students often have to borrow money to pay back the loans, and if they are unable to pay their debts or go into bankruptcy as a result of their debt burden, this will adversely affect their future, including their ability to find jobs and advance in their careers. If, on the other hand, they take jobs with low pay and because of their low salaries remain unable to pay their loans, it discourages some people from embarking on careers where the financial rewards are not great but the mission is important to society and the nation. As a former teacher myself, I have first-hand experience of that type of situation. If you become a teacher with a $30,000-a-year salary and you have to pay $6,000–$10,000 a year for your college debt, especially if you get a higher degree, that's a very serious challenge.

Yet another problem that we face is universities of uneven quality, because we don't have a national accrediting system: We have a regional accrediting system. In the absence of a steady flow of public and private funds, many higher education institutions rely on increased levels of enrollment as a way of meeting their budgets. This, naturally, affects quality. In addition, universities, by necessity, incur financial aid obligations, which they sometimes cannot fully meet because the more students they enroll, the more financial aid they have to provide. This situation is worsened by the fact that now, there is a new, major enterprise competing for students: proprietary, primarily for-profit organizations, along with online institutions such as Phoenix University and others, which have access to federal loans. These entities are expanding their reach exponentially. Currently, the U.S. Congress is investigating why a disproportionate amount of Pell grants are going to proprietary and online schools. Some argue that Pell grants should not go to these institutions at all, but those who want specific kinds of job training, such as beauticians and various kinds of technicians and so forth, argue that they should have access to the same kind of funding sources as other students.

So these are some of the problems. But there is still another that is among the most important of all, and that is the following: We all agree that what makes universities great is the quality of their faculties. I have always believed that the faculty is the bone marrow of the university. Students come and go, administrators come and go—even visionary leaders, though they be few and far between, come and go—but a university's faculty provides continuity. In that connection, the challenge is that many universities cannot afford to maintain or recruit high-quality faculty, nor can they have the same number of top-level faculty that they did in the past. As a result, they resort to replenishing their ranks with adjunct and part-time faculty. Part-time faculty size has increased from 22 to almost 40 percent in many universities, making the overall quality of their faculty questionable. I'm not referring to the Harvards, Princetons, Yales and others of that rank; I'm talking about those small colleges and public universities that cannot afford to maintain an excellent faculty roster and so must rely on part-timers in order to preserve themselves during difficult financial times. Remember, when you have part-time faculty, you save money, because you don't have to give them offices or provide benefits or sabbaticals or other types of resources. It's almost like piece-work is being introduced into higher education.

In addition, naturally, during times of financial crisis such as we find ourselves in now, another challenge that arises is that there is a growing impulse to do what is expedient, such as reducing the number of academic units required to graduate. Hence, I am not surprised that once again there are voices raised, asking, Why can't the time required for a B.A. and other degrees be reduced to three years? After all, some say, Oxford started with four years and then reduced it to three. Harvard copied the four-year system, and it has been with us since the beginning of the higher education system in the U.S., but why does it have to remain that way? Let's reduce it. Quality, depth and richness of education don't seem to factor into these suggestions.

This brings me to what may be the core crisis facing higher education today, and that is the onslaught of information that now accosts almost every human being in our borderless, always tuned in, always connected and interconnected globalized world. Perhaps nowhere is this flood of information more apparent than in the university—particularly in the United States. Never mind that much of the information is irrelevant to us and unusable. No matter, it still just keeps arriving in the form of books, monographs, periodicals, websites, instant messages, social networking sites, films, DVDs, blogs, podcasts, emails, satellite and cable television shows and news programs, and the constant chirping of our Blackberries and smart phones—which, by the way, I hope you have turned off, if just for now!

While it is true that attention to detail is the hallmark of professional excellence, it is equally true that an overload of undigested facts is a sure recipe for mental gridlock. Not only do undigested facts not constitute structured knowledge, but, unfortunately, the current explosion of information is also accompanied by its corollary pitfalls, such as obsolescence and counterfeit knowledge.

And if you will indulge me for sacrificing the English language for a moment, another phenomenon we are confronting is the "Wikipediazation" of knowledge and education. At least in part, this is a result of the fact that we are all both givers and takers when it comes to running the machinery of the Information Age, particularly the virtual machinery. I am talking, of course, about the Internet. Let me tell you about a notorious event involving Wikipedia that has come to represent how easily false information can virally infect factual knowledge. What has come to be known as the Seigenthaler Incident began in 2005 when a false biography of the noted journalist Robert Seigenthaler, Sr., who was also an assistant to Robert Kennedy when he was attorney general in the 1960s, was posted on Wikipedia. Among the scurrilous "facts" in the biography was: "For a short time, [Seigenthaler] was thought to have been directly involved in the Kennedy assassinations of both John, and his brother, Bobby. Nothing was ever proven."

This horrendous misinformation—represented as truth—existed on Wikipedia for 132 days before Seigenthaler's son, also a journalist, happened upon it and called his father. Seigenthaler, Sr. then had Wikipedia remove the hoax biography, but not before the same false facts had migrated to many other sites. Probably somewhere in the estimated 30 billion online pages, it still exists. Wikipedia has taken steps to address this problem, but estimates are that there may be somewhere around two million distinct sites on the Internet, with more being created all the time, and there is no central authority, no group, individual or organization to oversee the accuracy of the information they purvey.

Clearly, therefore, one of the greatest challenges facing our society and contemporary civilization is how to distinguish between information—which may be true, false, or some tangled combination of both—and real knowledge. And further, how is knowledge transformed into the indispensable nourishment of the human mind: genuine wisdom? As T. S. Eliot said, "Where is the wisdom we have lost in knowledge? Where is the knowledge we have lost in information?"

Today's universities—along with our colleges, libraries, learned societies and our scholars—have a great responsibility to help provide an answer to Eliot's questions. More than ever, these institutions and individuals have a fundamental historical and social role to play in ensuring that, as a society, we provide not just *training* but *education*, and not just *education* but *culture* as well, and that we teach students how to distill the bottomless cornucopia of information that is ceaselessly spilled out before them 24 hours a day, seven days a week, into knowledge that is relevant, useful, and reliable and that will enrich both their personal and professional lives.

This is not an easy task, especially in a nation where, as Susan Jacoby writes in her recent book, *The Age of American Unreason*, the "scales of American history have shifted heavily against the vibrant and varied intellectual life so essential to functional democracy. During the past four decades, America's endemic anti-intellectual tendencies have been grievously exacerbated by a new species of semiconscious anti-rationalism, feeding on and fed by an ignorant popular culture of video images and unremitting noise that leaves no room for contemplation or logic. This new form of anti-rationalism, at odds not only with the nation's heritage of eighteenth-century Enlightenment reason but with modern scientific knowledge, has propelled a surge of anti-intellectualism capable of inflicting vastly greater damage than its historical predecessors inflicted on American culture and politics."

What Jacoby so forcefully points out is that ignorance is absolutely *not* bliss when both the strength of our democracy and the future of our society are at stake. And it may well be, for not only are we distracted and overwhelmed by the explosion of images, news, rumor, gossip, data, information and knowledge that bombard us every day, we also face dangerous levels of fragmentation of knowledge, dictated by the advances of science, learning, and the accumulation of several millennia of scholarship. Writing about the fragmentation of knowledge and the advent of specialization, it was not so long ago that Max Weber criticized the desiccated narrowness and the absence of spirit of the modern specialist. It was also this phenomenon that prompted Dostoevsky to lament in *The Brothers Karamazov* about the scholars who "have only analyzed the parts and overlooked the whole and, indeed, their blindness is marvelous!" In the same vein, José Ortega y Gasset, in his *Revolt of the Masses*, as early as the 1930s decried the "barbarism of specialization." Today, he wrote, we have more scientists, scholars and professional men and women than ever before, but fewer cultivated ones. To put the dilemma in 21st-century terms, I might describe this as everybody doing their own thing, but nobody really understanding what anybody else's thing really is.

Unfortunately, the university, which was conceived of as embodying the unity of knowledge, has become an intellectual multiversity. The process of both growth and fragmentation of knowledge underway since the 17th century has accelerated in our time and only continues to intensify. The modern university consists of a tangle of specialties and sub-specialties, disciplines and sub-disciplines, within which specialization continues apace. The unity of knowledge has collapsed. The scope and the intensity of specialization are such that scholars and scientists have great difficulty in keeping up with the important yet overwhelming amount of scholarly literature of their own sub-specialties, not to mention their general disciplines. Even the traditional historical humanistic disciplines have become less and less viable as communities of discourse. As the late Professor Wayne C. Booth put it wistfully in a Ryerson Lecture he gave more than twenty years ago that still, sadly, sounds like breaking news from the education front: "Centuries have passed since the fateful moment…when the last of the Leonardo da Vincis could hope to cover the cognitive map. [Now] everyone has been reduced to knowing only one or two countries on the intellectual globe…. [In our universities] we continue to discover just what a pitifully small corner of the cognitive world we live in."

In that regard, I would add that this fragmentation of knowledge into more and more rigid, isolated areas is contributing to a kind of lopsidedness in the way education is organized and a growing disconnect between value-centered education and the kind of training that is aimed specifically at career preparation. What is hopeful is that there is a growing realization among the leaders of the nation's higher education sector that this lopsided system of education is both deficient and dangerous, that we need a proper balance between preparation for careers and the cultivation of values, that general and liberal education is the thread that ought to weave a pattern of meaning into the total learning experience, that unless such a balance is restored, career training will be ephemeral in applicability and delusive in worth; and value education will be casual, shifting and relativistic. I strongly believe that one of the great strengths of American higher education is that it is home for liberal arts education, which is a sound foundation for all the professions and professional schools.

In the words of Albert Einstein, "It is essential that the student acquire an understanding of a lively feeling for values. He or she must acquire a vivid sense of the beautiful and the morally good. Otherwise he or she—with his or her specialized knowledge—more closely resembles a well-trained dog than a harmoniously developed person." That is why I believe, and every year, whether I was a dean, president or provost of a university, I always reminded incoming freshmen to remember the famous line in Sheridan's *The Critic* (1799): "The number of those who undergo the fatigue of judging for themselves is very small indeed." It is the task of higher education to increase the number of those who do undergo that fatigue.

To sum up, it seems to me that by trying to reduce the requirements for a degree and at the same time expecting to be able to break down education into specialized parts—each part swollen to overflowing with endlessly and exponentially increasing amounts of data and information—we are going in absolutely the wrong direction. Why? Because all this pushing and pulling and compartmentalizing presupposes that somehow one's education will eventually be finished, that it will come to an end and an individual can say, "Now I've graduated, and I don't have to learn anymore." But, of course, you never graduate from your life, and hence, you never really graduate from learning. One's "formal" education is really just an introduction to learning, where the skills to go on educating oneself are acquired and inculcated into everyday life—because learning is a lifelong endeavor. In that connection, when I was president of Brown, one day I decided, as a joke or as an ironic act, to propose awarding two kinds of degrees, one certifying that you know the following subjects, the other one certifying the subjects that you know, but most thought it was a crazy idea because parents would say, "We paid you to educate our sons and daughters and, instead, you're giving us an uneducated person." So I decided that we'd just say the B.A. degree was, as I've described above, an introduction to learning, an undertaking that must be carried on throughout all the years of one's life.

In order to further make my point about lifelong learning, let me share this one last story with you. Some years ago, when asked to give a major speech to an illustrious gathering at Southern Methodist University, instead of a speech, I gave an exam. I said, "Imagine that you are the last person on Earth. Nothing is left, no monuments, no other human beings, no libraries, no archives, and hence, you are the best-educated person on the planet. Suddenly, the Martians land, and they want to debrief you, the last human being standing, so they can preserve the history of humanity and the civilizations of the planet Earth. They begin by asking you questions such as: "We heard that you had some objects that could fly, but that's such an antiquated mode of transportation, so can you explain to us the principles by which these objects were made to fly? After all, your society awarded Ph.Ds and MDs and all kinds of other degrees to people like yourself, so can you just prepare a schematic for us about these flying things? And we also heard that you had some kind of ships that could travel under water, but how was that possible? We also heard that you were able to phone each other, and despite mountains and oceans and so forth, you could talk to each other across thousands of miles; how did that work? And, yes, we'd also like to have the maps of all the continents, so can you draw them for us? Please include all the nations along with rivers, counties, capitals, and so forth. After all, we understand that you are an educated person, so these things should be easy for you."

Then I said to the gathering, still speaking on behalf of the head Martian, "There's another subject we Martians want to know about. We have a long list of the names of the religions that people on Earth followed, and they were well-represented in the United States. We don't quite understand the differences between these religions and why you argued about them century after century. Here is just part of the list we have: Hinduism, Islam, Judaism, Jainism, Sikhism, Shinto, Confucianism, the Baha'i faith, and then the different forms of Christianity: Catholics, Protestants, Baptists, Southern Baptists, Lutherans, Pentecostals, Evangelicals, Amish, Mormons, Jehovah's Witnesses, Seventh Day Adventists, Greek Orthodox, Eastern Orthodox, and Russian Orthodox. Could you please pick five of these and tell us where they agree and where they disagree?" Of course, there was dead silence in the audience. So I concluded my "exam" by saying, "I thank you for not being the last man or woman on Earth, because education is a life-long experience and endeavor, and I believe you might have some catching up to do!" In a way, perhaps, we all have constant "catching up" to do when it comes to finding ways to address the many challenges facing our colleges and universities. But we will find them, I am sure, because in the words of Henry Rosovsky, the economist and educator, in "higher education, 'made in America' is still the finest label." We all should have a hand in ensuring that continues to be true.

Endnotes

1. Humphries, Debra and Patrick Kelly. "How Liberal Arts and Sciences Majors Fare in Employment: A Report on Earnings and Long-term Career Paths." Association of American Colleges and Universities. 22 January 2014.

2. Marcus, Jon. "Humanities Majors Don't Fare as Badly as Portrayed, New Earnings Report Says." *HuffPost College*. www.huffingtonpost.com. 22 January 2014.

3. Humphries and Kelly.

4. Einstein, Albert and Max Born. *The Born-Einstein Letters 1916–1955* (London: MacMillan Press Ltd., 1971/2005).

5. Aoun, Joseph. "To Meet President Obama's Job Goal, Involve All Colleges." *Bloomberg Business*. www.bloomberg.com. 29 January 2014.

6. Delbanco, Andrew. *College: What It Was, Is, and Should Be*. (Princeton: Princeton University Press, 2012).

7. Delbanco.

THE AMERICAN UNIVERSITY AND THE GLOBAL AGENDA

Richard Levin
President, Yale University

Thank you, Michael [Reisman], for that very kind introduction. It's a great pleasure to be with you this evening and an honor to address members and guests of the Foreign Policy Association—an association that leads the way in promoting international understanding. I thank you for the opportunity.

I am an economist by training and profession. Years ago, in addition to teaching survey courses in microeconomics and industrial organization, I also taught courses such as "Political Economy of Oil" and "International Competitiveness of U.S. Manufacturing," reflecting a longstanding interest in the politics and economics of world affairs. Now I see these issues from the dual perspective of international economist and university president.

I suspect that you are not often inclined to put universities and foreign policy into the same sentence. So let me offer you a provocative hypothesis: namely, that the American research university is a highly effective instrument of U.S. foreign policy. It would be an even more effective instrument if our political leaders understood fully what a unique and powerful asset our country has in its great universities. I am going to state the case in six parts.

First, America's power, both hard and soft, derives from the strength of its economy, the current credit crunch notwithstanding. The strength of our economy depends in large part on our leadership in science, which in turn depends upon the strength of our research universities.

Second, the strength of our economy also derives from our capacity to innovate, which in turn depends upon the kind of education that America's top universities and liberal arts colleges provide.

Third, U.S. research universities are magnets for the most outstanding students from around the world. Those students either stay here or they go home. America wins either way. If foreign graduates stay, they strengthen the productive capacity of the U.S. economy. If they go home, they increase the capacity of their home economies, but they also serve as ambassadors for America and as advocates for openness, freedom of expression, and democracy.

Fourth, our nation's great universities are increasingly ensuring that American students gain exposure to the culture and values of another nation as a part of their educational experience. This offers the hope that our future leaders and engaged citizens will have greater global awareness in the future than in the past.

Fifth, our universities have broadened the conception of what constitutes a "student." Today we provide leadership education to specialized audiences around the world, to help them address challenges to global political and economic stability, public health, and the environment.

Finally, with respect to at least one important item on the global agenda—how to respond to the threat of global warming—our universities have become laboratories to demonstrate that solutions are technically possible and economically feasible. Let me discuss each of these points in turn.

LEADERSHIP IN SCIENCE

For decades, America's competitive advantage in global markets has derived from its capacity to innovate—to introduce and develop new products, processes, and services. That capacity depends in large part on America's leadership in science, and the principle locus of scientific advance has been our research universities.

The emergence of universities as America's primary machine for scientific advance did not come about by accident. Rather, it was the product of a wise and farsighted national science policy, set forth in an important 1946 report that established the framework for an unprecedented and heavily subsidized system in support of scientific research that has propelled the American economy. The system rested upon three principles that remain largely intact today. First, the federal government shoulders the principal responsibility for financing basic science. Second, universities—rather than government laboratories, non-teaching research institutes, or private industry—are the primary institutions in which this government-funded research is undertaken. This ensures that scientists-in-training, even those who choose industrial rather than academic careers, are exposed to the most advanced methods and results of research. And, third, although the federal budgetary process determines the total funding available for each of the various fields of science, most funds are allocated not according to commercial or political considerations, but through an intensely competitive process of review conducted by independent scientific experts who judge proposals on their scientific merit alone. This system of organizing science has been an extraordinary success, scientifically and economically.

Oddly enough, for political and cultural reasons, no other nation has successfully imitated the U.S. system of supporting basic science, the source from which all commercially-oriented applied research and development ultimately flows. In Europe, too, much research has been concentrated in national institutes rather than universities, divorcing cutting-edge research from training the next generation of industrial scientists and engineers. And in the U.K. as well as continental Europe and Japan, most research funding has been allocated by block grants to universities or departments, rather than by the intensely competitive process of peer-reviewed grants to individuals and research groups. As a result, our lead in science has been maintained. Even today more than 30 percent of scientific publications worldwide are authored in the U.S., and nearly half the world's Nobel Prizes in science go to Americans.

Our competitive advantage in emerging industries based on science—such as computers in the 1960s, software in the 1990s, and biotechnology today—should not be taken for granted. Yet federal funding in support of basic research has waxed and waned. The budget of the National Institutes of Health (NIH) was doubled between 1998 and 2003, a 14 percent annual rate of growth. For the past five years, the NIH budget has grown at an annual rate of less than 2 percent, failing to keep up with inflation. This means that much of the young talent we trained during the boom cannot get funding today. What we need to succeed as a nation is a steady, predictable growth in basic research at the rate of long-term average growth in GDP. If we do not do this, we are likely to lose our wide lead in biomedical technology, and we will fail to establish ourselves as the world leader in the other major area of emerging importance—alternative energy technologies.

LEADERSHIP IN INNOVATION

Our hard and soft power in foreign affairs depends on the strength of our economy. And the strength of our economy depends not only on having scientific leadership, as I have just argued, but also on our national capacity to translate cutting-edge science into commercially viable technologies. This capacity depends in turn on two principal factors: the availability of financial capital and an abundance of innovative, entrepreneurial human capital. Our highly decentralized financial system, despite its endemic cyclicality, of which we are today painfully aware, has unique advantages in encouraging investment in innovation. Funding for start-up companies in the U.S. is more easily available, and more adequately supported by value-added services, than anywhere else in the world.

And thanks to the kind of higher education we provide, the human capital required for innovation is more abundant and more effective in the U.S. than anywhere else in the world. Why? Because, at our best colleges and universities, we educate students to be creative, flexible, and adaptive problem-solvers, capable of innovation and leadership in science, business, and the professions. We are told constantly that China and India are training more engineers than we are. And it is true that we could and should invest more heavily in science, math, and engineering education at all levels to ensure that our graduates have the technical capacity to succeed. But if you look closely at China and India, you will see that their aspiration is to educate students who are more like ours—students with the capacity to think creatively and independently.

In the modern economy, many successful companies produce products or services based on technology or marketing strategies that didn't exist a decade or two ago. New scientific discoveries are made every day, and new theories displace old ones with relentless regularity. The radical changes in communications technology that we have experienced over the past two decades have opened up whole new industries and destroyed others. In such a world, knowledge of a given body of information is not enough to survive, much less thrive; scientists, business leaders, and government officials alike must have the ability to think critically and creatively and to draw upon and adapt ideas to new environments.

The methods of undergraduate education used by America's most selective universities and liberal arts colleges are particularly well suited to prepare students for a changing world. These institutions are committed to the "liberal education" of undergraduates. The premise underlying the philosophy of liberal education is that students will be best prepared for life if they can assimilate new information and reason through to new conclusions. Since any particular body of knowledge is bound to become obsolete, the object of a contemporary liberal education is not primarily to convey content, but to develop certain qualities of mind: the ability to think independently, to regard the world with curiosity and ask interesting questions, to subject the world to sustained and rigorous analysis, to use where needed the perspectives of more than one discipline, and to arrive at fresh, creative answers. While many other cultures favor passive education and technical mastery, we in America gain from a pedagogy that enlarges the power of students to reason, to think creatively, and to respond adaptively.

The elements of that pedagogy are undoubtedly well known to this audience: small classes with ample opportunity for student participation and exams and homework assignments that ask students to weigh conflicting points of view or to solve problems actively, rather than merely reciting facts or the opinions of authorities. For the past four summers, I have led a workshop for the leadership teams of China's top universities. The number one topic on their agenda is how to reform curriculum and pedagogy to reflect the best practices of American universities. Why? Because they see in the products of U.S. education, including those U.S.-educated Chinese who are coming to dominate their own faculties, greater creativity and an enlarged capacity for innovation. China's political leaders are encouraging this effort at university reform, because they recognize that creativity and the capacity to innovate are characteristics that China will need in order to compete when they can no longer rely on a steady stream of low-cost labor migrating from the countryside to industrial employment. It is a sad fact that China's leaders have a more sophisticated understanding of the decisive advantages of U.S. universities than our own political leaders.

EDUCATING INTERNATIONAL STUDENTS

Nearly one-quarter of all students who leave their home countries for higher education abroad come to the United States, and our nation's share of the very best students is much larger. Only the finest universities in the United Kingdom offer serious competition to the best institutions in the United States, although in recent years Australia and Singapore have made significant efforts to compete for strong international students. These countries made substantial gains in the first years after the passage of the Patriot Act, when failure of the Departments of State and Homeland Security to adjust rapidly to new requirements rendered many thousands of students unable to secure visas in time for the start of the academic year.

The problem with student visas has now largely been fixed, thanks to a felicitous high-level intervention. But it is seldom appreciated in policy circles how much America gains from this inflow of international students.

Nearly half of America's Nobel Prize winners in science have been foreign born. In the current debate about immigration policy, almost all the public attention focuses on the inflow of low-income immigrants from Mexico and the Caribbean. Outside Silicon Valley, Seattle, and Route 128, we hear too little about the difficulty our most technologically sophisticated companies are having in attracting sufficient highly skilled scientists and engineers. Much of the outsourcing of R&D undertaken by high tech firms is not driven by cost considerations, as is the outsourcing in manufacturing, back office work, and call centers. Instead, much R&D outsourcing is forced by the absence of qualified, highly skilled engineers and scientists with graduate degrees.

The annual quota for H-1B visas, covering foreign students who seek to remain and work in the U.S. after graduation, has been fixed for years at 85,000, and the annual allocation is typically exhausted within days at the start of each year. Recently, a new rule has extended the period of stay under an H-1B to 29 instead of twelve months. But the number of visas to be allocated has not increased. The demands of high-tech industry have been lost in the contentious debate about the illegal aliens and the immigration of unskilled workers.

There is no doubt that our nation would benefit from retaining more graduate engineers and scientists, and for them there's a simple solution: Scrap the H-1B visa, and staple a green card to the diploma!

As I mentioned before, our universities serve the nation well not only by educating those who stay in our country, but also by educating those who return to their home country. It's true that in some cases, we would gain even more by retaining highly skilled graduates. But it's also true that those who return home typically serve as ambassadors for American values, or at least they understand them. I have already cited one example: The pressures for curriculum reform and critical thinking in China, along with pressures for greater freedom of expression on university campuses, are coming in large measure from those educated in the United States. Again and again, I encounter international students at Yale who tell me that they have been astounded by the degree of openness and intellectual freedom they find in America. And when I travel abroad, I see senior leaders in influential positions whose views of the world have been transformed by their educational experience in the United States.

Sending Our Students Abroad

Increasingly, American universities are also encouraging domestic undergraduates to spend time in another country. Traditional junior-year abroad study programs remain widely available. They attract a large fraction of students at institutions like Dartmouth and Middlebury, but only a modest fraction of undergraduates at Yale. We have responded by offering every undergraduate at least one international study or internship opportunity either during the academic year or during the summer. And we provide the financial resources to make it possible. By mobilizing our alumni around the world, we have created a superb infrastructure of serious summer work internships in seventeen cities: Shanghai, Hong Kong, Singapore, Delhi, Accra, Cape Town, Kampala, Athens, Brussels, Budapest, Istanbul, London, Madrid, Buenos Aires, Joao Pessoa, Montreal, and Monterrey. In addition, we send hundreds abroad every summer for immersion language courses or Yale summer school courses taught at partner institutions. We expect that an increasing number of institutions will follow our lead in making an overseas experience available to every student and, eventually, in making an overseas experience a requirement for the Bachelor's degree.

I believe that a 21st-century liberal education requires not simply the capacity to think critically and independently, but also the capacity to understand how people of different cultures and values think and behave. The world has grown smaller, and nations have become more interdependent. Whatever profession they choose, today's students are likely to have global careers and deal regularly with collaborators or competitors who see the world differently. To be adequately prepared for such careers, exposure to another culture is necessary. And a single meaningful encounter with cross-cultural differences in one's formative years will typically make it possible to learn easily from subsequent encounters with other cultures later in life.

I also believe that providing American students with a meaningful overseas experience is the best way to escape the insularity and parochialism that too often influences American foreign policy. With international exposure, our students will not only become better professionals, but better citizens. By getting more U.S. students abroad, our colleges and universities will create a more informed citizenry and one capable of thinking about foreign policy issues with greater sensitivity and intelligence.

EDUCATING LEADERS TO ADVANCE THE GLOBAL AGENDA

Our universities serve not only those students who enroll full time in courses of study leading to undergraduate, graduate, and professional degrees; they are also increasingly engaged in the provision of short-term executive education. Many institutions, notably the Kennedy School at Harvard, make a substantive contribution to U.S. foreign policy by running short-term and even semester-length courses for foreign government officials. Recently, Yale has initiated a series of multi-disciplinary programs for senior governmental officials from China, India, and Japan. To cover effectively the complexity of the most important global issues, we draw upon faculty from throughout the university—from our professional schools of law, management, forestry and environmental studies, and public health, as well as our departments of economics, political science, and history. The "students" in these programs typically have the rank of vice minister or, in the case of India and Japan, member of parliament.

Education programs such as these have very high impact, because we are working with students who already occupy positions of significant power and influence. Even at America's finest universities, only a small fraction of our regularly enrolled students turn out to have a significant influence on the affairs of the nation and the world.

Such high-level programs have an effect similar to that of "track two" diplomacy, informal interaction among senior government officials. Only here the contact is not government-to-government, but U.S. experts-to-foreign governments. Even if the views of our academic experts do not always align with the position of our government, the foreign ministers and parliamentarians who attend these programs leave with a deeper understanding of American perspectives.

LEADING BY EXAMPLE

Let me point to one final, idiosyncratic way in which American universities can assist our nation in addressing the global agenda. The problem of global warming cries out for a multinational solution: reducing carbon emissions in a way that is equitable and efficient. Developing nations like China and India fear that serious limits on greenhouse gas emissions will unfairly constrain their future growth. Skeptics in the U.S. fear that controlling carbon will impose a large cost on our economy as well. And yet all recognize that if we collectively fail to take action, future generations will likely face much larger costs from economic dislocation and environmental destruction.

Universities have an important role in the effort to curtail global warming. Much of the work on climate science that has led to the detection and understanding of climate change was done within our walls, and we have been at the forefront of modeling the economic, social, and environmental impact of rising global temperatures and sea levels. We will also participate in developing carbon-free technologies such as solar, wind, and geothermal power, as well as in finding more efficient ways to use carbon-based fuels.

More recently, universities have begun to play a different role, taking the lead in setting standards for carbon emissions that are substantially more restrictive than those adopted by national governments. In 2005, Yale made a commitment to reduce carbon emissions to 10 percent below the 1990 level by 2020, which translates to a 43 percent reduction in our 2005 carbon footprint. This is a reduction in the range of what will be needed to keep global temperatures from rising more than 2 degrees centigrade by the end of the century. It is an ambitious goal. If the nations of the world were to negotiate a reduction of this magnitude in Copenhagen in 2009, we would be taking a giant step toward saving the planet.

And here's the good news. We believe that a reduction of this magnitude is not only possible but also relatively inexpensive. We estimate that we can achieve this goal at a cost of less than 1 percent of our annual operating budget, perhaps no more than one-half of 1 percent.

We have made this commitment because we believe that in so doing, we are being faithful to our mission as a teaching institution. We are leading by example. We have encouraged our sister institutions in the Ivy League to join us in setting a specific goal for reducing carbon emissions. And we are working on eliciting similar commitments from our nine partners in the International Alliance of Research Universities and from the 34 Chinese universities with which we have been working on curriculum reform and other issues over the past four years.

We have no illusion that the collective action of universities will have a measurable impact on global carbon emissions. But we do hope that our action will inspire others to believe that significant carbon reduction is feasible and not exceedingly costly. In leading by example, we hope to make a global carbon compact more likely.

CONCLUSION

Let me recapitulate. I have argued that America's universities are a highly effective instrument of U.S. foreign policy because they:

- Have given America decisive leadership in science;

- Educate students with the capacity to innovate;

- Educate international students who strengthen our nation by staying here or serving as ambassadors when they return home;

- Give U.S. students a deeper understanding of foreign nations and cultures;

- Prepare international leaders to tackle the global agenda; and

- Demonstrate solutions to global problems.

PRINCETON
IN THE WORLD

Shirley M. Tilghman
President, Princeton University

Christopher L. Eisgruber
Provost, Princeton University

Everyone is talking about globalization, and it is easy to understand why. People, products, information, capital, cultural artifacts, social trends, pollutants, and pathogens are all circulating throughout the world with dizzying speed. Domains from business to the arts, from politics to medicine, are becoming more intensely and self-consciously international than ever before. Local knowledge and regional differences remain important, of course. Yet, it is almost impossible to imagine how any contemporary community or ecosystem could be like the Galapagos Islands of Darwin's day, wholly buffered against influences from the outside world. Today, local traits and customs mix with and define themselves in relation to global forces and patterns of activity.

To flourish in this environment, Princeton—and, indeed, America's universities and colleges more generally—will have to find ways to meet the challenges of internationalization. Students will have to be knowledgeable about, and comfortable interacting with, cultures different from their own. Researchers will have to become more attentive to international issues and more sensitive to the international dimensions of domestic problems. Faculty will have to recognize that their potential collaborators and rivals will come from not only familiar institutions in the United States and Europe, but also a host of new, and newly vigorous, universities throughout the world.

Of course, globalization has been going on for a very long time, and so has Princeton's response to it. For example, the establishment of the Woodrow Wilson School for Public and International Affairs in 1930 specifically underscored the importance of international relations to the university's mission. More recently, when the university revised its unofficial motto in 1996 from "Princeton in the Nation's Service" to "Princeton in the Nation's Service and in the Service of All Nations," it did so to recognize that Princeton could not be a great teaching and research university unless it incorporated an international dimension into its mission. All of these changes, and the ones recommended here, reinforce Princeton's special role as a distinctively American university: They recognize that, in order to be a great American university, Princeton must integrate the national and international domains into a cohesive educational enterprise.

The accelerating speed of change in the world means that we must continually assess and enhance our effectiveness in the ways we engage the world. In 2003, after reviewing reports from an internal faculty committee and an outside review committee, we concluded that an integrated approach to international and regional studies was needed so that faculty taking global approaches to issues, such as trade and global governance, could benefit from the thinking of others who focus on specific regions of the world, and vice versa. The Princeton Institute for International and Regional Studies (PIIRS) grew out of these deliberations, with its mission to conduct collaborative, interdisciplinary research and teaching projects that help to integrate international relations and regional studies approaches. With the benefit of energetic leadership from its founding director, Professor Miguel Centeno, and his successor, Professor Katherine Newman, PIIRS is catalyzing new and exciting work in these fields.

If Princeton is to participate fully in the challenges and opportunities that await us in the years ahead, more changes are needed. Every department in the university, not just those specifically concerned with international topics, has the potential to embrace a more international outlook. For that reason, in 2006–2007 we requested two additional reports about how Princeton could improve its response to globalization. We convened a special faculty committee to prepare a confidential report on the broad topic of how to "develop a set of strategic priorities and specific measures that will enable the university to fully realize [its] aspiration to be an American university with a broad international vision." Jeremy Adelman, the chair of Princeton's Department of History, and Anne-Marie Slaughter, the dean of the Woodrow Wilson School of Public and International Affairs, agreed to chair the Committee, which included faculty members from every division of the university. We also asked Dean of the College Nancy Malkiel and Associate Dean of the College Nancy Kanach for specific recommendations about how Princeton could enhance its study abroad program.

The Adelman-Slaughter Committee and the dean of the college have proposed that Princeton embark on concerted efforts to enhance its international dimensions in ways that preserve and extend the university's traditional strengths. The Adelman-Slaughter Committee articulated a distinctive model of an international scholarly enterprise. The Committee's members envisioned a rich exchange of scholars, students, and ideas across international borders along fluid pathways defined by the research and educational interests of our community, not by inflexible investments in overseas campuses or specific regions of the world. The dean of the college encouraged us to embrace the idea that every Princeton undergraduate should incorporate an international experience into his or her Princeton career. These recommendations chart a course that Princeton must pursue if it aspires to sustain or enhance its standing in the world and provide excellence in teaching and research that will make a real difference in the decades ahead. We are pleased to endorse these proposals, and we are delighted to announce that Princeton will immediately begin fundraising to implement them.

PRINCETON'S DISTINCTIVE MISSION

As both the Adelman-Slaughter Committee and Dean Malkiel recognized in their reports, Princeton University has unique characteristics and strengths. In the words of the Committee, "Princeton is an outstanding research university with a deep commitment to superb teaching. It is distinctive in the breadth of its research excellence, the intensity of its engagement with students at all levels, and the close-knit character of its community." Princeton's response to globalization must build upon these attributes. We cannot simply borrow strategies that have been deployed by other American institutions, because we are different in several important ways from our peers. Princeton focuses more on fundamental research and on its undergraduate and doctoral programs, without large professional schools in law, business, and medicine that have played a leading role in international ventures at other American universities. Likewise, Princeton is smaller than many of its peers. Our size facilitates cross-disciplinary collaboration, but it also requires us to choose carefully when we decide what kinds of overseas programs we most want. Another constraint, at the undergraduate level, is Princeton's required independent work—junior papers and a senior thesis— that limit students' choices for study abroad. Perhaps most importantly, Princeton's ethos nurtures and depends upon a rich and demanding form of community. We insist that our faculty be present on the campus and in the classroom, and our students often develop such strong loyalties to the institution that they are reluctant to spend time away from it.

Because of these characteristics, the most successful ventures at Princeton have always been "bottom-up" rather than "top-down." They have emerged out of the scholarly expertise, interests, and passions of our faculty and the educational needs of their students rather than from a centrally designed administrative plan. Not surprisingly, the reports from the Adelman-Slaughter Committee and the dean of the college emphasized the need to stimulate and facilitate faculty-driven proposals to internationalize Princeton's research and teaching agenda. Such efforts will require more work and creativity than a one-size-fits-all university initiative, but that investment will be well justified: The resulting initiatives will be more likely to flourish in Princeton's unique academic culture.

"Networks and Flows"

The Adelman-Slaughter Committee offered a compelling vision for how Princeton can build on its strengths and core values to meet the challenges of globalization. Their recommendations were organized around three basic principles:

- "Internationalization should be nimble and flexible, avoiding heavy sunk costs in institutions." The Committee emphasized that Princeton's tradition is "to facilitate, not regulate." It counseled the university to avoid investments in satellite campuses that might ultimately do more to constrain than to enable valuable scholarly efforts. As the Committee wrote, "in the long run, we will be distinguished more by the research we promote than by our management of institutions that too often outlive their original inspirations."

- "The framework for internationalization should enable and support faculty-driven activity." In the international domain, as elsewhere, Princeton must permit research and teaching priorities to shape the ventures it launches. The Committee rightly observed that "research and exchanges work best at Princeton when the stakeholders are also the initiators and custodians of their efforts." It, accordingly, urged the university to "mobilize latent scholarly resources by encouraging faculty and students to reach out and realize ambitions that would otherwise remain in their filing cabinets or email directories."

- "Internationalization requires an infusion of leadership, resources, and commitment." The Committee called upon the university to raise substantial new funds to support international initiatives. It also highlighted the need for effective governance mechanisms and administrative leadership to ensure that these resources are well deployed and that the university presses forward the "major transformation" of policies needed to realize its international aspirations.

As the Committee noted, these three principles "share a common theme: the importance of investing in Princeton's general capacity for international exchanges and research, rather than concentrating on any particular region, country, or field of research." The Committee called upon the university to encourage "networks and flows" of faculty and students worldwide, lowering the barriers that inhibit our students and faculty from going abroad and scholars from other countries coming to Princeton. By bringing visitors from abroad, the university will nurture relationships between its own faculty members and students and their foreign counterparts. These relationships will lead naturally to research collaborations, and they will enrich the content and impact of the experiences that Princeton undergraduates and graduate students will enjoy when they go abroad. By increasing the "porosity" of the campus through increases in both export and import of people and ideas, we will ensure that Princeton's scholarly energy will be felt throughout the world.

STIMULATING NEW INTERNATIONAL PROJECTS AND PARTNERSHIPS

The Adelman-Slaughter Committee emphasized that if Princeton wishes to generate innovative research and educational projects that address the challenges of globalization, it must make substantial new investments to support such activity. Princeton must take steps to encourage faculty members to think about opportunities to steer their research and teaching in international directions. And it must ensure that when faculty members and graduate students design research projects with an international dimension, they can find institutional support for their efforts. The Committee highlighted several different kinds of resources that it regarded as crucial to the achievement of these goals.

BRINGING INTERNATIONAL VISITORS TO THE PRINCETON FACULTY

The Committee urged Princeton to create a new set of faculty positions that would bring to the campus a distinguished cadre of international scholars who would visit on a recurring basis. These "Global Scholars" would come to Princeton for visits of varying duration: some professors, for example, might come for one semester in each of three consecutive years; other professors might come for a shorter span—say, half a semester—in multiple years. While at Princeton, these professors would be expected to teach or co-teach courses; participate in ongoing workshops; and give at least one public presentation, in a workshop or lecture, each time they visited.

The Committee imagined that "the Global Scholars would bring vital new voices from abroad to our departments and classrooms. In addition, the program would inaugurate and sustain durable ties between Princeton and academic centers of excellence around the world. One faculty member in the humanities described these benefits of exchanges to the Committee: 'More doors would ultimately be opened for us abroad, and our own campus would look and feel and sound a little different, if we made greater room for bringing the best foreign scholars to Princeton.'"

The benefits of the Global Scholars program will be many and lasting. For example, when they return to their home countries, the Global Scholars will help to raise Princeton's profile there. Their visits to Princeton, moreover, will catalyze collaborations that will bring Princeton faculty members, graduate students, and undergraduates overseas. In effect, we will be establishing a vigorous form of academic free trade, in which a robust import policy will go hand-in-hand with a robust export strategy, and ideas will flow freely across international borders. The Committee emphasized that if the international visitors are to play this catalytic role effectively, they must be fully integrated into campus life. For that reason, the Committee insisted that the visitors should return to Princeton for multiple years so that they have a chance to attract a following among students and to build relationships with faculty members.

There is already precedent for the Global Scholars program that gives us confidence that it will have a significant impact on the campus. For example, the School of Architecture has hosted the distinguished Japanese architects Kazuyo Sejima and Ryue Nishizawa for multiple semesters. Likewise, the Department of German has brought Joseph Vogl of the Humboldt University and Juliane Vogel, from the University of Konstanz, to Princeton for multi-year visits. The German Department's visitors have catalyzed exactly the sort of international relationships that the Committee envisioned: Princeton's department is participating in collaborative ventures with both Humboldt and Konstanz.

The Committee recommended that the university aim eventually to have fifteen or more such visitors on campus each year. To achieve that goal, the university will need to provide short-term housing options that make it convenient for leading scholars to visit and live in Princeton. We have asked our executive vice president, Mark Burstein, and our vice president for facilities, Michael E. McKay, to begin evaluating options to meet this need.

FACILITATING INTERNATIONAL FLOWS OF GRADUATE STUDENTS

The Committee highlighted the critical role of graduate education in any plan for internationalizing Princeton. The Committee recognized that Princeton's graduate student body is already remarkably internationally diverse. Princeton should seize opportunities to capitalize on this diversity. The Committee also expressed an expectation that "much of the movement through our research networks will be conducted by younger scholars, post-doctoral fellows, and—especially—graduate students." The Committee counseled Princeton to provide resources to support international research projects of Princeton graduate students and to facilitate visits by foreign graduate students who might come to Princeton to collaborate on research or educational projects. These resources would include travel grants and fellowships for Princeton students who need to extend their term of study to do research abroad; funds to defray the costs of having visiting foreign graduate students; and short-term housing.

CREATING A GLOBAL INITIATIVES FUND TO NURTURE NEW INTERNATIONAL VENTURES

To launch international research and educational projects, faculty members need two kinds of support—financial resources to defray the costs of adding an international component to their research and teaching, and relief from burdensome administrative practices that too often impede foreign collaborations. The Committee recognized that, in general, Princeton's researchers must rely on external funding sources, such as competitive government grants, to support their projects. That principle must apply to international ventures as well as domestic ones, but supplemental funding will be needed. For example, government agencies like the National Institutes of Health do not permit their research training funds to support foreign students and fellows at Princeton.

The Committee described three examples of the kinds of projects that might benefit from the support of a Global Initiatives Fund:

- SEED GRANTS to catalyze important research initiatives based on international collaboration between Princeton faculty and colleagues overseas, with allocations based on peer review.

- SUPPORT FOR GLOBAL NETWORKS that enable Princeton graduate students to spend significant periods in partner institutions abroad conducting research under the guidance of senior foreign faculty who have committed to mentoring them, while reciprocal arrangements encourage faculty from partner institutions to visit Princeton to work in laboratories, present papers, participate in annual conferences, and spend their sabbaticals here.

- TRAVEL SUPPORT that permits our students and faculty to travel together to work for periods of time, ranging from a few weeks to an entire term, in foreign institutions and at field sites.

These categories describe valuable, compelling activities that fit well with Princeton's approach to education and research. However, we should be attentive to the Committee's wise counsel that internationalization at Princeton must be "nimble and flexible" and that we must avoid making dedicated investments in projects or institutions that are likely to "outlive their original inspirations."

For this reason, the newly raised Global Initiatives Funds should be configured to ensure that the university can respond vigorously not only to the specific challenges that globalization poses at the outset of the 21st century, but to ones that we cannot now anticipate but that undoubtedly will arise in the decades ahead. They should be flexible enough to provide needed funding for the Global Scholars Initiative, graduate student exchanges, seed grants for new ventures, global networks, and other ventures that might arise in the near or distant future. We will seek donor support to establish these funds on a permanent basis, but we are pleased to announce that, as a result of the extraordinary support from Princeton's alumni for the 2006–2007 Annual Giving campaign, the university will be able to launch these initiatives immediately with a budget in excess of $1 million per year.

OVERSEEING AND IMPLEMENTING OUR INTERNATIONAL INITIATIVES

The Committee recognized the critical importance of governance and administration to the success of its plan, and it made a number of specific suggestions to ensure that Princeton's efforts at internationalization will have the support they require.

PROVIDING FACULTY LEADERSHIP AND ADVOCACY

The Adelman-Slaughter Committee proposed the creation of a faculty governance board to oversee the university's international initiatives. Though this governing body will neither offer courses nor appoint faculty members, it should enjoy a status comparable to that of the university's major faculty councils, such as the Council on Science and Technology or the Council of the Humanities. Princeton will accordingly create a new Council on International Teaching and Research to continue to design and implement the international initiatives of the university.

The Council's responsibilities will include continuing the strategic planning process begun by the Adelman-Slaughter Committee; overseeing the distribution of new resources to support international visitors and projects; reviewing university policies for establishing international collaborations and partnerships; identifying changes to policies when such amendments are needed to encourage more international activity; and monitoring the university's progress in meeting its international objectives. The Council might also cooperate with other partners, such as department chairs and academic deans, to produce reports or recommendations pertaining to specific topics (such as, for example, language teaching) that are important to the internationalization of the university. Responsibility for the university's study abroad programs and international internships would remain under the auspices of the dean of the college, but the Council might assist the dean's office by, for example, helping to fund new educational projects overseas and assisting with the development of new study abroad programs (the Council would supercede the faculty committee that currently advises the director of the study abroad program). Members of the Council, who would be drawn from all four divisions of the faculty, will also serve as advocates for internationalization, both with their faculty colleagues and with the central administration.

Like the Council on Science and Technology, the Council on International Teaching and Research will consist of a director and an eleven-member Executive Committee. (The director will be one of the Committee's eleven members and will act as its chair.) The Council will include four ex officio members: the dean of the Woodrow Wilson School, the director of the Princeton Institute for International and Regional Studies, the director of the Study Abroad Program, and the associate dean for academic affairs and diversity in the Office of the Graduate School. The president will appoint members of the university faculty to the remaining seven seats on the Council and select one of those faculty members to serve as the Council's director. Members of the Council will ordinarily serve three-year terms, as will its director. Because the Council's work will have a substantial impact on the life and work of academic departments, two or more of its members should be sitting departmental chairs. At least in the Council's early years, its task will be sufficiently critical that the president and the provost should meet regularly with the entire Council.

Ensuring High-Quality Administrative Support

The Committee strongly argued that the university will need a new high-level administrator to implement the international initiatives, and we agree. The new administrator would serve as secretary to the new Council; collaborate with other Princeton administrators to make the university more hospitable to international ventures; ensure that the needs of international projects and visitors are considered when new policies are crafted; and help to negotiate agreements with foreign institutions. International ventures will often confront special problems, such as the need to hammer out complex agreements or contend with intricate government regulations. Solving these problems will require the expertise, persistence, and talent of an outstanding administrator.

Because the new administrator's responsibilities will span all units of the university, the logical place for the appointment is in the provost's office. By creating an associate or vice provost for international initiatives, Princeton will take a critical and necessary step forward in its efforts to become a more international university.

Reviewing and Revising Administrative Policies

The Committee observed that university policies might sometimes impose unnecessary barriers to the success of international projects. It drew specific attention to policies that might unduly restrict the flow of graduate students into or out of Princeton or that might interfere with the ability of faculty members to participate in international collaborations. The Committee also recognized, however, that many of these policies also serve legitimate university interests, and it recommended that the policies be revised only when doing so would serve the overall interests of the university. Identifying problematic policies and designing appropriate amendments will require sustained effort not only from the faculty Council and the new administrator in the provost's office, but also from every university office. Implementing change will also require resources: We will need, for example, to expand the operations of Princeton's Office of Visa Services.

Establishing a Home for International Activities at Princeton

The members of the Committee attached special importance to establishing a visible and central place or "hub" for international initiatives at Princeton that would bring together various centers, programs, institutes, and offices engaged in international initiatives. That "hub" is likely to be located in Frick Hall. The university has already indicated its intention to locate PIIRS in Frick Hall after the Department of Chemistry moves into its new building and, as indicated in the next section, the dean of the college is eager to locate the expanded Office of International Programs in Frick Hall as well. In that way, Frick would become a symbolic and practical focal point for faculty and students interested in any aspect of Princeton's international programs.

The Committee also highlighted the need to provide other facilities at Frick that will support the university's internationalization efforts, such as "classrooms capable of state of the art video-conferencing, to allow students working on a particular part of the world to engage directly with students directly from that area, and to allow those studying any problem to benefit from the insights of others abroad through faculty research networks." While the planning for Frick is in its early stages, and the building must answer a number of needs in the humanities and the social sciences, we are very supportive of the Committee's recommendation.

Improving Communication and Visibility

The Committee maintained that the university needed to provide not only a "physical center" for its internationalization efforts, but also "a virtual equivalent on the university's website, allowing students, faculty, administrators, and visitors to know exactly what is happening on campus." More generally, the Committee recommended that, as the Council on International Teaching and Research implements the plan for internationalization, it put together a public document summarizing the university's international initiatives.

It would be difficult to overstate the importance of this recommendation. At present, many of Princeton's international efforts are hard to discover. Indeed, some members of the Committee were surprised to learn of the extent of the faculty's engagement with international collaborations or that Princeton was already bringing to campus some multi-year foreign visitors comparable to the Global Scholars it envisioned. Princeton's internationalization program will become more cohesive and powerful if the university ties it together in a visible and easily comprehended website and publications. Faculty and students interested in international projects will find it easier to become involved, and administrators supporting those projects will have a better sense of their needs.

INCORPORATING INTERNATIONAL EXPERIENCES INTO UNDERGRADUATE EDUCATION

Because we had already asked the dean of the college for recommendations about how to expand Princeton's undergraduate study abroad program, we did not ask the Adelman-Slaughter Committee to address that topic. The Committee nevertheless underscored the importance of increasing the proportion of undergraduates who have a substantial experience abroad during their course of study at Princeton, and it considered an expanded and proactive study abroad office to be an integral and essential part of their agenda for "internationalizing" Princeton.

As Dean Nancy Malkiel said in a report to the Academic Planning Group last year, "Like other leading international universities, Princeton has a responsibility to produce globally competent citizens. Global competence—defined as a combination of substantive knowledge about international matters, an empathy with and appreciation of other cultures, foreign language proficiency, and a practical ability to function in other cultures—should be a part of every Princeton undergraduate's education." She concluded that Princeton should begin to set an expectation for all students, regardless of their field of study, that they should incorporate an international experience as part of their education.

Princeton has already done much to expand its study abroad programs in recent years, but we can do better still. Indeed, when we speak to alumni about Princeton's international initiatives, they are especially enthusiastic about seeing the university improve its study abroad programs. Many alumni express regret that they did not go abroad during their time at Princeton, and some of them complain—with unfortunate accuracy—that Princeton in the past put too many barriers in the way of students who sought to add an international component to their experience. Those who did go abroad, on the other hand, often regard that experience as one of the most valuable components of their Princeton education.

The critical question about study abroad is not whether to expand Princeton's offerings, but how to do so. Some other universities—Stanford and Chicago are notable examples—have established "mini-campuses" at overseas locations. Programs of this kind have advantages: for example, they maximize the sponsoring institution's capacity to ensure the quality of the curriculum it is offering. They also offer students a familiar, comfortable option for studying abroad, which potentially encourages more students to go abroad. On the other hand, such programs also have countervailing disadvantages. Precisely because they create mini-communities of students from the host university, they shelter students from the full-blast experience of being embedded within a foreign culture.

At Princeton, our most successful study abroad programs have emerged out of the creative efforts of dedicated faculty and supportive departments. The Department of Ecology and Evolutionary Biology has sponsored a popular program that takes students to Panama to study the rich ecosystem of a tropical rain forest. Princeton-in-Beijing has a long and much admired track record for educating students in Chinese intensively during the summer. PIIRS recently created a summer seminar that sent Princeton students to Hanoi where, under the leadership of alumnus Desaix Anderson '58, they were exposed to a dazzling array of perspectives on Vietnam's culture and America's history of involvement with it.

The dean of the college recommended that Princeton should create a wide variety of options for students, during term time or in summer, in courses that yield academic credit or in summer internships that provide valuable experiences of a different kind. Her report envisioned "a future in which 20 percent to 25 percent of our larger graduating classes of 1,300 students will have studied abroad during term time, as many as 40 percent will have studied abroad during the summer, 20 percent to 25 percent will have held summer internships or employment abroad, as many as 10 percent will have done senior thesis research abroad, and another 10 percent will have participated in summer service opportunities abroad. (In some cases, students will have engaged in more than one of these activities.)" Of course, the actual distribution of students among these opportunities is likely to vary, and we might, for example, see an increasing number of students selecting internships rather than more traditional study abroad options. Princeton must be ready to accommodate such changes: The main message from the dean of the college is that, if we are to maximize the number of Princeton students who go abroad as part of their education, we must be flexible about how they go abroad.

Princeton students might also go abroad even before they begin their freshman years. We have seen growing interest from students in the possibility of taking a "gap year" between their high school and college careers. A gap year devoted to public service in a foreign country would bring special advantages: It would enable students to experience another culture, participate in the benefits of civic engagement, and enter Princeton with a richer, more seasoned perspective on their classroom studies.

New resources will be needed to realize the program envisioned by the dean of the college. The resources must include funds to encourage faculty members and departments to design new study abroad programs; to support these new programs and expand existing study abroad and international internship programs; and to provide financial aid for students who could not otherwise afford to study or work abroad. These investments will have to be substantial if Princeton is to provide its students with the education needed to make them competent leaders and citizens in a globalizing world.

An infusion of resources will be necessary but not sufficient. Careful planning will be essential. For example, a successful study abroad program will both enhance and depend upon instruction in foreign languages at Princeton. We are fortunate that Princeton has excellent leadership and talent in the departments responsible for teaching languages. Nevertheless, as the Adelman-Slaughter Committee observed, we will need to revisit Princeton's programs in this area on a regular basis as the demand for particular languages changes with time. In this domain, as in others, Princeton's approach should be driven by the scholarly commitments of its faculty and the educational needs of its students, rather than by inflexible investments in regions or facilities.

The success of Dean Malkiel's proposal will also depend upon strong leadership and increased administrative capacity. While the idea of going abroad is exciting and attractive to some students, it can seem unfamiliar, difficult, and even frightening to others. We must do everything we can to ensure that going abroad while at Princeton seems attractive and easy to arrange. In particular, we must make the university's administrative support for study abroad and international internships more visible and robust. We will need significant additions to the office staff to advise students, assess external programs, and collaborate with departments to create new opportunities for students to study abroad. We are pleased that the extraordinary success of Princeton's Annual Giving campaign last year has enabled us to accelerate the expansion of the office's staff.

Finally, to assist students who may be bewildered by the array of departments and programs on campus that sponsor international programs, it is essential that we create the impression of "one stop shopping" for international experiences. This service should include not only the opportunities that we have already mentioned, but access to information about other valuable post-graduation experiences, such as those offered by Princeton-in-Asia and Princeton-in-Africa. As noted earlier, Dean Malkiel proposes that the Office of International Programs should have a visible presence on campus and help to create a "hub" of information and opportunities for students, ideally co-located with PIIRS in Frick Hall, and we concur.

Conclusion

Globalization presents universities with great opportunities and challenges. It generates a fascinating new array of problems for researchers to analyze and students to study. It calls upon universities to rethink their missions and practices so that they can supply the leadership and analysis needed to solve problems with an international dimension. It demands that universities prepare their students to become worldly cosmopolitans. And it promises to generate strong universities around the world that can be partners and that will also be rivals to their American peers.

Yet globalization also presents risks for universities. We have already seen some institutions stumble by trying to extend their educational practices too rapidly or in ways that are not faithful to their core values. If Princeton is to flourish in the 21st century, it must meet the challenges of globalization in a way that is both vigorous and consistent with traditions and practices that define our scholarly community. The Adelman-Slaughter Committee has mapped an approach to globalization well adapted to Princeton's distinctive commitment to an intense scholarly community of teaching and research. The Committee's ideas constitute a coherent and powerful approach that will, in its own words, transform Princeton into "a center for a multitude of scholarly networks humming with activity and effectively responding to changes in scholarship and the vagaries of world affairs, while creatively defining the cutting edges of global research." That is the right international vision for Princeton, and we should pursue it.

MIT's Approach to International Engagement

L. Rafael Reif
President, Massachusetts Institute of Technology

This article describes MIT's approach to international engagement. It starts by explaining why MIT engages internationally and then shows how—appropriately for our entrepreneurial community—MIT has many approaches to international engagement, not just a single, centrally coordinated "international strategy." It then explains our present approaches to these engagements, followed by a description of MIT's funding model, a few examples of today's many international activities, and a brief summary of some of the risks of engaging—or not engaging—internationally. The article ends with an evolving vision of MIT that connects many of our international activities to MIT's enduring global themes: bringing knowledge to bear on the world's great challenges and educating the global leaders of tomorrow. In our international activities, as in all we do, the overriding intent is to make MIT stronger and to reinforce MIT's position as one of the leading science and technology academic institutions in the world.

Many of the criteria discussed in this article are applicable to our domestic activities as well. The focus, however, is on MIT's present international activities and their benefits to MIT. Of course, we also want our partners, collaborators, and sponsors to benefit as well from their engagement with MIT.

It is important to recognize, at the start, two important realities:

MIT's TALENT COMPOSITION IS INTERNATIONAL. MIT, like other leading institutions of higher education in the U.S., has benefited tremendously from its ability to attract talented students, faculty, and staff who, for a variety of reasons, choose to leave their home countries to come to the U.S. MIT has been an institution open to international talent for a long time. At present, over 40 percent of our graduate students, over 70 percent of our postdocs, and about 40 percent of our faculty were born outside the U.S. This international profile has benefited, and continues to benefit, MIT and the U.S. enormously.

MIT's PROBLEM-SOLVING AMBITIONS ARE GLOBAL, AND WE CANNOT SOLVE THE MOST IMPORTANT WORLD PROBLEMS ALONE. MIT certainly focuses on problems important to the U.S. For example, MIT conducted the "Made in America" study in the 1980s and has launched the recently announced initiative on Production in the Innovation Economy. But MIT has also focused on global problems, addressing concerns that go beyond the geographical boundaries of the U.S. (e.g., MIT's Energy Initiative). In order to do the latter, MIT has been collaborating with individuals and entities inside and outside the U.S. These collaborations benefit the U.S., MIT, and our partners.

I. WHY DOES MIT ENGAGE INTERNATIONALLY?

MIT faculty members have been engaging internationally for a long time. Why? Because they find collaborators they want to work with, and/or laboratory facilities they want access to, and/or research and education opportunities they find attractive (e.g., an appropriate region to test new ideas for greatest impact or to access data), and/or research sponsors they do not find in the U.S. In addition, MIT academic leaders—deans, department and program heads, center and lab directors—sometimes initiate international activities when it benefits their units and when the activities can be integrated into the larger intellectual context of the units. MIT academic leaders also want to provide educational opportunities to prepare their students to become global leaders. The MIT central administration becomes involved in international activities when it is important to provide a larger, broader MIT context. Regardless of how an international activity is initiated, our faculty and students have benefited significantly from a variety of such interactions. In recent years, the opportunities and motivations for international engagement have expanded considerably, with several factors helping to explain this trend, including:

RELEVANCE. There was a time when MIT and other U.S. academic institutions worked solely on problems of interest to the region and/or the nation. Of course, MIT faculty members still focus on such issues. But in general, our faculty want to work on the most important challenges of the day, and many of these challenges extend beyond national interest to global importance. To quote from MIT's mission statement: *"The Institute is committed to generating, disseminating, and preserving knowledge, and to working with others to bring this knowledge to bear on the world's great challenges."* The world's great challenges do not have national boundaries. By engaging internationally, we can (i) monitor progress of worldwide efforts, (ii) learn from others at the same time that we extend our own expertise, (iii) provide global network opportunities for MIT students and faculty, and (iv) enable our faculty and students to connect with MIT alumni, global companies, and our partners worldwide. Moreover, even though the U.S. will continue to be a source of inspiration for new ideas in research and education, many creative ideas will emerge or be implemented first elsewhere. Consequently, it is essential to MIT's continuing strength that our faculty and students remain closely engaged with the increasingly interconnected and expanding world of ideas and innovation.

TALENT. At present, several nations are trying to emulate the U.S. academic system of education and research, and they are moving toward closing the gap by increasing their investments in these areas. American institutions, including MIT, have benefited significantly from being situated in the strongest economy in the world, and this has helped them attract some of the world's most talented scholars and researchers. As the economies of other nations strengthen and as these nations invest in their local institutions, their ability to attract the best international talent will increase dramatically.

We are already beginning to experience difficulties in retaining talent at MIT against competition from international institutions, reflecting an increase in competition for young talent globally. International activities make it possible for the institute to stay connected and engaged with excellent talent worldwide and increase our opportunities to attract some of this talent to MIT.

EVOLVING EDUCATIONAL VISION. We need to educate our students to understand the world in order to prepare them to compete globally and to become the global leaders of tomorrow. Our students' exposure to the international community that comprises MIT strengthens their understanding of the world, as well as their education as future global leaders. It also is important to provide our students with opportunities for meaningful international experiences abroad, and close faculty involvement is necessary to ensure that international components of a course of study conform to MIT educational standards and expectations. In addition to educating our own students, it is important for MIT to contribute to the education of future global leaders who may not be able to attend MIT. The U.S. and the world benefit from the kind of education that MIT provides, and we should carefully consider opportunities to integrate our educational expertise into our international activities.

FUNDING. It is prudent and beneficial to diversify and expand MIT's funding sources. Not only is this a good policy, but it is also a natural evolution reflecting a more international and globally connected institution. As with talent, these funding sources are increasingly found overseas. For example, the institute's sponsored research expenditures coming from international sources nearly quadrupled over the last ten years to $96 million in FY2010. This corresponds to an increase in the proportion of total campus-sponsored research expenditures funded by international sources from approximately 7 percent in 2001 to about 15 percent in FY2010.

II. WHEN REFERRING TO "MIT'S INTERNATIONAL STRATEGY," WHO IS MIT?

Only a handful of individuals can make a commitment or sign a formal document on behalf of MIT. Nevertheless, MIT has about 1,000 faculty members, including more than thirty heads of academic units and more than fifty directors of interdepartmental labs/centers/institutes/initiatives, five school deans and three deans for students and education. In addition, MIT has an office for Resource Development, including directors of foundation and corporate relations. When any one of these individuals (or offices) speaks with an international entity or individual (whether public, private, government, commercial, or industrial), the international entity or individual often assumes the conversation is being conducted with "MIT."

Consequently, even though many members of the MIT community, including our alumni, would like to see a greater degree of coherence in our international engagements, and would expect this coherence to flow from the central administration (i.e., from the president, provost and/or chancellor), the reality is that most of our engagements are neither initiated by, nor explored in coordination with, the central administration.

Hence, in a dynamic and entrepreneurial community such as ours, it is not possible to speak of *the* "MIT International Strategy" if that refers to a coherent set of activities taken up by MIT faculty, departments, and schools in response to a cohesive, centrally coordinated strategy. On the contrary, marching in lockstep in this way would not be desirable, as the best ideas at MIT are those that originate with, and flow from, the students, faculty, and staff. On the other hand, the central administration does have a coherent global strategy and an approach to international engagement that is consistent with the exciting and entrepreneurial nature of our community.

III. MIT's Approach to International Engagement

MIT faculty and academic leaders are free to pursue engagements and seek access to collaborators, facilities, and sponsors that will benefit them and their partners, whether in the U.S. or abroad. In supporting these initiatives, MIT expects that the engagement be consistent with our policies regarding faculty commitment to MIT and with MIT's mission, principles, and values. When dealing with international activities on any level, it is particularly important to assess the reputational risk to MIT before starting an engagement and to monitor this risk continuously during the engagement. Moreover, it is also important to recognize that regulatory issues applicable to international engagements add additional layers of compliance, complexity, and cost.

As mentioned earlier, in addition to faculty and academic leaders, the central administration occasionally pursues international initiatives that reflect a broader or more formal commitment on an institutional level, particularly those that offer our faculty and students access to (i) talent (i.e., students, postdocs, faculty, other researchers), (ii) ideas and collaborations, (iii) facilities and research infrastructure, (iv) research and educational funding, (v) opportunities to educate future global leaders, and (vi) opportunities to work on the world's great challenges. Usually such initiatives involve some level of partnership with a foreign university (or group of universities), foundation, or government agency and come with a strong expectation of lasting benefits to MIT as well as to our partners. By and large, the central administration takes a proactive role in launching or shaping international activities when these are in support of a larger strategic goal for MIT.

How does the MIT central administration choose where to engage? Ideally, the potential international engagement ought to offer most of the following:

- Intellectual content of high interest to our faculty
- Talent, ideas, and resources

- Expectation of long-term commitment
- Potential for long-term impact
- Potential to integrate research and education
- A partner that values science and technology (S&T)
- A partner that values knowledge creation and applications
- A partner that recognizes the impact of S&T on the economy and society
- Scale of engagement that involves multiple disciplines
- Engagement in a current and/or future regional hub for innovation
- Engagement in a region with significant MIT alumni presence and the potential for involving them
- Engagement consistent with MIT's values and principles

Consistent with MIT's mission to *"work wisely, creatively, and effectively for the betterment of humankind,"* MIT should also support initiatives that pursue, where appropriate, activities that include a service dimension in underprivileged countries or regions that could greatly benefit from MIT's expertise, while at the same time providing MIT faculty and students with challenges to solve important problems.

The MIT central administration has practiced both a responsive and a proactive approach to international involvement. At this time, we are proactively exploring possible opportunities in China, India, Russia, and Brazil, complementing perceived faculty interest in these countries.

We recognize, however, that there is limited capacity for such engagements of significant breadth and that there are opportunity costs associated with these activities (e.g., participating in a large engagement in a given country may prevent us from participating in an important and desirable engagement in another country).

One way that we assess and monitor our international engagements is through MIT's International Advisory Committee (IAC), which is co-chaired by Associate Provost Philip S. Khoury and Vice President for Research and Associate Provost Claude R. Canizares. The IAC assesses international engagements by focusing on (i) consistency of the engagement with faculty's commitment to MIT, (ii) alignment of the engagement with MIT's mission, principles, and values, and (iii) reputational risk of the engagement to MIT. The IAC also seeks to learn from past and ongoing activities in order to apply that experience to future activities.

The IAC sponsors faculty Working Groups engaged in designing possible strategies by countries and regions. A recent example is the "MIT-Greater China Strategy" report (available at: web.mit.edu/provost/reports/Final-GCSWG-Report-August-2010.pdf). These IAC Working Groups advise the administration and provide regional guidance to faculty interested in working in specific regions.

In short, MIT's approach to international engagement can be summarized as follows: (i) activities that emerge from academic leaders, faculty, students, and staff take many forms but should be consistent with MIT's mission, principles, and values, and the MIT central administration plays an important role ensuring that this is the case, and (ii) activities initiated by the central administration are guided by a coherent strategic vision that strengthens MIT and is consistent with the entrepreneurial nature of our community.

IV. Funding Model

With few exceptions, research and education sponsorships at MIT cover all (i.e., direct and indirect) project-related costs (exceptions include a few not-for-profit U.S. sponsors). Similarly, international sponsors also are expected to cover all direct and indirect research and education costs. However, larger-scale international sponsorships, particularly those initiated by the central administration, are typically asked to provide financial support beyond direct and indirect costs. Why is that?

International activities often require our faculty to travel away from MIT, creating an absence on campus that usually needs to be addressed. Moreover, due to their complexity, these activities typically require additional oversight, and in some instances governance commitments. Some large international engagements may require the active participation of members of MIT's central administration and ongoing support from MIT administrative offices such as finance, research administration, and technology licensing. As we engage in institution building overseas, we should seek resources to renew and strengthen MIT, i.e., to fund our own institutional renewal.

As a result, international sponsorships initiated by the central administration are typically asked to contribute to MIT's endowment in addition to covering all direct and indirect project costs. Some of this endowment could be used, for example, to create new faculty lines to offset the additional call on faculty time.

As indicated in Section III, some members of our community also work in regions of the world that significantly benefit from MIT expertise but that cannot afford to fund the engagement. MIT believes these activities are important as well and is exploring ways to provide seed funds while the interested faculty members seek more stable support. There may also be cases where our strategy would be best served by MIT providing an initial investment of resources to help develop collaborations with particular countries, leading to possible longer-term engagements that would conform with the funding model for larger-scale projects described above.

V. MIT's International Activities: A Few Current Examples

As noted at the beginning, MIT has engaged internationally for a long time, whether participating in research collaborations or in institution building. An article by S.W. Leslie and R. Kargon ("Exporting MIT: Science, Technology and Nation-Building in India and Iran," University of Chicago Press on behalf of History of Science Society, 2006, pp. 110–130) describes MIT's role in the establishment of the Indian Institute of Technology in Kanpur (IIT/Kanpur) and the Birla Institute of Technology and Science (BITS) in Pilani in the 1960s, as well as the Aryamehr University of Technology in Iran in the 1970s. Why do MIT faculty engage with people and entities elsewhere, not just elsewhere in the U.S., but abroad as well? The answer is simple: because it benefits our faculty, it benefits our students, and it benefits society.

Our international involvement today comes in different forms, and its expanse is breathtaking. It covers a broad range of activities, from interactions with a partner/collaborator/sponsor to faculty activities in regions where the necessary research infrastructure is available and to a variety of student internships. This section highlights only a few current examples of research and educational collaborations, student internships and exchange programs (of course, the classification used here is arbitrary and not thorough). The examples below are a mix of faculty-led initiatives and initiatives driven by the central administration.

Research Collaborations. There are many individual MIT faculty collaborations with researchers in other institutions in the U.S. and abroad. There are also individuals and groups of MIT faculty engaging elsewhere in collaborations that provide access to research facilities we do not have at MIT. An example of the latter is the research our high-energy physicists have been conducting at CERN [European Organization for Nuclear Research]. In fact, numerous examples of spectacular research done by our physics faculty at the facilities of the SLAC [Stanford Linear Accelerator Center] laboratory in California and of Brookhaven National Laboratory in New York underscore the point that our faculty go wherever necessary to access the facilities (and collaborators) they need for their research. In the case of CERN, those facilities are outside the U.S.

A new model for global engagement emerged with the establishment of the SMART [Singapore-MIT Alliance for Research and Technology] Center in 2007 in Singapore.

The SMART Center offers our faculty, students, and postdocs the opportunity to collaborate with talented researchers in Singapore and elsewhere in Asia who have complementary expertise; it also provides access to Singapore's complementary facilities and to research issues that benefit from study in the region (e.g., local infectious diseases).

EDUCATION COLLABORATIONS. Just as MIT faculty helped establish new universities elsewhere in the 1960s, they continue to do so today. The Masdar Institute (MI) in Abu Dhabi, established through the Technology and Development Program in 2009, is a graduate-level institution dedicated to energy and environmental sustainability. The Singapore University of Technology and Design (SUTD) will matriculate its first students in April 2012 and will offer a multi-disciplinary curriculum focused on design. MIT faculty participate in these institution-building activities partly driven by their sense of mission, but also partly to engage in activities they find intellectually stimulating, such as developing new curricula (which also benefit MIT) and integrating state-of-the-art research with the education of future global leaders unable to attend MIT. Moreover, MIT faculty benefit from opportunities and resources to carry out research in important fields (e.g., sustainability and design).

STUDENT INTERNSHIPS. An example of an international program with a focus on MIT students is MISTI (MIT International Science and Technology Initiatives), based in the Center for International Studies, which connects MIT students (and faculty) with research and innovation around the world. By working closely with premier international corporations, universities, and research institutes, MISTI matches hundreds of MIT students annually with internships and research opportunities abroad. In addition, MISTI provides funding for MIT faculty to jump-start international projects and encourages student involvement in faculty-led international research. Another example is D-Lab, which fosters the development of appropriate technologies and sustainable solutions within the framework of the International Development Initiative. Like MISTI, D-Lab seeks to give students deep and meaningful experiences and is committed to making a long-lasting impact in the communities where they work. To this end, D-Lab provides an opportunity for students to engage in fieldwork and maintains strong relationships with partner organizations.

STUDENT-EXCHANGE PROGRAMS. An example of this kind of program is the Cambridge-MIT Exchange, which provides MIT and University of Cambridge undergraduate students the opportunity to study for one year at the partner institution.

An example of an activity that combines research, education, student exchanges, and internships is the Global SCALE (Supply Chain and Logistics Excellence) Network, established in 2008 in the Center for Transportation and Logistics. This network currently includes logistics centers in Spain (Zaragoza), Colombia (Bogota), and at MIT.

These are just a few examples of the tremendous breadth of engagements that our dynamic and entrepreneurial faculty, students, and staff participate in, as well as initiate.

Examples that MIT does not include in its portfolio at this time are satellite campuses and conferring MIT degrees elsewhere. We will come back to this in Section VII.

VI. Risks of Action and of Inaction

There are several risks of action, among them:

Reputational. For example, as a result of MIT

- Not fulfilling its obligations and/or commitments, and/or
- Not meeting its collaborating partner's expectations, and/or
- Not understanding or anticipating mismatched expectations.

Political or cultural. For example, as a result of

- U.S. foreign policy, and/or
- Host country shifts in political conditions, and/or
- Host country cultural differences.

In addition to these risks, there is the important issue of faculty workload. With increasing global engagements, the load on our faculty may increase. A possible solution could be an increase in the size of our faculty.

There are, of course, several risks of inaction. Among them is the risk of jeopardizing MIT's position as the place (or one of the top places) "where the action is" in science and technology. It is clear that outstanding S&T international talent gravitates toward major centers of activity, i.e., where the future is being invented and where the most creative, novel, and groundbreaking research is being carried out. MIT is one of those places in the world, attracting outstanding talent. MIT should continue to work on the most important problems our nation is facing, and it should continue to work on the world's great challenges. The latter suggests that MIT must engage globally to continue to attract some of the best international talent. Inaction not only risks our ability to continue to attract the best talent to

MIT, but also risks the ability of our faculty and students to stay engaged with many of the most innovative ideas being generated worldwide. The risk of inaction is that, over time, MIT may lose the S&T preeminence it enjoys today.

VII. An Evolving Vision

As already stated, it is MIT's responsibility to prepare our students to understand the world and to engage and succeed in a globally competitive environment in order to become the global leaders of tomorrow. At the same time, it is important for MIT to consider expanding its educational reach and participating in the preparation of future global leaders who are unable to attend MIT.

At present MIT is neither establishing satellite campuses nor conferring MIT degrees elsewhere. Instead, a possible alternative model for extending MIT's international involvement is to establish a global network of research and educational institutions that focus on science and technology and that share MIT's values and principles. These institutions would be located in present or future regional hubs of innovation.

Examples might include MIT's SMART Center in Singapore, MI in Abu Dhabi, and SUTD in Singapore. These institutions, whether established as part of MIT (e.g., SMART) or in collaboration with MIT (e.g., MI and SUTD), could potentially become part of a network of institutions that will not only enable MIT students, faculty and staff to engage globally, but will also enable MIT to contribute to the education of future global leaders attending those other institutions. Moreover, in the future, the education of an MIT student may combine time at MIT with time at one or more institutions that are part of this "MIT global network." This strategy allows MIT to (i) strengthen local institutions in geographically diverse regions, (ii) interact with, and participate in the education of, student talent in those institutions, (iii) provide unique opportunities to prepare our students to understand the world and to compete globally, and (iv) collaborate with complementary expertise and in complementary facilities to solve the world's great challenges. All these activities, when properly funded and administered, strengthen MIT. MIT's Sloan School of Management is already assisting partner schools to become leading institutions in their home countries and exposing MIT faculty and students to collaborations with counterparts from those countries.

MIT could further expand its participation in the education of future global leaders by offering credentials for learning MIT content online. MIT students could participate in this mode of education while attending the "MIT global network" of institutions or doing internships abroad. In other words, this would benefit not only students who cannot attend MIT, but also MIT students spending time elsewhere.

VIII. Summary

MIT faculty, academic leaders, and the central administration pursue mutually beneficial engagements in the U.S. and abroad. They do so because these engagements allow access to talent, collaborations, ideas, facilities, and/or funding. Furthermore, in line with MIT's mission, they allow us to work *"with others to bring this knowledge to bear on the world's great challenges."* These engagements strengthen MIT's ability to continue to attract and retain some of the best international and domestic talent. They also allow MIT to better prepare our students to understand the world, to compete globally, and to become the global leaders of tomorrow. As part of our institutional strategy, we should consider expanding our role globally, such as by participating in the education of future global leaders who are unable to attend MIT. MIT's global engagement will become more important with time and will reinforce MIT's position as one of the leading science and technology academic institutions in the world.

Bringing Cornell to the World and the World to Cornell

David J. Skorton
President, Cornell University

Beginning with its founding, Cornell University has been international in scope and aspiration. Included in Cornell's earliest classes were students from Canada, England, Russia and Brazil. By the early 1900s, Chinese students were a significant presence on our campus. In the 1920s, Cornell's first major international project, the Cornell-Nanjing Crop Improvement Program, launched an important relationship with China, which contributed to the development of a generation of Chinese plant breeders and improved food production—accomplishments that still resonate in China today. Ezra Cornell's determination to found an institution where any person can find instruction in any study, as expansive a goal as any in the history of higher education, included the assumption that the dream would not be limited to New York or to the United States.

Over the decades, Cornell's international programs expanded geographically and into new academic areas, building on the university's longstanding excellence in a broad range of disciplines, from the physical and mathematical sciences and engineering to agriculture, the life sciences (including animal and human health and disease), the social sciences, the arts and the humanities. On the Ithaca campus, the international component of many courses increased, the numbers of international graduate and undergraduate students expanded, and the colleges hired faculty with international roots. Off campus, Cornell expanded its educational roles, with dual-degree and joint-degree programs and with linkages to academic institutions around the world to foster student and faculty exchange and scholarly research. At Weill Cornell Medical College, there has been a growing emphasis on global health, including significant overseas health care, research and educational activities. The university (including Weill Cornell) now has over 200 agreements with institutions in 81 countries. Across the university, faculty students and staff members have addressed important issues including nuclear proliferation, food insecurity, poverty, human rights, global health and water availability.

In short, Cornell developed into a globally respected institution of learning, discovery and creativity that excelled at both international studies (understanding the world and its peoples) and international engagement (utilizing education, research and academic partnerships to effect positive change in the world). Most of Cornell's international programs contain elements of both these overlapping areas, with learning, discovery and engagement informing and strengthening each other.

The positive effects of this international involvement are clear, whether viewed from East Hill or from the other side of the globe. In my 2007 commencement address, I called on Cornell and other U.S. universities to take international involvement even further—to develop a new type of Marshall Plan that would reduce global inequalities through capacity-building partnerships with universities in developing countries—and we have made significant progress along these lines. In fact, it may be argued that our faculty, staff and students have acted as if Cornell were the land grant institution to the world—and that orientation can and should be an essential part of our mission in the years ahead.

Despite this long history of distinction, in recent years, considering the interdependence of people and nations in the 21st century, insufficient attention has been paid to international studies and international engagement at Cornell. This is not to say that we have failed to make progress in many areas. Cornell is still widely respected as an international powerhouse and is a magnet for students and scholars from scores of countries each year. Faculty excel in work involving every continent and in both developed and developing countries.

But the world of university-based international studies and engagement is changing, and Cornell must respond aggressively or risk being left behind. More important, without a clear and strategic vision of its international role, Cornell faculty, students and staff risk becoming less relevant globally at just the time when challenges such as global climate change, nuclear proliferation, infectious diseases, trade regulation and many others require international collaboration and when all of us need the skills to live and work effectively across cultures and national borders. Internationalization is not and should not be an end but a means by which to focus selected areas of Cornell excellence in education, discovery and engagement.

This white paper represents a personal view of Cornell's past, present and potential future role in international studies and engagement. It is not meant to be comprehensive, but it is meant to sound an alarm that the entire worldwide Cornell family needs to heed in order to maintain and enhance one of the defining characteristics of this institution. I believe there is some urgency in the need to confront these challenges, and in this paper I include a call for expeditious planning across the institution and also indicate the need for immediate action in a few specific areas.

THE CLIMATE FOR INTERNATIONALIZATION AT U.S. UNIVERSITIES

There is growing recognition on university campuses across the world that internationalization is important in every aspect of higher education. If we are to educate students for global citizenship, we must offer them language study, an understanding of history and of cultures beyond their own, and meaningful international experiences. We must equip them to live and work in a world whose chief problems transcend national boundaries.

Although many U.S. colleges and universities have long emphasized international education and research, the recently sharpened focus on internationalization has arrived at a challenging time. University resources nationwide declined along with the global economy starting in 2008. Federal and state governments have retreated from funding education in general as well as specific programs like the Fulbright-Hays program and National Resource Centers. On many campuses language programs and library collections and staff have suffered deep cuts in resources. And, after September 2001, movement across borders in many areas became more difficult.

Against this background, here are a few national trends in internationalization efforts. These trends are in addition to the very robust faculty-initiated research interactions among U.S. scholars and their counterparts in universities worldwide. Cornell has hundreds of such interactions.

INTERNATIONAL EXPERIENCES

U.S. student participation in traditional study abroad and other kinds of international experiences has, according to the Institute for International Education, more than doubled over the past decade. The number of U.S. students studying abroad fell slightly in 2008–2009, after rising steadily since about 1990. This reflects a decline in short-term study (summer, January term, or eight weeks or less during the academic year); students going for longer periods increased slightly. As noted below, Cornell lags behind other U.S. institutions in the rate of student participation in international experiences and clearly needs to improve.

JOINT AND DUAL DEGREE PROGRAMS

This model involves establishing joint programs with colleges in the host country—often with provision for students from both institutions to spend time on each other's campuses. In joint or dual degree programs, the U.S. university typically works closely with the partner institution in the host country toward immediate delivery of enhanced postsecondary education in the host country, while at the same time working to increase the partner institution's—and therefore the country's—internal capacity to deliver higher education. In addition to dual and joint degrees, such partnerships can include faculty mentoring in the host country, development of research capacity or other goals. As of 2008, 38 percent of U.S. graduate schools had at least one joint or dual degree program with international universities (up from 29 percent the previous year), and 31 percent planned to start one in the next two years, according to the Council of Graduate Schools.

Both joint and dual degree programs have advantages but significant challenges as well. Joint degrees can be particularly problematic. Any changes in these offerings at Cornell should reflect strong faculty commitment and long-term capacity.

ESTABLISHMENT OF CAMPUSES ABROAD

In this model of internationalization of higher education, the complete curriculum is set up by the U.S. university, and faculty are hired by and work within the faculty of the parent school. Tuition paid by students from the host country and other funds from the local or national government flow to the U.S. university, often with subcontracts or other funds channeled back to the host country in order to purchase goods and services locally. Specifics vary from partnership to partnership, but a common basic precondition is budget neutrality or better for the U.S. university.

This arrangement certainly increases the availability of education and services in the host country. This approach does not by itself increase the capacity of universities in the host country to deliver education and to perform needed research. The intention is that such capacity will develop over time, as graduates of these institutions become the next generation of leaders within their own countries. A common concern with this approach is the assumption that the U.S. university model can function appropriately in other cultures with only minimal modifications.

The number of international branch campuses has increased substantially in recent years. Nearly 80 percent of international campuses, about half American, have opened in the last decade.

Cornell has been at the forefront in establishing complete international campuses, having opened Weill Cornell Medical College-Qatar in Doha, part of the ambitious project of Education City, over a decade ago. Although this campus is very successful, and Cornell is frequently approached to consider opening other campuses in a variety of fields and locales, I do not believe that it is in the near-term interest of the institution to establish more such campuses in the next five years. However, Cornell should consider establishing additional significant strategic partnerships as well as offices in a few strategically important cities.

Examples of Current International Programs at Cornell

Below I highlight a few examples of Cornell's international programs to give a sense of the scope of our efforts. In the context of Cornell's broad excellence in international studies and engagement—in Ithaca, nearby Geneva, New York City, Washington, Rome and elsewhere—these choices by no means imply that programs not mentioned are less worthy.

Einaudi Center for International Studies

The Mario Einaudi Center for International Studies catalyzes and supports activities that advance international studies at Cornell. Founded in 1961 to stimulate, support and coordinate Cornell's far-flung research, teaching and outreach with an international focus, the Einaudi Center is the umbrella organization for eighteen interdisciplinary programs across the university. The Center's mission continues to evolve as it takes over functions from other units of the university, such as the Fulbright Program and the cross-college undergraduate concentration in international relations; provides international travel grants for graduate students, as well as seed and small grants for faculty; and serves as an incubator for new initiatives.

Area Studies Programs. According to federal enabling legislation, area studies is a program of comprehensive study of the aspects of a world area's society or societies, including study of history, culture, economy, politics, international relations and languages. Area studies programs transcend traditional academic, professional and national boundaries. Area studies faculty are drawn from the traditional liberal arts and from applied disciplines, with the goal of promoting the teaching of languages, history, culture and politics; offering undergraduate concentrations and graduate minors; and making expertise and research available worldwide, particularly through the advanced training of area scholars.

Among many area studies programs at Cornell, three—the Southeast Asia Program (SEAP), South Asia Program and East Asia Program— are Title VI/National Resource Centers (NRCs). The Southeast Asia Program is the oldest continuously supported NRC in the United States. It is nationally prominent in promoting advanced foreign language training, area and international knowledge in the liberal arts, and applied disciplines focused on Southeast Asia (Brunei, Burma, Cambodia, Indonesia, Laos, Malaysia, Philippines, Singapore, Thailand and Vietnam). SEAP also offers outreach to regional K-12 and post-secondary schools/teachers and is known for its academic publications focused on the region. It supports the Cornell University Library's Echols Collection, the largest library collection of its kind in the world.

INTERNATIONAL RELATIONS MINOR. Cornell offers dozens of courses in many departments and several colleges that provide a strong grounding in the international relations field, including courses in government, economics, history, rural sociology, modern languages and linguistics, international comparative labor relations and others. The international relations minor, offered through the Einaudi Center, is open to undergraduates enrolled in any of Cornell's seven undergraduate colleges.

CLARKE PROGRAM IN EAST ASIAN LAW AND CULTURE

The Clarke Program brings a broad interdisciplinary and humanistic focus to the study of law in East Asia. It prepares Cornell law students for the complexities of international legal practice by providing them with a richer and more subtle understanding of Asian legal systems. It aims to foster new levels of collaboration between legal scholars and scholars in other disciplines with interests in East Asia. The program also seeks to train a new generation of scholars in the United States and Asia.

CORNELL INTERNATIONAL INSTITUTE FOR FOOD, AGRICULTURE AND DEVELOPMENT (CIIFAD)

Established in 1990 with partners in Africa, Asia and Latin America, CIIFAD initiates and supports projects that contribute to improved prospects for global food security, sustainable rural development and environmental conservation around the world. Its initiatives include the System of Rice

Intensification, Integrative Graduate Education and Research Traineeships focused on food systems and poverty reduction, an agricultural program in Zimbabwe, and Student Multidisciplinary Applied Research Teams that assist organizations in developing countries.

DURABLE RUST RESISTANCE IN WHEAT

Cornell leads a global project to combat a deadly wheat pathogen that poses an imminent threat to global food security, particularly in the poorest nations of the world. Funded by the United Kingdom's Department for International Development and the Bill & Melinda Gates Foundation, the project involves partnerships with national and international research centers and laboratories, universities, and scientists and farmers from more than forty countries.

AGUACLARA

AguaClara is a program in civil and environmental engineering that is improving drinking water quality through innovative research, knowledge transfer, open source engineering and design of sustainable, replicable water treatment systems. Cornell students have developed a cost-effective technology that provides water that meets U.S. Environmental Protection Agency standards without requiring electricity. The first AguaClara plant began producing clean water for the Honduran community of Ojojona in 2007. Since then, full-scale municipal plants have been added in four other areas. Among the program's goals is the expansion of operations in the developing world beyond Honduras. Those working on the project, both graduate students and undergraduates, can receive course credit for their involvement.

GLOBAL HEALTH PROGRAMS

NIH FOGARTY INTERNATIONAL CENTER. With the support of an NIH Fogarty International Center grant and university funds, a multidisciplinary undergraduate, professional and graduate curriculum has been developed by six Cornell colleges: Weill Cornell Medical College, Human Ecology, Engineering, Veterinary Medicine, Arts and Sciences, and Agriculture and Life Sciences. For undergraduates, Cornell offers an interdisciplinary global health minor, including field experience abroad. For Weill Cornell medical students, global health has been integrated into the curriculum, and international electives have been strengthened. A global health track has been added to the MS program in clinical epidemiology and health services research.

WEILL CORNELL MEDICAL COLLEGE-QATAR (WCMC-Q). Established in 2001 as a joint venture between Cornell University and the Qatar Foundation, WCMC-Q is the first medical school in Qatar and the first institution to offer a U.S. MD overseas. It offers an integrated program of pre-medical and medical studies leading to the Cornell University MD degree. Teaching is by Cornell and Weill Cornell faculty, including physicians at Hamad Medical Corporation who hold Weill Cornell appointments. WCMC-Q has graduated four MD classes, the largest being the 31-member Class of 2011, which included graduates from sixteen different nationalities. The WCMC-Q premedical program can accommodate sixty students per year, and the Foundation program prepares students for the pre-medical program with intensive English, math and science courses.

JOINT AND DUAL DEGREE PROGRAMS

The Cornell School of Hotel Administration's Master of Hospitality Management degree is offered jointly with Nanyang Technological University in Singapore. Students in this program can apply to spend the entire twelve months of their program on Cornell's Ithaca campus or to spend six months each in Ithaca and in Singapore. Students who opt for the two-campus program receive joint degrees granted by both institutions and signed by both university presidents. In addition, Cornell offers a dual degree program in food science with Tamil Nadu Agricultural University in India and a dual degree in law with partner universities in Europe.

CURRENT STATISTICS ON INTERNATIONAL STUDENTS AND SCHOLARS AT CORNELL

As of fall 2011, Cornell's Ithaca campus enrolled over 3800 international students, about 18 percent of our total enrollment and the highest percentage in a decade. International students accounted for 9 percent of our undergraduates, 24 percent of professional students (Law, Johnson School, Veterinary Medicine), and about 42 percent of our graduate students. These international students represent more than 120 countries, with China (1,024), South Korea (540), Canada (505), India (477) and Singapore (102) the most common countries of origin. In November 2011, the Institute of International Education released a report that places Cornell among the top 25 campuses with the most international students.

At Weill Cornell Medical College, there are currently five MD students from four countries (Canada, Mexico, Japan and Greece), while the Weill Cornell Graduate School of Medical Sciences enrolls 32 international students from twelve countries out of 62 students in the 2011 entering class. In addition, 644 international students applied to Weill Cornell Medical College for a clinical elective through the Office of Global Health

Education, and 152 of them were placed in an elective of their choice.

Some expected and some disconcerting trends are evident in the Ithaca data: Not surprisingly, the number of students from both East and South Asia has increased dramatically, especially since 2005, but the number of Africans has been essentially level since 1996. Far fewer students from Europe, Oceania, Latin America and the Caribbean have enrolled since 1996. Since 2007, the number of students from the Middle East has increased, but current numbers still are lower than those in 2000. These fluctuations have many causes, but availability of financial aid at both the undergraduate and graduate levels is important. An encouraging trend is that several emerging economies are investing in graduate education and undergraduate exchanges, which likely will increase the number of students from China, India, Brazil and Indonesia at Cornell.

TITLE VI GRANTS (NATIONAL RESOURCE CENTERS) AND AREA STUDIES

The de-emphasis of area studies as a national priority has been detrimental to the vitality of area studies programs at Cornell and nationally. Recent cuts in Department of Education funding for NRCs have added further urgency to rethinking the role of area studies at Cornell.

As mentioned above, currently, Cornell has three National Resource Centers: East Asia, South Asia, and Southeast Asia. In the past we have had as many as six. The Institute for European Studies recently lost its status as an NRC, as did the Latin American Studies Program. Cornell also has four Foreign Language and Area Studies fellowship programs (in the three Asian areas and European Studies). Following is a sampling of other universities with NRCs and FLAS programs.

	NRCs	FLAS
University of Wisconsin	8	8
University of California, Berkeley	8	7
Indiana University	7	8
University of Washington	7	7
University of Illinois	6	6
Columbia University	5	6
University of Michigan	5	5
Yale University	5	3
Harvard University	4	4
University of Pennsylvania	4	4
Ohio State	4	4
University of Chicago	4	4
Cornell University	3	4
Michigan State	3	3
Stanford University	3	3

Among the Ivies, Dartmouth, Brown and Princeton have one or none of these programs.

Faculty Attrition: Recent and Expected

Cornell has suffered numerous faculty retirements and losses in international studies in recent years for a variety of reasons, with some areas harder hit than others. Moreover, as is the case for the faculty and staff in general, additional retirements are on the horizon. Faculty renewal in international studies and international engagement is a critical need if Cornell is to enhance its stature in the most strategic international areas.

International Experience Statistics

About 27 percent of Cornell students earn academic credit for international experience at some point in their Cornell careers. According to Open Doors 2011, a report of the Institute for International Education, at least forty U.S. doctoral institutions have higher undergraduate participation rates than Cornell. Of this group, fourteen have participation of 50 percent or more, including Dartmouth, Yale, Georgetown, Tufts and Notre Dame. Many smaller institutions send a higher proportion of their students abroad. At least 24 institutions (most of them small) send more than 70 percent of their students abroad at some point during their undergraduate careers.

According to Open Doors 2011, the leading fields of study for U.S. students studying abroad are the social sciences (22 percent of those studying abroad), business and management (21 percent), humanities (12 percent), fine or applied arts (8 percent), physical/life sciences (8 percent), foreign languages (6 percent), health professions (5 percent), education (4 percent), engineering (4 percent), math/computer science (2 percent) and agriculture (1 percent).

The Future of Internationalization at Cornell: The Urgent Need for a University-wide Dialogue and Plan

There is an urgent need for an expeditious university-wide discussion and plan for the future of internationalization at Cornell. This plan should be faculty-led and the faculty appointed by the provosts jointly, including scholars from both the Ithaca and WCMC [Weill Cornell Medical College] campuses. Topics to be considered in the plan should include all those raised in this white paper, as well as others identified by the group.

While a thoughtful, full consideration of the future of internationalization at Cornell by its faculty is the sine qua non of a robust, sustainable plan, recent attempts at planning have failed to produce the needed guidance in some urgent areas. While awaiting the deliberations of the planning group, I believe we need to move forward immediately on the following changes:

PRIORITY NO. 1: PARTNERSHIP IN STRATEGIC FACULTY RECRUITMENT

We have a particular need to hire faculty in international studies and international engagement, especially in view of faculty we have already lost and expect to lose to retirement. For example, of the seventy faculty designated as International Professors in the College of Agriculture and Life Sciences, twenty already have emeritus status and another twenty are in their sixties. Similar trends exist in other colleges with strong international programs.

The International Professor designation, mostly in the contract colleges in Ithaca, could be considered for expansion across the university. Regular meetings, both physical and virtual, of International Professors would inform Cornell's international community of new initiatives and opportunities, help coordinate the university's international course offerings, and identify faculty positions essential to international programs.

Although I am fully supportive of the long and very successful authority given to departments and colleges in faculty recruitment, the provosts should play a larger than usual role in identifying the areas of greatest need and should supply financial incentives to hire such faculty. Specifically, the provosts, in partnership with the deans in Ithaca and department heads at Weill Cornell Medical College, should enunciate specific goals for faculty renewal relevant to internationalization. Consideration might be given to scholars who teach and do research on languages and culture and to those emphasizing problem-solving and capacity-building in the developing world, as well as global health. Cluster recruitment should also be considered.

PRIORITY NO. 2: MORE, AND MORE EFFECTIVE, INTERNATIONAL EXPERIENCES FOR STUDENTS

Cornell needs affordable opportunities for students to have at least some international experience, whether through Cornell Abroad, other overseas study programs, well-designed internships or service learning. Our goal should be to ensure that no less than 50 percent of Cornell undergraduates have an international experience by the time they earn their degrees.

Another possible aspiration could be for Cornell to rank among the institutions with the highest percentage of graduating seniors in the U.S. who have an intensive international experience; these students could be those who have spent three months or more living in another country, who are competent in at least one language other than English, or who join the Peace Corps or a similar global service organization after graduation. A mechanism for achieving that goal might be to expand the Einaudi Center's successful graduate research travel grants program to undergraduates who intend to carry out research abroad, with preference given in appropriate fields to students working within the subject area of a faculty member's research.

Also needed is a reorganization of the Cornell Abroad office, coupled with a new financial model and introduction of more Cornell-led initiatives. The provost in Ithaca may wish to appoint a specific task force to investigate best practices elsewhere and make recommendations for restructuring international experiences and financial aid for students studying abroad. International experience is only one mechanism for better preparing global citizens and should be coupled with an increased emphasis on the study of languages and cultures across the undergraduate curriculum.

Priority No. 3: Access to Cornell for International Students with Financial Need

An increase in international students would greatly benefit all our students as we seek to prepare them to live in a multicultural world. But need-based undergraduate financial aid for international students is extremely limited, and we need more focused resources in this area. Some progress on aid for international students is being made in the current philanthropic campaign, but a greater emphasis is required.

Priority No. 4: Newly Conceptualized Institution-wide Academic Leadership in International Studies and Engagement

In the finest tradition of academic decentralization that has served Cornell so well for nearly 150 years, the senior university leadership has limited ability to effect change in our international efforts. However, some enhanced coordinative function will be necessary to achieve the goals of a new era of internationalization at Cornell. The Ithaca provost should in particular consider recasting the vice provost for international relations as a new position with responsibility for a wider portfolio.

What could be considered is a centralized unit that is strongly integrated with college programs and with the efforts of the senior vice provost for research, graduate school dean and vice provost for undergraduate education to administer Cornell's international education and research programs in order to reduce duplication, ensure uniform interpretation of pertinent policies and improve the academic quality of international experience programs.

In addition, an international advisory board that includes Cornell alumni, representatives of the diplomatic and development communities, the private sector and academics could provide guidance on the design, implementation and assessment of Cornell's international programs.

PRIORITY No.5: SEED RESOURCES

In order to encourage significant progress on internationalization at Cornell, I call on the provosts and deans of Cornell's campuses to allocate some additional funds for these priorities and for other international initiatives. In particular, including funds I will allocate from a modest discretionary pool available to the president, I suggest the Ithaca campus provost allocate additional resources for a total of $15 million over the next five years for renewing Cornell's commitment to being international in both scope and aspiration. We will also increase substantially the international component of the current philanthropic campaign.

CONCLUSION

Cornell University has a long, distinguished and proud tradition of excellence in both international studies and international engagement. Expeditious establishment of a small, respected intercampus planning group is imperative, as is action on the priorities listed above, to strengthen our international programs for the future.

THE GLOBAL UNIVERSITY

John Sexton
President, New York University

I am a teaching university president. For as long as I've been an adult—if you consider a 17-year-old to be an adult—I've needed the classroom to maintain my vital organs. This is my 55th year of teaching, and all through my time as dean and all through my time as president and now in my time as both at New York University, the last 28 years, I've always taught a full faculty schedule. I've never understood people who call it a teaching load; I've never viewed it as a load. I've viewed it as a tremendous privilege: Opening up students' potentialities and viewing them is one of the great joys of my professional life.

I arrived at this conference a few hours ago, because Sunday is the first day of the week in the [United Arab] Emirates, and I teach two classes every couple of weeks in Abu Dhabi. My classes at New York University are on Tuesdays, so I have to get back there. Usually I have a wonderful rest to prepare me for the week: Give me a plane, don't give me any food, don't give me any wine, and give me something flat. It can be the floor and a fourteen-hour flight, and it's heaven. No Internet: You can write, you can think, and you can sleep. I end up coming back as if from a spa. But when this presentation was proposed, I couldn't resist it. So I took the 2:40 a.m. flight from Abu Dhabi to Istanbul, and I have to get the flight back this evening so that I can be back for class tomorrow.

I think that one of the things that brings us all here to Istanbul is this extraordinary university, Boğaziçi University. I've known of it from a distance. You would have to be somehow numb as a human being not to have Istanbul on your list of favorite cities. It's such an extraordinary place, especially for people who have a kind of uber-gene, a cosmopolitan gene in the classic Greek sense of the word "cosmopolitan." Boğaziçi University has just had its 150th anniversary, and NYU is coming up on our 200th anniversary. There must have been something in the water of great thinkers—interestingly, thinkers from outside academe—in that period in the early 19th century.

NYU's founder is Albert Gallatin, who was Jefferson's and Madison's secretary of the treasury and then the ambassador to France and then the ambassador to the United Kingdom—England at the time. When he was ambassador to England, he became very close friends with Jeremy Bentham. They looked at the universities of their day, and they said: Things are happening that require a completely new vision of what a university is.

Gülay Barbarosoğlu [rector of Boğaziçi University] is right that the university is a well-tested entity. Never forget that it is well-tested. With all the fads and changes that come, be careful. There are 85 institutions in the world today that exist structurally the way they did 500 years ago. You can name a few: the English Parliament, the Vatican, take eight off the board, because there are eight cantons in Switzerland. So I've given you ten of 85. Seventy of the remaining 75 are universities. Of course, none of them is an American university. So think about that for a second.

There's something powerful in the concept of a university. People think of me as an academic lawyer, because I was the dean of NYU's law school for fourteen years. But before I went to law school, I was the chairman of a religion department, and my first doctorate is in religion. Perhaps there are two things that distinguish us from other beings: What theologians call the soul or spirit is one of them. But what we know distinguishes us from other beings is the mind: thought. And that's what universities do: They advance thought. We inculcate the capacity to think: That's the business of a university from the Bodhi Tree to Socrates to today.

Albert Gallatin and Jeremy Bentham said that the time had come to change, but they didn't truck with the fundamentals: They didn't truck with the core. They looked at the great universities of their countries. For Bentham, it was Oxford and Cambridge; for Gallatin, it was the Ivies. They shared certain characteristics: They were available only to the elites; they were highly theoretical; and they were typically way out in the country.

I want you to visualize Washington Square Park and the arch that was put up for the 100th anniversary of George Washington's inauguration. Obviously, it wasn't up yet in the 1820s. There were some red houses just behind it, the summer homes of the wealthy from New York City who came out to the country. Everything behind them was farmland. Columbia University was way out in the country, and the city grid was not yet laid down. Fourteenth Street and above it is where New York, Manhattan Island, begins to make sense. If you go below 14th Street, you really have to know a native, like me, because the streets are like spaghetti, intersected and twisted around. There is actually one intersection of West 10th Street and West 10th Street, so no matter which way you go, you're on West 10th Street.

What Gallatin and Bentham said was that major changes are occurring: democracy, the Industrial Revolution, and the emergence of the merchant class. Let's face it: It took a while to get to women, and it took even longer to get to minorities. But changes pressed them to say that we need a different form of education. Cities were beginning to become the centers of activity, so universities should be, in their words, "in and of the city." Universities should produce practical knowledge. New York University's first chaired professor was Samuel Morse, who, by the way, was a professor of fine arts when he invented the telegraph and Morse code in our university building. The first picture of a human face was taken by John Draper, our second professor. They created a new concept of the university.

I look at the founding 150 years ago of what I'll call BU [Boğaziçi University]—this is, the European BU. I understand that there is a great BU in Boston, Boston University. But back to your founding: If you go to the statement of purpose and the mission of your university as laid out by Cyrus Hamlin and Christopher Rheinlander Robert, it is really the same kind of idea—practical, useful knowledge and connectivity. You carry it through with your notion of sustainability today.

You'll recognize in my remarks here the theologian in me. Theologians are trained to think in at least centuries and sometimes millennia. Looking at what's going on in the world through that lens, you ask the question that every university has to ask, even if times are less turbulent than the tectonic changes of today. The world is in tumult in some very fundamental ways. One could say that we are at a major inflection point. My family and I like to go into the wilderness, and we were at the North Pole, working our way along on an icebreaker and passing a glacier that was 120 miles long. Some of the glaciers we saw had migrated to the North Pole from what we would call the Caribbean. Somewhere along the vast billions of years of history that are represented in a sight like that or a sight like the Grand Canyon, humankind, relatively recently, appears. We are a glory of creation, no matter what your view is on how it happened or how it evolved. It could be that after all those hundreds of thousands of years of work by our predecessors to get us to the point where we are today, this century could be the one in which we screw it up.

We are at an important inflection point. And, of course, we all agree and are united by the fact that universities are going to play an important part— I would argue the most important part—in resolving the issues of today in the right way. If universities are going to do this, it's very important that we understand right at the top that when we talk about universities like those represented by the people at this conference, we are talking about a small percentage of the overall higher education symphony. We should keep in mind that higher education is a symphony orchestra of various educational types. Matching students with the right part of the orchestra is an important component of the common enterprise of higher education. We would be right to argue that awareness of the world should come through all parts of the orchestra: That's part of the scales that the musicians in the orchestra should be playing.

However, we are talking about the leading 200 to 500 universities in the world, out of the tens of thousands of universities that exist. Some of them are in intimate settings like the one we are in now, or even smaller. The largest class in NYU Abu Dhabi is a class of twenty students, which I taught yesterday. Other classes are massive, with hundreds of thousands of students online. The variety is important, wherever you are in the orchestra and whoever is given the privilege, which we are given, of describing and telling the story of what a university is.

Universities are places where people like us can do what I call evocative leadership: You can tell a story. Theologians know the power of mythos—not myth in the way that Americans use the word to mean a falsehood, but myth as a deeply experienced truth that sometimes can be expressed only through a story and not within cognitive categories. Our job is to create a story that is both recognizable and aspirational for our universities, to tell that story, and to call people to the story. To do that, you have to spend a lot of time noticing what special contributions your university can make. We are in a privileged position in universities that we lead. It's a very special place to be. Arguably, it's the most important place, because what happens at the leading universities of the world will permeate throughout the rest of the orchestra.

The Jesuits have a phrase for this, and business people have a phrase: value proposition. But since we are educators, we are not allowed to use that phrase. So we use Latin. The Jesuits call it *Ratio Studiorum*, and it works for everything. You have to know what your *Ratio Studiorum* is for each class that you teach; each course, which is an ensemble of classes; and each major. It's another way of saying what we should ask ourselves, as individuals, every day. Everybody in this room won the lottery: We were born smart. We had nothing to do with that: It just happened to us. But this imposes an obligation to use our talent and what comes from it in a useful way. Am I living a useful life? That's the question we have to ask ourselves. When you are the president or leader of a university or a dean of a school or in charge of a single classroom, the answer to that question, at least with regard to our professional life, is very much tied to the question of how NYU is useful or how BU is useful. The answer can't just be that we're going to be "better" or "more excellent": That's not enough. What is the contribution we are making to the common enterprise of higher education?

How can we think about this topic in the context of this conference? I am going to start by saying that there are two big trends animating my thinking. I was a reluctant president. The trustees wanted me to be president of NYU for about four years before I wanted to be president. It's a fulfilling life, and I think that I'm being useful. Before I left NYU law school, where I knew I was doing good, helping to create humanitarian and humanistic lawyers, I had to figure out what there was about NYU, as opposed to just another good university, that would be useful.

At the same time, New York Mayor Mike Bloomberg asked me to do something unusual. It was right before his election for a second term as mayor. He was driving the people around him crazy: They couldn't believe he was convening all of his commissioners for two days on Staten Island. The mayor was notable for going to islands without saying where he was going. This particular island was just over the Verrazano-Narrows Bridge and isn't seen as such a glorious place to go as, say, Bermuda or St. John. But the mayor was off on the island, and there I was, given the job of asking, "What will it take to make New York City a world capital city fifty years from now?"

It's a thought exercise. The first big trend that I began to notice about five or six years earlier was that a "network of idea capitals" was developing. There was a network, and there were different leagues. If you think of this as English soccer, for example, there is a Premier League that is developing. Some cities will get relegated down to the next league, and so forth and so on. The idea capitals are developing: Let's say there are twelve or sixteen of them in the world. They are magnets for talent, and they will be magnets for talent going forward.

I began to notice this in recruiting faculty. Many of us in this room are involved in recruiting faculty. Now if you're recruiting a great neuroscientist, what the neuroscientist wants is other great neuroscientists, right? You've got to have a critical mass of people. They want to talk to people about their passion, neuroscience. So you do cluster hiring. You want to have a good couple of dozen neuroscientists around. But most of them, in fact, are among the most healthy-minded faculty, and they are able to become part of a common enterprise, a team. They don't want to talk only to neuroscientists. Also, by the way, they have spouses and kids and families, and all of a sudden that understanding becomes important. I always want to know about the family and what is going to create happiness at the dinner table.

Urbanologists in the 20th century said that great world cities are brought together by F.I.R.E.: finance, insurance, real estate. The concept that I'm going to offer you today is that in the 21st century, F.I.R.E. is a necessary but not sufficient condition to be a magnet for talent. What is necessary is I.C.E. as well: the intellectual, the cultural, and the educational environment that attracts smart people. F.I.R.E. and I.C.E.: That was the theme I began to hit with Mayor Mike Bloomberg and his people. It became a theme in my thinking about what was happening in the world as these idea capitals develop.

Daniel Patrick Moynihan was asked in the 1960s in India: How do you create a world-class city? He said, "Create two world-class universities and wait 200 years." If you think about it, universities are a critical element of F.I.R.E. and I.C.E., because they are both consumers of I.C.E. and producers of I.C.E. I feel this very much in the role that we are playing in the Emirates: Yes, we have NYU Abu Dhabi, a liberal arts college and a research university with all kinds of faculty research going on. But it is equally important that we run about thirty conferences a year there. We have what we call the NYU Abu Dhabi Institute, with a series of two or three speakers a week. It becomes part of the cultural fabric of the city, as Abu Dhabi becomes one of these premier-league idea capitals. That is my first concept, and it's relatively benign.

For a nice analogy, let me go—with my Jesuit European background— to the Italian Renaissance. If you had said to Leonardo or to Michelangelo, "You can only do your art if you do it only here in Venice," you would not have gotten them to come to you, right? They were part of an intelligentsia, a creative class, a gifted class that wanted to circulate among Milan and Rome and Venice and Florence and so on. Just freeze that thought for a second. Think of this premier league of idea capitals together. By and large, the modern university says, "You can only do your art if you do it in Venice." We say to our faculty members, essentially: You have to stay *in situ*. It's ironic, because universities have always operated beyond sovereignty.

As two of you here today said, the issues go beyond sovereignty. But even when the issues were more local, and even in disciplines that are more local, there is always a world network. I am blessed in my life with a friendship with an extraordinarily bright person who was, for my mind, a terrific leader: Gordon Brown. We were having breakfast once, just the two of us, and he knew more about NYU than he should have. He said, "I love this idea you have of a circulating world," a phrase I had offered to him. I said, "You know, Gordon, universities have always operated beyond sovereignty." He always came with a pad, and he wrote it down, saying, "I love that phrase, beyond sovereignty. I'm going to use that phrase." And I remember saying to him, "Mr. Prime Minister, this is why your polls are in the tank." I said, "John, president of a university: okay to say 'beyond sovereignty.' Gordon, head of government: not a good idea to say 'beyond sovereignty.'" But he taught me something. He said, "You're wrong. The network is going to be developing regardless. And the key question is: Will London, will New York, will Istanbul, will Abu Dhabi, will Shanghai be premier-league stops? What role will they play?" The force is there.

The second force is that the world is miniaturizing: It's growing small. We call this interdependence or globalization. Some of us have been thinking about this since we picked up in college, back in the 1960s, the writings of the great Jesuit theologian Teilhard de Chardin, who talked about how it was inevitable. Now, he saw it theologically, and he took up the doctrine of biological evolution, even though at the time Catholicism and Christianity widely saw evolutionary biology as an attack on their theories of creation and the evolution of the world. Teilhard took it up and said: No, no; it's a wonder, and it's a metaphor for spiritual growth.

I'm not here to preach to you; I'm going to say that this is a metaphor for a progressive view of the world. Teilhard would summarize it by saying that species emerge, then they diverge into a multiplicity of forms—the wonderful biological diversity that we love—and then there comes a convergence into what he called "Omega Point," which for him was foreshadowed by Christ and the capacity to love deeply and completely sacrificially. Put that aside. What is the metaphor, in a broad view, for the evolution of human society? It's the emergence of humankind essentially into a tribalistic consciousness and a divergence into the great individuality that is expressed nowhere better than in Greenwich Village, New York, where if you chose to fully tattoo yourself, strip stark naked, and walk through the park, no one would notice.

But the world is miniaturizing. We are all in each other's faces, and gating strategies are not going to work. Just say the word ISIS or the initials ISIS: Gating strategies don't work. The question is going to be—and this is the deep question of this century, I think—how are we going to respond to this miniaturization?

We have the potency of the idea capitals to provide thought and connectivity and elevation of humankind. But we're very good at "other-ing." Do we ever notice that it's an accident of birth that made me a Yankee fan and made my brother-in-law a Red Sox fan and also me a Catholic and him a Jew? All of the other things we use to separate ourselves, be they geographical or these things that we call nation-states, are other ways to team up. The whole way we've come to talk about education and economic activity is competitiveness. It's as if we are in a camp, and we are divided into groups by flags. Instead of viewing knowledge as a positive-sum game, we have this deep capacity to "other." So what are we going to choose? Are we going to choose, on one hand, a clash of civilizations or, on the other hand, a more—what I was taught to call—ecumenical view? Pope John XXIII taught us that even if we maintain our own faith, we are better off if we understand the faiths of others and incorporate them from their vantage points. The man under whom I did my doctoral dissertation in 1963 was the world's leading expert on a single medieval Christian theologian, St. Anselm. By 1983, I was celebrating him at the United Nations for the publication of his sixty-volume work on world spirituality, which addressed 25 different faith traditions. He was still a Christian, but he could understand faiths in depth. If you want the ecumenical movement, if you want Teilhard and John XXIII in a metaphor, it's learning to view the world not through the one window you're given, but through the many facets of a diamond. And it's not relativism at all. It's classic cosmopolitanism. And it's characterized by something Americans aren't very good at practicing: deep humility.

So those are the big trends. Now I'm going to describe to you NYU's response to them. I offer one example, but I don't offer it as universal. My view is that this will be seen as a premier form of higher education. Twenty to 25 years from now, there will probably be a dozen schools worldwide that will be practicing what I'm going to describe. This is kind of full monty: We're in, all in. There will be others that will use different approaches to it, and I'll give you some outlines for that. The buzz-phrase is "make the world your major."

You want to come and study economics? We've had three Nobel laureates in economics in the last ten years. You'll get a great education in economics or theater or history or business or whatever you want. But then you're going to get, on the experiential level and the thought level, an education in being an instrument in the creation of the community of communities. This view of the world is not homogeneity, but a community of communities. Like the elements of a watch, each part is identifiable but interlocking in a whole that's greater than the sum of its parts. That's the Teilhardian view of the next stage of human development.

Taking the theology out of it, we are a community of communities celebrating simultaneously the wonder of the diversity of creation and the joy it gives us to be able to see through those many facets of the diamond and, on one hand, the commonality among us and, on the other hand, the common enterprise of being human. This is not competitive; it's a positive-sum game.

Very quickly, let me start by saying what NYU's global network university is not. It's not a branch campus system. With a branch campus system, you've got headquarters, and you've got branches. It's the French Foreign Legion: You send off folks, and maybe you'll never see them again—but they are over there; they've got your uniform on. There are varying levels of quality. Some of it is, frankly, designed simply to bring revenue back to the mothership. We are not an international, global footprint like IBM. I've talked with people at IBM, and they feel that they are very much siloed in their various enterprises.

The best phrase I've been able to come up with to describe what we are is an organic circulatory system that creates a new structure for the university and that is present in the premier-league idea capitals of the world. We are not in all the capitals, but we are on every continent. You circulate, and it is all about quality. I read, and I take seriously, the dangers described by the dean of Harvard Business School. This system, in my view, is the best way to maintain quality, and it's an inerasable talent magnet for a disproportionately high share of the high-talent people in the world. They don't want to just do their art in Venice, or their spouses don't, or they don't want that world for their children, or whatever. If you can give them the capacity to circulate—faculty, students, and staff—it's a talent-magnetization.

Now I'm going to take you very quickly through its evolution, the 1.0. I was named president in May 2001, before 9/11. The case for it escalates following 9/11. But before 9/11 there was simply an accident of my being involved with two friends. They are a fellow named Dan Doctoroff, who later became deputy mayor in New York and is a brilliant guy who had just finished running the financial side for Mayor Mike Bloomberg, and Jay Kriegel, who was deputy mayor under John Lindsay, a great mayor of New York thirty years earlier. The two of them had decided that they wanted to get the Olympics to New York, and I was the third wheel. They came up with the punch line for the Olympic bid, and I said to them, "I don't care if we get the Olympics; you've created a view of what New York is, the mythos that we should be using to describe this city." It was this: "Come to New York, the world's second home. Every team will have a neighborhood."

Think of the power of that. I stole the phrase, with their permission. We are located at Washington Square with no campus. Half of our buildings are not next to other NYU buildings. There are no gates. Suddenly, thanks to Dan and Jay, I said, "Wait a minute. Our cacophony and our complexity, the facts that we don't do big-time sports and it's all micro-communities: This becomes a learning opportunity." And then you've got New York City. You can hear the prayers, the language, taste the food, hear the music of every country in the world by getting on a subway. So we started running buses on Saturdays and Sundays. There were buses in front of the library, and kids could get on a bus and go to wherever. There is an old timer there with a restaurant who is happy to give you a discount meal. He has got a map, and he is talking in another language, and the music is playing. If you do that on Saturday and Sunday for fourteen weeks every semester, you can visit 200 countries by the time you graduate.

This is not Epcot City; this is the real stuff. New York is the first ecumenical city: 40 percent of the citizens were born outside of the United States. New York City's public school system is the first in the world that can say that it educates kids from every country in the world, kids born in those countries and not only descendants of people born there. The people in those New York neighborhoods may be Irish, like my ancestors, or Italian or Turkish or whatever. If you ask them what they are, they'll say New Yorkers. New York is the first uber-community, a community of communities. So you'll be teaching that.

The next logical thing, 2.0, is: Okay, it's nice to visit the Italians in Little Italy, but shouldn't we take them on, on their turf? It's all about getting out of your comfort zone. It's the second major, in addition to economics. You are getting the world as your major, building a community of communities. Second, you open up a study-away site in Florence, a real study-away site, because it's about quality. The courses and the faculty: They're all NYU courses and NYU faculty. You've got an internship program there; you've got extracurricular activities; and you've got all of the student life things that are important these days to student wellness. You've got to be able to say to their parents that they're going to be safe.

When my daughter went to Yale, she faced heavy headwinds against studying away. When my wife died suddenly in Katie's first week of her second semester of freshman year, she said that she wanted to be home with her brother and me and asked Yale if she could take four courses with award-winning professors at NYU. The answer was, "We only allow two courses to be taken away, because it's the Yale way. Yale is wonderful, of course, and she got a great education. But only two courses? Being a law professor, I use the Socratic method. I asked the dean whom I was dealing with whether Yale takes transfer students. "Yes." I thought that was the end of it and that I didn't have to ask the next question. But the result was that Katie took two courses, and no more than two courses, at NYU and then had go back to Yale, because she wanted to return as a sophomore. She went back to Yale during the summer to take two courses in a Yale building and taught by New Haven high school teachers, but it was the Yale way. And when she went to study away in Prague, she was in a hostel, and a Yale professor was there for the summer. When she was mugged on the streets of Prague, there was no one to whom she could turn. Thank God we have a study-away center for NYU there that could mobilize.

You develop a network, that's 2.0: the study-away sites. We now have—and I'm going to do some double counting—fifteen study-away sites with high-quality courses and pathways. If you're a pre-med, you can't go to all fifteen, but there are five where you can get organic chemistry with a first-rate teacher. Or if you're a Tisch student in dance, there are three where you can go. The departments at schools and units have taken ownership: This is the quality part. If it's a circulatory system, as opposed to a branch campus system, the person who takes Economics 101 in London is going to be in my Economics 201 class. I care about who's been appointed to teach the course and what the content of the course is, because that course is going to be articulated into my department and will be part of my major. There are fifteen study-away sites on six continents.

3.0: We looked at the system and asked: If we want to be the first ecumenical university, where is the Arab and Muslim component? Then the question became: Can we do it? We started looking and discovered an extraordinary leader, Mohamed bin Zayed, in Abu Dhabi. I met with him to talk about a study-away site, and he said: I've read your stuff about idea capitals, and I want to make Abu Dhabi the idea capital of the Gulf. Would you consider creating a full presence of NYU: A to Z for students, with study-away and students from anywhere in the world?

Until two years ago, about half of my faculty thought we were in Abu "Dubai," which proves the need to be there. I've been privileged to know many heads of government, heads of state, but Mohamed bin Zayed is as close to Plato's philosopher king as I've seen. Thinking fifty years ahead, his father, a Bedouin who had never been in a classroom, said, "The key to the future is the education of our people and the education of the world." And Mohamed bin Zayed said to me that he wanted to create a university that's fully integrated into NYU, starting with a liberal arts college and building graduate and research programs for a research university of liberal arts and undergraduate education. And he said to do it for the best students in the world and to find them wherever they are. And we found them.

The first class was brought in five years ago. We only wanted 100 students. We had recruited the president of Swarthmore to be the dean, who is called the vice chancellor there. Al Bloom had gone over there, and we brought in the first class. Al said to us, "You're going to get a 60 percent yield. That's what Swarthmore gets, so if you want a class of 100, make 180 offers." But we got a class of 150, with SAT numbers and grade point averages as good as Harvard's in the very first year. That class graduated last May. We had a 90 percent return on our offers of admission last year. There were 15,000 applications for 150 spots, and the kids applied from all over. We graduated 140 kids last May from 48 countries. The median kid speaks four languages, and 31 of them came from families in which, until we brought one member of the family in for graduation, the family member had not been more than five miles from home.

Just to give you one example that's important to my thesis: A young man named Musba, who homeschooled himself until the 8th grade in a tribal village in Ethiopia, walked five days to Addis Ababa and persuaded the international school to accept him. They found out six months later that he was living in a cardboard box, a home he had built for himself, with no water or electricity. They gave him housing, he graduated first in his class, and then he graduated *magna cum laude* from NYU Abu Dhabi last year. It's just extraordinary. Out of the 140 kids who graduated, three of them are right now in Rhodes College, Oxford. Think about that for a second: the first graduating class and three graduates go to Rhodes College. Abu Dhabi was 3.0.

We have two doorways through which a kid from the Bronx can choose to come in: from New York, and encounter predominantly Americans and massive cacophony, and from Abu Dhabi. We just moved to a new Abu Dhabi campus. We will be expanding to 2,000 undergraduate and 1,000 graduate students. On the former campus, we had 700 students from every sector of society and representing 102 countries. It's a tight community, and you can't avoid people: Community there is easy.

And then the Chinese came to us and said, "We want to do the same thing." That's how NYU Shanghai happened. It is fully government-supported there as well. We are the first American university to be licensed as a Chinese university, so we get Chinese funding for our research competitively, and the campus they built was just completed. It's a million square feet right in the heart of Pudong, and they're building us a dorm, which will be another million-square-foot building. The Abu Dhabi campus is 3 million square feet, with 21 buildings, and it is fully operative now.

The Chinese campus is a third doorway. Half of the class is Chinese, but students can't apply unless they are in the top 60,000 of the 12 million Chinese high school graduates, so they are in the 99.9th percentile. We do two days of interviews for everybody who comes into Abu Dhabi or Shanghai.

In closing, I'll offer this: There are going to be many ways to do this. I came here on a Turkish airplane that was an Etihad plane and a JetBlue plane, so there's going to be code sharing. That's one way of doing it: not simply massive open online courses (MOOCs) and alliances, but deep partnerships; remember that quality control is going to be key. At the other end of the spectrum is the old kind of study-away, which was academic tourism: You use your elective subjects, and it's not integrated; you may not get credit in your department, but you are in Paris for a year, whether you go to class or not. That's kind of passé. But there is a significant way to do it less aggressively than we've done it, which I call code sharing.

I believed it about the United States, but what Abu Dhabi has proven is this: There is talent out there, unless you're a racist and you think that the smartest 3 percent of people in the world are in the United States or that they are only in one segment of society. We're really in danger as we go through what's called here in Europe the massification of higher education: relegating the poor, the unconnected, the uninformed to online degrees that the elites will never want for their kids.

We have to develop ways to search for talent that is out there and bring them into the 200 to 500 universities that I started out talking about. There are ways to do it. I am the chairman of the Board of something called the University of the People. If you are a high school graduate, you are fluent in English, you have access to the Internet, and you are abjectly poor, you are in. It is not a MOOC—we use MOOC and online open source materials—but there is a curriculum; there is an exam at the end; and there are 32 people in a class and peer-to-peer and volunteer teachers. You take your courses, and you get your degree. If at the end of the first year kids have excelled in the University of the People, we will bring them in for interviews. I was teaching yesterday a freshman whom we found through the University of the People, an Afghani woman. This is what we, as the higher education enterprise, have to do as we go forward.

Globalization and the Responsibilities of the University

John J. DeGioia
President, Georgetown University

It is a privilege to be here at the National University of Singapore—one of our world's great universities, a leader in engineering, the life sciences and biomedicine, the social sciences, and natural sciences. "May our noble aspiration bring Singapore success," notes the National Anthem of Singapore, and I've no doubt that through the outstanding work of your fourteen faculties and schools, the National University of Singapore has certainly done so, while also advancing the boundaries of knowledge and contributing to the betterment of society.

The work that you do here to promote knowledge and human development—as well your university's motto, "Towards a Global Knowledge Enterprise"—resonates deeply with efforts in which we are engaged at the university I have called my home for more than three decades. We, too, are striving to evolve into a truly global university. To be a global university requires a different way of engaging with our world; it requires that we recognize that global means multilateral, multinational, and multicultural. It is why we were so happy to join with the National University of Singapore, and ten other leading universities from six continents, to establish our Center for Transnational Legal Studies in London. It is why we participate in student exchanges between our two law schools and—beginning this fall—our schools of public policy.

The work to evolve into increasingly global universities is imperative in our increasingly globalized world where nations are more interconnected, individuals more interdependent. Perhaps nowhere is the increasing pace and growing importance of globalization more obvious than here in Singapore—which, according to the Globalization Index (a collaboration between *Foreign Policy* and A.T. Kearny), is recognized as the most globalized nation on earth.[1]

In a world increasingly defined and characterized by globalization, I believe there are urgent questions that we must address from the perspective of the university. We are unique institutions, and I believe we bear a special responsibility in responding to the forces of globalization. What are the responsibilities of a university in responding to globalization? Have we achieved a consensus regarding the phenomena of globalization? If we have, do we know how we are to respond? And do we have a sense of the moral responsibilities that emerge in a world shaped by these phenomena?

I wish to begin with a working definition of these multifaceted phenomena. I offer nothing original here. I believe the term globalization captures the convergence of forces that include new information, communication and transportation technologies that create unprecedented opportunities to be engaged, connected, and present in different parts of the world. I agree with President Lee Bollinger of Columbia University, who delivered the inaugural S.T. Lee Lecture here at the Lee Kwan Yew School last fall, when he said: "Globalization is first and foremost an economically driven phenomenon."[2] Globalization is driving greater integration of markets and is expanding the opportunities for trade in goods and services between and among nations.

But what kind of response does globalization demand? These forces have provided for extraordinary economic growth. China is considered the case study of how a country can benefit from participation in a globalized economic system, with more than 300 million Chinese moving out of poverty in the past generation. But globalization is also blamed for increasing inequalities across nations. The rich are getting richer, the poor, poorer. Half of the world still lives on less than two dollars a day, more than a billion on less than one dollar a day. Globalization is regarded as a source of fragmentation, division—and implicated in this growing inequality. And there is also growing consensus that our international institutions are not designed to cope with this new context. Our most significant institutions are the products of a post-World War II context and are insufficient to respond to the emerging challenges of our time: climate change, nuclear proliferation, pandemics. New structures are needed. No one has provided more significant global leadership in addressing this need for new structures of global governance than Kishore Mahbubani [dean of the Lee Kuan Yew School of Public Policy], and I have learned much from his example.

Today I wish to bring the issue of globalization into the context of the university. It is within the context of the university that I believe we can find the resources for addressing the questions of moral responsibility. Specifically, it is the very "ethos" of a university that we can bring to bear on the challenges posed by globalization. By "ethos" I mean "the characteristic spirit" that animates the identity and purpose of the university.[3] In my remarks, I wish to recast the framing of globalization within that ethos of the university.

The "characteristic spirit" of the university is to seek the betterment of humankind. Consider these words from the mission statement of this university:

"The NUS mission comprises three mutually reinforcing thrusts:
1. Transformative education that nurtures thinking individuals who are alive to opportunities to make a difference, are valued members and leaders of society, and global citizens in diverse settings.
2. High-impact research that advances the boundaries of knowledge and contributes to the betterment of society.
3. Dedicated service, as a national university, that adds to social, economic, and national development."[4]

How can we harness the forces of globalization in the service of these three themes? I believe first and foremost, we must assert ourselves, animated by the values that are so present here in this academic community, and work to reshape the very meaning of the term "globalization." I believe our understanding of globalization is too limited, too constrained. I don't believe our understanding of globalization should be defined simply by economic terms and market considerations. Instead, globalization should be understood as a force through which we can further advance the betterment of humankind.

Globalization poses new challenges and new opportunities, and perhaps the most significant is how to interpret the reality we are experiencing. Animated by our ethos, I believe our universities offer important resources for reframing our understanding.

I wish to suggest four areas for reflection that resonate with the ethos of the university. It is my hope that by engaging these four areas of reflection, we might open up and broaden our understanding of the meaning of globalization.

The first responsibility of the university is the development of the intellect of the young people who come to our campuses. The ethos of the university includes, in the words of my colleague at Georgetown, the distinguished historian John O'Malley, a recognition of the "preeminence of truth and the dignity of the quest for it."[5] We seek to instill the habits of mind that will sustain this quest. We seek to nurture thinking individuals who are alive to opportunities to make a difference.

No one has captured the ethos and identity of the university more than John Henry Newman, who in one month will be beatified by Pope Benedict XVI. Newman wrote, in the lectures that became *The Idea of the University*, that the purpose of university education is the "real cultivation of mind," that is, "the intellect...properly trained and formed to have a connected view or grasp of things."[6] By "connected view," Newman means the ability to develop a "comprehensive view of truth, in all its branches, of the relations of science to science, of their mutual bearings, and their respective values."[7]

Newman is committed to the idea that we can aspire to what would have been called in the 19th century "Universal Knowledge," a belief in a unity of knowledge which is within the grasp of a cultivated intellect. We seek to understand each of the disciplines but also the relationships of the disciplines to one another.

Newman's conception of a "unity of knowledge" would not be held in our contemporary academy. Our practices of disciplinary specialization and the sheer complexity of what we now know make the thought of such integration implausible. But what if, in our pursuit of new concepts that could guide us in responding to globalization, we re-examine this key insight of Newman: that the purpose of university education is to grasp the truth and the connection between and among the disciplines?

Coming from a very different perspective than Newman, the distinguished biologist E.O. Wilson raised just this prospect at the end of the last decade. What if we could establish as an element of our intellectual agenda this challenge of integration of knowledge, the exploration of the potential for what Wilson called "consilience"? What if globalization could come to be understood as an effort at seeking consilience?

A second responsibility of the university entails the formation of character. We use different words to capture this idea. At Georgetown we describe this aspect of our mission as educating "women and men to be responsible and active participants in civic life, and to live generously in service to others."[8] This idea is captured beautifully in the words of the NUS mission statement: "individuals who are alive to opportunities to make a difference, are valued members and leaders of society, and global citizens in diverse settings." This idea is deep in the ethos of the academy, with roots in the humanism of the Renaissance. The great formulators of this aspect of our ethos, Erasmus, Bruni, Petrarch, sought to ensure a focus on citizenship, on civic responsibility, on the formation of character. The locus of this work is in the disciplines we call the humanities.

Could we imagine an ideal like that articulated in your mission statement of global citizenship—of global civic responsibility? What would it look like? And what kind of preparation might be required for such citizenship and for such responsibility?

We offer the very best settings in the world for the living of these questions. We are the homes to the most extraordinary young people, with access to the best that has been thought and written and connected to one another in ways that are unprecedented in the history of our world. For our students, globalization means connectedness. It means access to ideas. It means an ability to participate in the construction of knowledge and the building of communities.

How do we understand the nature of the interior lives of our young people? How are they making sense of our world and their place in it? What effect are new technologies for connecting with one another having on their ways of making meaning in their lives? How are their imaginations being formed, and how do they understand the depth and breadth of their possibilities?

An important insight for us to consider was provided in April by Adolfo Nicolas, the superior general of the Jesuit Order, in a speech to a gathering in Mexico City of educators from Jesuit colleges and universities from throughout the world. He noted, "We need to understand this complex new interior world created by globalization."[9]

This interior world—the conscience and imagination that emerges— shapes the nature of one's engagement in the world. Can we imagine a global citizen? Can we ensure that our engagement with the humanities provides our students with the resources to inform an interior life capable of emerging with a sense of responsibility for others in the world?

Beyond the humanities, we offer other resources that contribute to an understanding of responsibility. This leads me to a third set of reflections that emerge from the ethos of the university and that I hope can expand our conception of globalization. There has been a development that has been underway now for the past two decades, a development that has the potential to transform the way we understand the nature of our responsibilities to one another. This development is best captured in the series of publications that will celebrate their 20th anniversary this year.

Beginning in 1990, the United Nations has produced an annual *Human Development Report*. The intellectual father of this initiative is the Nobel laureate Amartya Sen, who over the course of his career has developed a set of ideas that is transforming the way we understand our responsibilities to one another. We refer to this set of ideas as the Human Development and Capability Approach. This Approach seeks to address the underlying economic, social, and political conditions that enable each of us to fulfill our promise and potential. This is "an approach to development in which the objective is to expand what people are able to do and be."[10]

The animating concepts were established in the very first *Human Development Report*. Human development was defined as "both the process of widening people's choices and the level of their achieved well-being."[11] The core idea: "The purpose of development is to enhance people's capabilities."[12] What is meant by capabilities? A capability is the "freedom to promote or achieve what [one] values[s] doing and being."[13] It is the freedom to engage in the practices and activities that one values doing and for which there is a value doing. It is through these activities that one achieves "well-being" or "human flourishing." The question that Sen asks and that is at the heart of the Human Development Approach is: Do you have the capability to engage in the activities, the practices, what Sen calls the "functionings," that matter most to you? Do the social, political, and economic structures provide you with the framework to achieve this capability?

For so much of the modern era, we have considered our responsibilities to each other within the poles of utilitarianism and duty-based theories— between the poles of Mill and Kant. For so much of the modern era, in our understanding of political economy, this has translated into a focus on GDP. The Human Development and Capability Approach asks us to consider a different way. Again, in the words of the first *Human Development Report*: "The basic objective of development is to create an enabling environment for people to enjoy long, healthy and creative lives. This may appear to be a simple truth. But it is often forgotten in the immediate concern with the accumulation of commodities and financial wealth."[14] It is lost with a focus on GDP.

This idea of human development deeply resonates with the ethos of the university. Can you imagine an account more focused on the betterment of humankind? I believe we need to embrace this new understanding of our responsibilities to each other for full "integral" development. It would be invaluable if we could support efforts to expand an understanding of globalization that accepts this understanding of human development. But beyond that, could we imagine, in the exercise of our institutional agency, the university playing a deeper role in this work of human development?

This is a challenging question. Let me offer one example from my own context of how challenging this can be. Colleagues of mine at Georgetown, at our Center on Education and the Workforce, led by the distinguished economist Anthony Carnevale, issued a report this summer entitled "Help Wanted, Projections of Jobs and Education Requirements Through 2018." Their report projected both job and employment growth in the United States in the coming decade. They project that the U.S. economy will produce 22 million jobs by 2018. But nearly two-thirds of all jobs that will need to be filled in this decade will require some postsecondary education. Their key finding: We "will under-produce postsecondary graduates by approximately 3 million by 2018."[15]

Job creation is an element of human development. Leaders of colleges and universities have long accepted a role for our schools in supporting regional economic development. In the words of the NUS mission: "Dedicated service, as a national university, that adds to social, economic, and national development." The findings of my colleagues, however, point to what is something more of a structural issue. In the next decade in the United States, given current patterns, we will not produce enough graduates for 3 million jobs requiring postsecondary education.

The challenges are more acute in other parts of the world. Unemployment is above 25 percent in South Africa; 20 percent in Nigeria and in Spain; 13 percent in Ireland; and between 17 and 20 percent in Estonia, Latvia, and Lithuania. In the United States, we have our highest rates in two decades. The fifth volume of the *Arab Human Development Report* estimated that 51 million new jobs must be created in the Arab world by 2020. This will be the largest group of young people entering the work force in the Arab world, and current projections will not meet these needs.

How do universities respond to these kinds of structural needs? We teach, we do research, we care for patients in our academic medical centers, we provide service, usually in our local communities and in some cases in different parts of the world. We play a role in supporting regional economic enterprise. In a few special circumstances, we are creating some businesses that evolve from the research in our laboratories. But we are now engaged in the world in ways that would have been unimaginable just a few years ago. And a new understanding of our responsibilities to one another is emerging in the logic of human development. Can we find ways to contribute to addressing structural constraints to human development? We have an opportunity to expand both our understanding of the nature of globalization and our understanding of the nature of our institutional agency.

A fourth set of reflections: I believe we are uniquely capable of expanding the conception of globalization to capture a greater capacity for understanding one another across boundaries and differences. Our campuses have long been "melting pots," with students and faculty coming together from throughout the world, creating academic communities shaped by a common commitment to learning, scholarship, and research. Can we draw from this characteristic of our campuses and commit to deepening our efforts at mutual understanding?

There is one area I wish to propose that, I believe, is of critical importance at this time. Can we consider the possibility of more deeply engaging our religious traditions in the work of the academy? I don't mean simply as objects of study—we have pursued the formal study of religion for nearly 150 years in our universities. I mean engaging the intellectual dimensions of our religious traditions on their terms, bringing them into the discourse that takes place in the contemporary academy. I make this recommendation, particularly in the context of expanding our conception of globalization, for two reasons: First, our world has become much smaller. Those with different faiths are in much more proximate contact with one another, both physically and through advances in communications technology. We can no longer ignore those of a different faith. We need to know each other at ever deepening levels. If a significant part of an individual's identity is animated by faith, we need to be able understand the dimensions of that faith.

Second, our religious traditions are the repositories of deep wisdom. As we seek to explore the impact of globalization on the interior lives of people, these wisdom traditions offer important resources for self-understanding and mutual understanding. For too long, we have cut off from academic discourse the insights of these traditions.

I wish to offer one last comment. As I prepared these remarks, it was impossible not to be deeply moved by the confluence of disasters that are hitting our sisters and brothers in different places around our world. At one point this past week, 557 wildfires raged over a 1,740-square-kilometer region southeast of Moscow. In China, more than a thousand lives were lost in Gansu province as a result of mudslides. A third of Pakistan was under water, a submerged area as big as the United Kingdom. Fourteen million Pakistanis have been affected; 2 million are homeless. At times it seems that we have to be prepared to consider "crisis management" as an aspect of everyday life. If we are to understand the nature of our moral responsibility in a context of globalization, we must acknowledge that our academic communities must be prepared to engage these issues. Animated by a "characteristic spirit," we need to learn how to work together, how to learn together, to determine how we, all of us, understand the nature of this world in which we live and our responsibilities for it.

Globalization provides unprecedented opportunities to better humankind. The ethos of the university, our "characteristic spirit," is to seek the betterment of humankind. We need to enrich our conception of globalization. There is work that is properly that of the university that can enrich our understanding of globalization.

Is it possible that one day, when people think of globalization, the ideas that will come to mind are the search for consilience, for the unity of knowledge? Is it possible that globalization will entail a commitment to global citizenship and global civic responsibility? Could globalization come to capture the idea of integral human development and articulate the expectation that in the exercise of institutional agency, the university would play a role in such development? Could globalization mean a capacity to know one another more deeply, to understand one another and the deepest sources of our commitments with empathy? Could globalization come to mean an understanding of a more profound responsibility we have for our world and for one another?

Now is the time for us, for our communities of learning, to step in and offer our contribution to our understanding of globalization—an understanding that has, at its core, an acknowledgement and appreciation of the inherent human dignity of every individual in our global community.

Endnotes

1. "The Globalization Index." *Foreign Policy.* 163 (2007):70. Print.

2. Bollinger, Lee. "Universities for a Global Society." National University of Singapore. 27 October 2009. Keynote address.

3. "Ethos." *Oxford English Dictionary.* 2nd ed. 1989.

4. "NUS Mission." http://www.nus.edu.sg/aboutus/vision.php. National University of Singapore, Office of Corporate Relations. 1 August 2010.

5. O'Malley, John W. *Four Cultures of the West* (Cambridge, Massachusetts: The Belknap Press of Harvard University Press, 2004) 79.

6. Ker, Ian. *The Achievement of John Henry Newman* (Notre Dame, Indiana: University of Notre Dame Press, 1990) 20. My emphasis.

7. Ker, 3.

8. "University Mission Statement." http://president.georgetown.edu/sections/governance/missionstatement. Georgetown University. 1 August 2010.

9. Nicolas, Adolfo. "Depth, Universality, and Learned Ministry: Challenges to Jesuit Higher Education Today." Remarks for "Networking Jesuit Higher Education: Shaping the Future for a Humane, Just, Sustainable Globe." Mexico City, 23 April 2010.

10. Severine Deneulin and Lila Shahani, eds. *An Introduction to the Human Development and Capability Approach: Feedom and Agency* (London: earthscan, 2009) 23.

11. Deneulin and Shahani, eds., 26.

12. Deneulin and Shahani, eds., 26-27.

13. Deneulin and Shahani, eds., 31.

14. Deneulin and Shahani, eds., 41.

15. Carnevale, Anthony P., Nicole Smith and Jeff Strohl. "Help Wanted, Projections of Jobs and Education Requirements Through 2018." Center on Education and the Workforce. 1 Aug 2010.

CREATING A WEB OF GLOBAL ENGAGEMENT

John A. Fry
President, Drexel University

Our greatest challenges today are global, testing the limits of current technologies and demanding ingenuity, agility, even audacity in addressing them. Problems posed by rapidly growing economies in some parts of the world and crippling poverty in others, climate change, human and information insecurity, growing demands for sustainable sources of energy, and the potential of deadly pandemics require complex global solutions spawned by innovative research and collaborative approaches.

As key institutions for knowledge creation and innovation, research universities are not only perfectly positioned to take the lead as global actors in addressing these challenges, they are also obliged to do so. They must prepare students to engage globally, to work across countries and cultures, navigate global markets and, ultimately, develop global solutions to the world's problems. Universities must internationalize their research initiatives and their academic partnerships, taking advantage of the opportunities for forging connections presented by new technologies and increasing openness in communication and steering the turbulent waters of competition and rapid change.

Research universities have clear advantages as global knowledge leaders, but they must consider their strategies for engagement carefully—driven by mission and institutional culture.

A Natural Source of Globalization

Universities have long been among the most international of communities. To draw from the example of Greater Philadelphia, where I work, more than 13,000 international students and faculty members study and teach at the region's colleges and universities each year. Thousands of our students study abroad, and our institutions establish partnerships around the world. Faculty members routinely engage globally through international research networks, digital resources, publications, and conferences.

Universities are also consistently developers and early adopters of the new technologies that have made it possible to collaborate across borders. At Drexel University, for example, we are one of twenty direct connectors to Internet2, the advanced research technology community founded by American universities and networked internationally with partners in fifty-plus nations. We also host ipl2, a public service learning and teaching environment built from the collections of the Internet Public Library and the Librarians' Internet Index.

Through these human and technological connections across the globe, colleges and universities are well positioned to respond to globalization and encourage global thinking. The strategic question for academic leaders becomes: What's the best path or paths of engagement for an institution committed to enhancing its global impact?

Branch Campus versus Collaborative Hub

As easy as it is to say we must continue engaging globally, it is a formidable challenge to establish a meaningful presence in geographically and culturally diverse locations. Different models for engagement, driven by reputation, finances, and vision have emerged for doing so by many of the world's most distinguished universities.

Attempts by existing universities to establish new, stand-alone units or "branch campuses" abroad—in essence, exporting the brand of the institution from one continent to another—have met with varying degrees of success and face serious challenges. The "global campus" presents enormous costs of infrastructure and staffing, and cultural differences are not easily overcome. Even for schools with worldwide name recognition, building a presence from scratch and maintaining it has proven difficult.

When an American university finds the right partner, however, whether another university, a research organization, or even in some cases a municipal entity or corporation, it opens the doors to a number of potential positive outcomes. Global research collaborations benefit from a broader range of perspectives and expertise; educational partnerships expand offerings to students; cross-cultural awareness and understanding deepens; prospects for recruiting new students increase; and opportunities for internships, local symposia, and interdisciplinary knowledge creation grow. This defines the vision for global engagement at Drexel University.

We have chosen at Drexel to focus on developing international partnerships organized around innovative research and teaching, with partners who have complementary strengths and mutual interests. These intellectually-driven hubs provide platforms for interdisciplinary research and education and project-based scholarship, and they serve as incubators for new ideas and commercialization. Often they are catalyzed by existing faculty relationships that grow organically, thus creating broader university opportunities. The existing connections, manageable scope, and value of a local partner with local knowledge invested in mutually beneficial outcomes make such initiatives a promising route to global impact. Based on this approach, we welcomed global partners to our campus to celebrate an inaugural Global Innovation Partnership Week in October 2012. Participants included researchers and investment partners from China, Israel, and Turkey, along with representatives from regional industry, economic development agencies, and investment groups. Representatives of Coulter Translational Partnership Universities—members of an elite group, including Drexel, that have received a Wallace H. Coulter Foundation endowment for translational biomedical research—also participated during this now annual Global Innovation Partnership Week.

Creating a Successful Collaboration

Successful global engagement should mirror an institution's mission and priorities. Here at Drexel, our research enterprise is especially committed to translational research—work that intentionally moves discoveries from the lab to market—while our approach to education is grounded in learning from actual experiences. Our best partners tend to have a similar focus. Together, we have created several related models for expressing these approaches to creating and transmitting knowledge, in some cases working together to create life-saving solutions.

Our burgeoning joint Drexel University-Hebrew University of Jerusalem Institute for Drug Research Hub, for example, has four improved drug-delivery methods on the track to market. Discoveries are focused on ameliorating multiple sclerosis, epilepsy, asthma, and skin cancer. In addition to developing products to address pressing needs, this Drexel-Hebrew University Hub, animated by annual symposia and ongoing research collaborations, has created opportunities for sharing ideas, building partnerships, and fostering greater cultural and social understanding—engaging faculty and students in cutting-edge research and truly immersive international experiences.

In China, Drexel has joined with the Shanghai Advanced Research Institute (SARI), an organization created by the Chinese Academy of Sciences and the municipal government of Shanghai. SARI's vast campus is growing in Pudong, and Drexel has established an active collaborative research and meeting space within it. The joint Drexel-SARI Center sponsors ongoing joint research collaborations and educational partnerships, as well as providing research co-ops (six-month intensive residencies for undergraduates), and joint symposia.

Universities sharing similar approaches to education can also use international collaborations to grow their academic footprint through dual degree programs. Drexel has established a dual Ph.D. in translational research with Shanghai Jiao Tong University and a dual Master's degree in environmental engineering with Peking Graduate School for Energy and Environment in Shenzhen, China. This growing trend in international higher education creates opportunities for sustainable collaboration among faculty and students in addressing global challenges and advancing cultural understanding.

Drexel is known for experiential learning, fostered by one of the nation's oldest and largest co-operative education programs. Here, students alternate in six-month cycles formal classroom education with professional engagements in corporations, various non-profits, government agencies, or research. Extending Drexel co-op globally is one of our strategic priorities. While study abroad is a powerful learning experience, studying and working abroad can provide unique, valuable preparation for future success. Our international innovation partnerships help us identify new opportunities for real-world professional experience for our students. For example, Drexel's first co-op student at the Joint Drexel-SARI Center in Shanghai worked on developing a nanomaterial-based platform for anticancer drug delivery for brain tumor treatment. Extending our vision for global co-op, we are working with partner co-op institutions around the world, aided by our membership in the World Association for Cooperative Education, to form a worldwide web of co-op institutions. This approach promises to open global co-ops for students from all the partners, enacting our vision of students from various countries circulating globally, according to interest, discipline, geographic concentrations of corporations, or simply cultural curiosity.

Meeting Critical Challenges

No one strategy for achieving globalization will work for every institution. But strong partnerships and initiatives that extend the home campus's locus and strengths are essential. At Drexel, we are building our collaborative global partnerships by nurturing existing faculty research relationships, while also encouraging and facilitating faculty mobility and collaboration across borders.

In a new, related approach to global connectedness, we are also expanding the partnership model by working with new "technoparks," designed to encourage multi-institutional collaborative innovation and proliferating in places such as Turkey, China, and Israel, where we are building strong research and educational partnerships. I had the opportunity to visit several Turkish technoparks, and I was struck by the creative forces generated by high-density, high-impact communities of science and technology leaders linked with entrepreneurs. Those visits helped inform Drexel's vision for an "innovation neighborhood" around our University City campus in Philadelphia. Again, our vision has global reach: Through partnerships, we aim to open our innovation neighborhood globally, inviting those from similar neighborhoods throughout the world to consider our site as a good place to locate, even as they may beckon Philadelphia innovators and entrepreneurs to expand to their sites.

Beyond its cultural and commercial advantages, the "innovation neighborhood" will thus serve as a home away from home—a base in a vibrant city—for our partner institutions, driving local economic growth through global engagements. Its implementation will help us fulfill our commitment to enhancing the economic potential of our home, Greater Philadelphia, by increasing the region's global connections. By linking our international collaborative centers and our "innovation neighborhood," we are most likely to meet an essential goal of successful university globalization: high impact with multiple, sustainable, and shared benefits.

Drexel's approach to engaging globally through partnerships expresses our mission and institutional culture. A Drexel education aims to create professionals ready to enter a global workplace as effective global citizens prepared to be nimble, innovative, open to new opportunities and the perspectives of others. Drexel's long-standing commitment to experiential learning and creating useful knowledge is enhanced by its approach to global engagement. Launching a global web of partnerships, in line with our core beliefs, promises to enable our graduates to foster new approaches to addressing the world's most intractable problems. At its fullest, our global vision will create a worldwide innovation web, driving global connectedness and at the same time regional economic development. Already, we have begun to see positive results from our global web. We are eager to continue its development.

Teach for California, Research for the World

Janet Napolitano
President, University of California

It is a great honor to be invited to come before the Commonwealth Club. It has such a rich tradition, providing a platform for a steady stream of national and world leaders. It was before the Commonwealth Club that Woodrow Wilson laid out his vision for a League of Nations. FDR stood before this club as a presidential candidate and offered his prescription for a fair way out of the Great Depression. Martin Luther King, Jr., Audrey Hepburn, Barry Goldwater, Bella Abzug—it's been a wide-ranging and eclectic lineup that's come here to discuss the most pressing issues of the day. And I offer a toast to you: May that tradition continue for another 110 years.

So what about tonight? Tonight, you are getting one of California's newest citizens. Like so many Californians, I came here from some place else—most recently Washington, D.C., but before that Arizona, via New Mexico, via Pittsburgh, via New York City, where I was born. As I noted when I was appointed to serve as the 20th president of the University of

California, I am a non-traditional choice. My background is in law and in public service, not in higher education.

That said, I do not enter this new realm as a total stranger. My father had a Ph.D. in anatomy and was dean of the medical school at the University of New Mexico. One of my fondest childhood memories was hunting on the campus grounds for blue-tail lizards, while Dad was in his lab checking on experiments. These lizards have detachable tails, and he would pay me and my siblings a nickel for every lizard's tail we brought him. (I don't think he really needed the lizard tails—he just needed a creative way to distract us so he could work in peace.) My mother's degree was in zoology. My sister's degrees are in audiology. And my older brother is a Ph.D. at Sandia Lab in Livermore. Put simply, I come from a family of scientists.

As governor of Arizona, I kept my focus on education, including funding for all-day kindergarten and a new medical school and fighting to ensure that our universities, even in tough budgetary times, had the resources they needed to pursue their own vision of excellence. Now, to be clear, my father's service as a medical school dean, my family's background in science, my own record as an undergraduate at Santa Clara and as a law student at the University of Virginia—none of that by itself qualifies me to lead the greatest public research university in the world. I believe my selection was, in good measure, a result of my experience running large, complex institutions, such as the third largest department of the federal government and the state government of Arizona.

I made clear from the start that my learning curve at UC would be a steep one. But I have faced steep learning curves before. And I have found that the upward trajectory can be accelerated by taking a couple of steps early on. The first is to dive into the budget. Budgets offer the most direct road map to what truly matters to an organization. And they show where opportunity for new priorities or fresh initiatives might be lurking in the budgetary weeds. Since arriving in California, my bedtime reading has been book after book of numbers—numbers, numbers, numbers. These days, I dream in numbers. I don't count sheep to fall asleep; I count unrestricted funds and FTEs [full-time equivalent individuals].

I've also instigated a top-to-bottom efficiency review of the Office of the President. My understanding is that my predecessor did a terrific job of trimming and tightening, but there is always room for improvement. Our obligation, as public servants, is to stay constantly on the prowl for possible savings. The search for efficiencies is the administrative equivalent of painting the Golden Gate Bridge. The work never ends.

The other essential immediate step in taking the helm of an institution like the UC system is to listen and learn. This requires some discipline, because the natural instinct of any leader is to jump right in, to hit the ground running with grand initiatives that signal intent. The problem is that "ready-fire-aim" is rarely a productive approach. The first thing you need to know is what you don't know. Then, from that honest platform, you can begin to build your base of institutional knowledge. And so I have been out and about. Much of my first month as president has been spent visiting the constellation of UC campuses. Merced. San Diego. UCLA. The Berkeley Lab. Santa Cruz. Davis. Irvine. I've been everywhere. Well, almost everywhere. Riverside, UCSF, Santa Barbara and Berkeley will come soon.

Of course, the end of this initial journey won't mean I've learned all that there is to learn about UC. That would be a silly and even a dangerous notion. I expect, and I truly hope, that I will be learning something new every single day I serve as president. But I've already learned enough to state, without equivocation, that UC is special. We're here to teach, to transmit knowledge, to research, and to create knowledge. And we do it better than anyone else. We teach for California, and we research for the world.

I'd like to share with you a few highlights encountered on my travels to date and also a few impressions. My very first night on a campus was at UC Merced—and I do mean "night." I sat in on a biology class. Merced doesn't have a lot of classroom space. Classes start early and run late, six days a week. This one started—started—at 9:15 pm. I saw two dozen students squinting into their microscopes, hours after the sun went down. That tells me two things. First, these students are hell-bent on getting their educations. And second, we need to build more classrooms. When I think about those students, all I hear is Ray Liotta whispering, "If you build it, they will come."

At UC San Diego, I met the brain whisperers. These are the scientists answering President Obama's call to map the activity of the human brain. They're creating the technology we need to map the brain down to single cells, within the timescale of a millisecond. They're doing it across academic disciplines—from neuroscience to chemistry to nanoscience. And they showed me that collaboration is a big part of the spirit of a public research university.

I spent one night in a living laboratory at UC Davis. It's called West Village, and it's the largest planned zero-net-energy community in the country. On the ground floor, they're researching batteries, conservation, water. On the next floor up, faculty, students, and staff live and work side by side in structures that make use of the green technologies being explored on the floor below. It's a mini-ecosystem with a lot of solar panels. And it's going to show the world that zero net energy is practical on a large scale.

At UC Santa Cruz, I toured the campus's marine lab. It's one of the jewels of the university. I was invited to pet a shark, but I'd just arrived from Washington, and I'd had my fill of sharks. So I petted a dolphin instead. The Long Marine Lab has become a major hub of marine research worldwide. The professor who runs the lab, Gary Griggs, has taught and researched at Santa Cruz for more than forty years. One of his students was Kathryn Sullivan, who became an astronaut and was the first woman to walk in space. Professors like Gary don't just do research. They also teach. He told me, and he will tell anyone, that there is no toggle switch delineating research from teaching. It is not an either/or proposition. The blend of teaching and research is its own phenomenon. It's the magic mix that leads both to creating new knowledge and to educating students, not just instructing them.

UCLA let me drop in on a women's basketball practice. Standing beside me was Rafer Johnson, the Olympic gold medalist and an UCLA alum. He's one of California's—and the country's—greatest track athletes. Rafer had a story to tell about why he chose to attend UCLA in the 1950s. As you might imagine, he had many options. But he wanted to be a student body president. So he made a point of visiting the student resource centers on every campus trying to recruit him. UCLA, he said, was the only one with a photo of an African-American student on the wall. The rest is Bruin history.

I think Rafer's story tells us something about how diversity really works. The history of UC shows how great public research universities can be vehicles for social advancement. Thousands upon thousands of UC alumni were first-generation immigrants and the first in their families to attend college. Today, 45 percent of our freshmen are first-generation college students. One out of three is from an underrepresented minority group. And more than 40 percent of all UC students are low-income. Four of our campuses have more low-income students than all eight Ivy League universities combined.

There is a subset here that deserves special mention: undocumented students. These Dreamers, as they are often called, are students who would have benefited from a federal DREAM Act. They are students who deserve the opportunity to succeed and to thrive at UC. I know this issue well. I testified before Congress in support of the DREAM Act and in support of comprehensive immigration reform. When the DREAM Act failed to get cloture, I instituted a plan called Deferred Action for Childhood Arrivals, known by its acronym DACA. To date, almost 600,000 students have qualified for DACA. So let me be clear: UC welcomes all students who qualify academically, whether they are documented or undocumented. To help meet the special needs of Dreamers, I am making an announcement here tonight. I am setting aside $5 million—right now, for this year—to support these students with resources like trained advisers, student service centers and financial aid. Consider this a down payment, one more piece of evidence of our commitment to all Californians. UC will continue to be a vehicle for social mobility. We teach for California; we research for the world.

I'm often asked why I decided to come to UC at this time. It's a fair question. The answer rests in how California, across its history, has so often managed to lead the world to new ways of thinking, to new ways of conducting itself as a society. As California goes, so often goes the world. This was clear to me in Arizona. And it was clear to me in Washington. What I came to realize, however, is that it's also true that as the University of California goes, so goes California. The two grew up together, forming a symbiotic relationship that literally altered their shared future. Put another way, California would not be the society it is today without the University of California. The opposite is also true.

And so, in my view, I have taken on a high-stakes proposition. Not to go all Tom Friedman on you, but the world around us is changing—profoundly and undeniably. Irresistible forces of transformation are converging on many fronts at once: technical, environmental, economic, political, demographic, you name it. The changes are global in their sweep, but a real and present fact of everyday life in every locale. And that includes California. We live in a crossroads moment. And where we end up is not predestined.

Will we find new ways to work and live together and to:

- Build a prosperous, hopeful society that embraces diversity, not runs from it?

- Harness technology for the benefit of all and not just for the fortunes of a few?

- Protect the environment, even as our growing population places ever greater pressures on its resources?

We can shape the answers to these and other fundamental questions. We can shape the future. Once more, California can show the world the way. And the one big reason why it can, I am here to tell you, is the University of California and its time-tested power to provide a fulcrum on which the state can pivot toward a brighter day.

At the state's first Constitutional Convention, pioneers still brushing dust from the goldfields off their trousers were expressing the hope that they might create a university of their own. In time, with help from President Lincoln's Morrill Act of 1862, they built the University of California. And they built it to their own specifications, California specifications. To quote Daniel Coit Gilman, one of the earliest and most influential UC presidents: "It is not the University of Berlin nor of New Haven which we are to copy…, but it is the University of this State. It must be adapted to this people, to their public and private schools, to their peculiar geographical position, to the requirements of their new society." Amen!

In the early 20th century, it would be UC research that would lead California's transition from simple farming practices to the monolith known as modern agriculture. Californians, once confined to growing only what the rains would allow, learned to produce more crops with greater yields than the world had ever seen come out of one place. And we are doing it still. As food insecurity looms as perhaps the single most daunting global issue of our time, California's export, not just of crops, but also of the science and expertise needed to grow them, will become ever more vital. But California won't deliver for the world without UC.

Another example: Fifty-some years ago, as the first Baby Boomers were coming of age, UC President Clark Kerr and Governor Pat Brown led the way to the creation of California's Master Plan for Higher Education. As part of this, the university soon opened three new campuses. It enrolled thousands more Californians of all backgrounds. It laid the groundwork for a well-educated and active citizenry that has benefited the state ever since. And it led to a revitalized version of the California Dream.

I could go on. The growth of the aerospace industry, the intellectual seeding of Silicon Valley: These and many other phenomena can be traced back to particular moments when the university and the state worked together for the benefit of all Californians and ultimately, for the benefit of people around the world. So again, UC teaches for California, but it researches for the world. The significance of this dynamic equation will only grow. That's why I came here to serve. My intent is to be the best advocate possible for what this university and this state can achieve together.

UC, like California, simply cannot afford to stand still. If you're standing still in California, you're falling behind. We have a dynamic institution and a dynamic state, living together in a dynamic time. This means that at UC, excellence in research and education must be more than just maintained, must be more than a catchy phrase: It must be real, and it must be accelerated.

This is why, in two weeks, I'm going to be coming to the UC Regents with some big ideas for their consideration. In the meantime, however, I've heard enough to know that if we are to remain a premier research university, we must increase our support for post-doctoral fellows and graduate students. Our post-docs are key researchers in our labs and teachers in our classrooms. Tonight I'm announcing a $5 million increase in the President's Postdoctoral Fellowship Program. And to help fill the post-doc pipeline, I am announcing tonight an additional $5 million to recruit the world's best graduate students to our campuses. Graduate students and post-docs are the essential links between teaching for California and researching for the world. They are our future faculty members. They are our future innovators. They are our future Nobel laureates. They merit our additional support right now.

Some of my ideas are even larger in their reach and will take more time in the greenhouse. You'll hear more about them at the regents meeting in November and in the months after that. Moving the university forward in innovative new ways is critical, and not just because of the technological, environmental and economic forces at play today. It's also because there is a tremendous demographic shift unfolding around us.

In California, there is a new generation knocking at the door. This generation might look and speak a bit differently than the students of Clark Kerr's time. After all, a majority of California K-12 students today hail from diverse, historically underrepresented groups. But they still qualify for UC at a ratio far below that of their peers. This must change. This is a moral imperative. The California Dream, and all that the phrase invokes, must not be allowed to die off with the Baby Boomers. And, again, the University of California represents the state's best shot at making this happen. Make no mistake: These students share the same dreams as those who came before them.

This morning, I visited Oakland Technical High School. It's not far from UC's central office, my new home away from home. I met with students in Oakland Tech's leadership classes and with students in the school's African-American Male Initiative program. Then I spoke at a rally for 500 students. They came from a range of backgrounds, with distinct family demographics and distinct interests. But when I looked out into the auditorium, all I could see was one vast sea of hope and yearning, their faces lit up—absolutely lit up—with the idea of making their way to the University of California. When I say UC teaches for California, I'm talking about serving the hope and aspiration that was so palpable in that auditorium. I'm talking about transformation, one student at a time. And let's be clear, all Californians have a stake in this. Affordability, accessibility, diversity: These give California the citizenry and workforce it needs to be a global leader, always pushing forward and upward.

Academic excellence at the university must remain paramount. It is crucial as we teach for California. It is also crucial as we research for the world. I know that the connection between teaching and research and its impact beyond campus borders can sometimes be difficult to grasp. So let me put it this way: When thinking about academic excellence, the question to ask is, "Who benefits?" The answer is everyone, everywhere.

Consider Randy Schekman. He's a UC Berkeley professor who was just awarded the Nobel Prize for Physiology or Medicine. Randy was educated at UCLA and Stanford, but we don't hold the latter against him. Randy has taught at Berkeley for more than three decades: freshman seminars, post-doc supervision, you name it.

Years ago, he started researching yeast and the transport and secretion of proteins in cells. Like all those engaged in basic research, exactly where the quest would lead could not be known as he set out. The potential applications are rarely clear. Where it led eventually was to discoveries that have since changed how the world treats hepatitis B and diabetes and soon, perhaps even Alzheimer's.

Teach for California, and research for the world. This is the reason UC must thrive as a public enterprise. California and the university that proudly shares its name can show the world the way to a society that is more prosperous, more enlightened, different in many ways than it was in the past, but not in its essence: a society where hope and opportunity are not just words; they are realities.

THE NEW POLYTECHNIC: ADDRESSING GLOBAL CHALLENGES, TRANSFORMING THE WORLD

Shirley Ann Jackson
President, Rensselaer Polytechnic Institute

It is a high honor to be invited to Vassar College to deliver the inaugural Pauline Newman '47 Lecture. I thank the faculty in your distinguished multidisciplinary program in Science, Technology, & Society for this privilege. Judge Newman is a pioneer—and not merely because she was one of the first female research chemists in American industry, as well as the first woman to be appointed to the U.S. Court of Appeals for the Federal Circuit. The arc of her career is utterly forward-looking, and I hope that all the students with us today take guidance and inspiration from it. Allow me to summarize: After graduating from Vassar College, Judge Newman earned a Ph.D. in chemistry from Yale University. However, she found the experience of working as a research chemist in industry not entirely satisfying and, after a few years, she resigned her position and traveled to Paris for an adventure.

Upon returning to New York City, in definite need of employment, she accepted a position writing patent applications. This was the kind of work, she has said, that was typically "done by either failed scientists or failed lawyers." However, Pauline Newman was quite the opposite of a failure. Her interest piqued by her patent work, she attended law school, receiving an LL.B. from New York University School of Law, and became an expert in patent law and policy. Eventually, she helped to persuade the U.S. Congress to create the U.S. Court of Appeals for the Federal Circuit—which has nationwide jurisdiction over international trade legal issues, government contracts, and patents, as well as other subjects—and in 1984, Judge Newman was appointed to that court. Her opinions in all these areas have been influential and much admired for their fairness.

Hers has been an extraordinary career, but one with which we are familiar at Rensselaer, where a number of our alumni and alumnae have moved from science and engineering to become prominent figures in intellectual property law. They include the chairman of the Rensselaer Board of Trustees, Judge Arthur Gajarsa, who received a Bachelor of Science degree in electrical engineering from Rensselaer in 1962, before studying economics and then the law. Judge Gajarsa served fifteen years alongside Judge Newman on the U.S. Court of Appeals for the Federal Circuit. He says this about her: "She is brilliant, her opinions matter—even her dissents often being upheld by the U.S. Supreme Court—and she is a very nice person."

As the president of Judge Gajarsa's alma mater—the oldest private technological research university in the United States—I especially appreciate Judge Newman's work in the field of intellectual property, which has guided the growth of technology-intensive industries. In other words, Judge Newman used the insights and knowledge she garnered as a scientist to do incisive work in another sphere of influence, that of the law. In the process, she has helped to change the world around us, encouraging the movement of discoveries and innovations into the marketplace and toward the improvement of lives around the globe.

Increasingly, as Judge Newman did, it is critical that we draw on the perspectives of multiple disciplines to gain a multi-dimensional view of the world in order to make progress.

Today we are at a watershed moment, one that requires a fundamental rethinking and repositioning of the nature of pedagogy and research in the academy. Three factors lend some urgency to this.

- First, the fact that the challenges we face are increasingly complex, interconnected, and global.

- Second, the consequent need to create graduates who are true global citizens and true philomaths, while addressing questions many in our society have about the value of higher education.

- Third, the rise and ubiquitousness of technologies that magnify the power of the individual, that connect us in new ways, while enabling collaborative endeavors not possible before.

Interestingly, a proper context for this required rethinking is both historical and modern. The historical context is framed by the original definition and purpose of the liberal (or liberating) arts, while the modern context derives from what today's challenges demand and what new technologies both drive and support. Let us examine each of these factors in turn.

First: interconnected global challenges. This past January, I had the great privilege of attending the World Economic Forum Annual Meeting 2015 in Davos, Switzerland. Davos draws 1,500 of the most influential people in business in the world, as well as more than 300 heads of state and government leaders. From these leaders, I heard a great deal of concern about the stability of societies around the globe, given the threats we face at this moment. These include, of course, new geopolitical tensions and the rise of radical non-state actors. They include climate change, pandemics and other health-related challenges, the global competition for natural resources, and growing income inequality in both developed and developing economies.

Each of these challenges impacts the others, and indeed, the survival of human civilization. Climate change, of course, exacerbates issues surrounding our food, water, and energy supplies. It also is likely to increase the spread of vector-borne diseases, such as malaria. It influences our national and global security. For example, vast reserves of petroleum, natural gas, and mineral wealth in the Arctic, made accessible by melting sea ice, are likely to be a source of new geopolitical tensions.

Climate change also is likely to worsen the inequalities between rich nations and poor ones, as it undermines food and water security at the lower latitudes. Even within a single geography, the risks of severe climate events are greater for those with fewer economic and educational advantages.

Vulnerabilities intersect!

Recent history shows us that when there is a triggering event, intersecting vulnerabilities can, and do, result in cascading consequences. Consider, for example, the Great Sendai earthquake of 2011 in Japan—and the subsequent tsunami, with its destruction of electrical, transportation, and housing infrastructure, as well as loss of life—coupled with the meltdowns at the Fukushima Daiichi Nuclear Power Plant, the resulting environmental contamination, the long-term risks of cancer from radiation exposures, as well as worldwide economic effects. The very interconnectedness of our systems and societies leaves us vulnerable to such domino effects.

Another example of interlinked complexities is the threat to global food security represented by Colony Collapse Disorder. In the U.S., Colony

Collapse Disorder was first recognized when, in the fall of 2006, beekeepers began reporting dramatically high losses of their hives. The European honey bee is a key component of agriculture throughout the world. Fifty-two of the 115 leading global food crops depend on honey bee pollination for fruit or seed set. Eight and a half years after being recognized as a grave threat, the "cause" of Colony Collapse Disorder has not been fully determined. Researchers are concluding that Colony Collapse Disorder is likely caused by a multiplicity of factors including pathogens, parasites, stress factors in the management of bees—including beekeepers moving them great distances to pollinate different fields and environmental stressors—and exposure to pesticides, even at sub-lethal levels. Again, this is a web-like challenge that cannot be properly addressed without expertise in fields that range from bee genetics to data science to agriculture and environmental policy.

Clearly, large, networked challenges such as these, and others, cannot be addressed by even the most brilliant person working alone, nor by a single discipline, sector, or nation. Collaborations on a grand scale are required, and colleges and universities, as we educate future leaders and convene brilliant scholars, have an obligation to seed, and to support, new approaches to teaching, learning, and problem-solving.

The second factor that creates urgency to redefine what we offer in higher education is the fact that, at this moment, there are more and more citizens, and even some thinkers in higher education, who question the value of a liberal education—indeed, of any form of higher education without immediate practical application in terms of jobs. There are concerns about access and cost, completion/graduation rates, demonstrated educational outcomes for students—and with the rise of online approaches such as MOOCs [massive open online courses]—and even the continued benefits of a residential model of education. These concerns must be addressed and rooted in what we value as a society and how we see ourselves in the world.

Finally, the advent of remarkable new technologies, especially those enabled by advances in computation and artificial intelligence, not only support individual learning, but especially support multi-disciplinary collaboration in education and research. And the avalanche of data generated by the "internet of things"—by everything from smart phones and cameras; to low-cost genome sequencing; to instrumented running shoes, automobiles and tractors, biomedical devices, watches—offers us the raw materials for a new understanding of the world.

In fact, data can be considered as a great new natural resource. But a resource is as a resource does. What we do with any resource—what we do with data—matters. The students here today, no matter what field they enter professionally, almost inevitably will find themselves collaborating with experts in the tools of data collection and analysis.

Of course, the idea that higher education should freely cross and bridge disciplines is not a new one. Vassar College, for example, has offered interdisciplinary courses for a century. Vassar also consistently has expanded its reach into emerging disciplines, such as cognitive science, where it was the first institution in the world to offer an undergraduate degree, and computer science, where it was one of the first liberal arts colleges in the nation to purchase a computer on which students could learn. Of course, we all know that Vassar is the alma mater of Rear Admiral Grace Hopper, one of the great pioneers of computer science.

Although the founding vision of my university was to educate young people in "the application of science to the common purposes of life"—and indeed, we retain our scientific and technological perspective in everything we do—we long have offered an education that is as panoramic as it is tightly focused.

In 1851 Benjamin Franklin Greene, our third senior professor and first director, renamed the then-Rensselaer Institute, the Rensselaer Polytechnic Institute. "Polytechnic" means "many arts," and this change coincided with a radical broadening and deepening of the curriculum. Professor Greene established departments of rhetoric and philosophy and argued that Rensselaer students should receive a "scientific, literary, philosophic, artistic" education before they embarked upon their studies in "applied science or art." As a result, Rensselaer students were educated, even then, for intellectual agility as well as technical proficiency. In a young country being transformed by new technologies—by trains, bridges, telegraphs, and photographs—they were prepared to lead.

We are re-envisioning the meaning of polytechnic within the context of modern challenges and opportunities, while drawing on the meaning and teaching of the original seven liberal arts of classical antiquity. They consisted of the Trivium—grammar, logic, and rhetoric, first taught together as foundational subjects in ancient Greece; and the Quadrivium—arithmetic, geometry, music, and astronomy. Arithmetic was about numbers; geometry: numbers in space; music: numbers in time; astronomy: numbers in space and time. The intent was to train the mind how to think, not what to think. The focus was on teaching the art and science of the mind, as well as the art and science of matter. This is not so different than what our educational intent is today.

Today we speak of The "New" Polytechnic that supports promising areas of interdisciplinary research and learning and that uses the most advanced tools and technologies to unite a diversity of perspectives. The New Polytechnic draws on the grammar (natural language processing), the logic, and the rhetoric of thinking machines (sentient digital agents) and of social networks. The New Polytechnic is predicated on the absolute necessity of educating our students in multi-disciplinary and collaborative thinking and linking our researchers—in the arts, architecture, the humanities, the sciences, and the social sciences, as well as in engineering and the applied sciences.

As such, The New Polytechnic is a fresh collaborative endeavor across disciplines, sectors, and geographic regions, which serves as a great crossroads where talented people from everywhere meet, connect, and take on the hard problems. Engaged in by a broad spectrum of participants, guided by societal concerns and ethics, The New Polytechnic ultimately facilitates novel and effective approaches to global challenges.

History teaches us that no one can predict from which fields transformative ideas will arise—ideas that will change lives on a grand scale. What we can do, in higher education, is to create the conditions for serendipity by bringing together diverse groups with a multiplicity of perspectives and disciplinary backgrounds.

Allow me to offer an example of The New Polytechnic in action. Until recent decades, the remarkable diversity of the microbial world was concealed from scientists, because so few species could be isolated from their environments—and their interdependent communities—in order to be cultured in a laboratory and studied. In fact, microbes are still so unexplored that they often are called "the dark matter of life." However, with the advent of metagenomics, or the ability to sequence genes directly from an environmental sample, the curtain has been lifted on—as microbiologists like to say—who is there and what they are doing.

The potential applications for this work in terms of human health are enormous. You may well have heard this interesting statistic: In the average human body, the number of bacteria alone that have colonized us represents ten times the number of human cells. Each of us serves as an ecosystem (like a microbial coral reef) for an astonishing and supple range of microbes that varies over time, and varies among us, depending on factors that include environmental exposures. In fact, an imbalance in the diversity and composition of our microbiome is implicated in many diseases, including allergies, asthma, diabetes, obesity, and some cancers. To explore and exploit new tools and technologies in this arena, a very diverse group of Rensselaer faculty recently joined forces to create a Microbiome Informatics Team. They intend to lead in measuring, understanding, and even "engineering" microbial communities within the context of their environments and functions.

Just as metagenomics reveals microbial communities with many unexpected members, our Microbiome Informatics Team includes an array of experts whom you might find surprising. Of course, it includes two microbiologists, Professor Karyn Rogers of our Department of Earth and Environmental Sciences, who studies the relationship between the geochemistry of an environment and the microorganisms found there; and Professor Cynthia Collins of our Department of Chemical and Biological

Engineering, who studies microbial communities and "engineers" them using synthetic biology.

Our Microbiome Informatics Team also includes Architecture Professor Anna Dyson, who is the director of our Center for Architecture, Science and Ecology, where research is being done in next-generation building systems, including indoor environments that use consortia of plants and microbial communities to filter toxins and release probiotics.

The Team also includes a mathematician, Professor Kristin Bennett, to help identify patterns in the metagenomics and environmental data, and Professor Deborah McGuinness, our Tetherless World Senior Constellation chair and professor of computer and cognitive science. Professor McGuinness is developing web-based tools for integrating and exploring disparate geochemical and microbial datasets, in order to find the correlations within them.

Professor McGuinness and others are part of a university-wide initiative we call The Rensselaer Institute for Data Exploration and Applications, or The Rensselaer IDEA. The Rensselaer IDEA brings together our strengths in web science, high-performance computing, data science and predictive analytics, and immersive technologies—and links them to applications at the interface of engineering and the physical, life, and social sciences, in order to expedite scientific discovery and innovation.

And significantly, our Microbiome Informatics effort includes two professors from our School of Humanities, Arts and Social Sciences, who are cultural anthropologists, to offer a qualitative dimension to the findings of the group and to help this diverse team cross barriers in language and practice that divide the disciplines. They are Professor Kim Fortun, whose research focuses on the ethnography of environmental problems, and Professor Michael Fortun, whose research focuses on the culture surrounding genomics.

Ultimately, the Microbiome Informatics Team intends to improve human health by determining which probiotics in the environment help to prevent diseases, by "engineering" microbial communities as alternatives to traditional pharmaceuticals, and by finding new targets for personalized medicine. This is how progress is made.

Just as we strive to bring together different ways of thinking among the teams of collaborators we gather at Rensselaer, we also are striving to bring together different kinds of thinking machines in order to address complex global challenges.

Computers, indeed, are beginning to reflect the myriad ways that we humans perceive, learn, and discover. As long as we are aware of the ethical questions their development and use may engender, such tools are a great cause for optimism. At Rensselaer, we have the most powerful supercomputer at an American private university, a petascale IBM Blue Gene/Q system, which is an Advanced Multiprocessing Optimized System, whose acronym AMOS harkens back to our co-founder, Amos Eaton. AMOS is able to perform more than a quadrillion floating point operations, or mathematical calculations, per second. That is a thousand million million, or 10 to the 15th power, operations per second. It also has massive data storage capabilities. Supercomputers are particularly good at the modeling of large systems, such as the climate of the earth, or very intricate ones and determining how, out of trillions of possibilities, a chain of amino acids, encoded by our genes, folds itself into the shape that determines its function as a protein.

However, not every problem takes such a form. The senior vice president who oversees the key growth units of IBM, including IBM Research worldwide, Dr. John E. Kelly III—who also is a Rensselaer alumnus and trustee—has dubbed the supercomputers of today "brilliant idiots." They are excellent at performing the calculations they are programmed to do. But unlike humans, they are not good at learning from experience and adapting to their environments, and they are not adept at finding the single valuable insight within an unruly flood of non-mathematical data.

Cognitive computing—or computing by machines able to make inferences from data and to teach themselves—add to our capabilities in another way. You may be familiar with the IBM cognitive computing system Watson, which in 2011 was victorious over the best human champions in *Jeopardy!* Watson is able to absorb enormous amounts of natural language data, such as scientific papers, kitchen recipes, or blog posts. It can find valuable correlations within that data and generate hypotheses from it for human experimentation and exploration. We are very proud that many of the key figures in the development of Watson are Rensselaer alumni—including Dr. Christopher Welty, who was a professor in the Computer Science Department at Vassar before joining IBM and then Google. We were the first university worldwide to receive a Watson computer for research.

Now our scientists are working to extend cognitive computing to the entire world of open data on the Web, to make these intelligent systems even more nuanced.

Another example of the work in artificial intelligence being done at Rensselaer is Cogtio. Cogito is a robot imbued with sensing and reasoning ability and whose "mental" capabilities were developed at the Rensselaer Artificial Intelligence & Reasoning Laboratory, which is directed by Professor Selmer Bringsjord, head of our Cognitive Science Department. Cogito was created to study self-consciousness in machines. Given the classic "mirror test" used to measure self-awareness in animals and babies, Cogito is able to recognize itself in a mirror. If there is a mark on its forehead, Cogito understands that it does not belong there and decides on its own to remove it. Now Professor Bringsjord has moved on to a more sophisticated test of self-awareness. Told that it has been given either a pill that mutes it or a placebo, a robot is asked which pill it has been given. Initially, it responds, "I don't know." Hearing itself, it realizes that it has not gotten the pill that renders it dumb, and it answers correctly.

Researchers at Rensselaer, and elsewhere, also are investigating neuromorphic computing, or computing that mimics the architecture and function of the human brain, in order to gain some of the brain's advantages. In conventional computation, data is pulled from memory, processed, and then the result is sent back to storage before the next operation is addressed. This shuffling creates bottlenecks, tremendous excess heat, and is extremely expensive in terms of energy usage overall.

The human brain, on the other hand, has a networked architecture of neurons—the cells that transmit impulses—and synapses—the points between cells where signaling occurs—that allows the brain to distribute information processing in an extremely energy-efficient way. It has been estimated that for a conventional supercomputer to simulate the communication occurring at the 100 trillion synapses in the human brain—at the same speed as the brain—the combined power consumption of Los Angeles and New York City would be required. Our brains, on the other hand, currently are powered by the soup, salad, or sandwich we ate for lunch.

Neuromorphic computing also aspires to achieve the resilience of the human brain, which can lose neurons without compromising the entire system; has the ability to learn without being programmed; and has the ability to learn through our senses, as well as through our reason.

Neuromorphic processors that mimic neurons and synapses are much more adept at analyzing sensory data than conventional processors. This includes image processing to determine, for example, which activity in a crowded airport terminal, transmitted by a camera, is cause for concern.

Our scientists at The Rensselaer IDEA are exploring hybrids among all these types of computing so that our endeavors can be assisted by a holistic intelligence more like our own.

Rensselaer researchers are improving not merely on machine perception; they also are devising new ways to assist human perception. Sometimes the best way to understand what the data is telling us is to see it, to hear it, or to feel it. At Rensselaer, we are very focused on immersive technologies that enhance our sensory intelligence, including data visualization, haptics, and augmented reality.

We have a magnificent platform for this: Our Curtis R. Priem Experimental Media and Performing Arts Center, or EMPAC, which is not merely a remarkable place for the performing arts, but also is a locus of cutting-edge research in human-scale immersive technologies. We are in the process of developing, in partnership with IBM, The Cognitive and Immersive Systems Laboratory@EMPAC. Initially, this laboratory will focus on creating Situations Rooms—interactive environments that automatically respond to their occupants by listening to and watching them. A Situations Room will help collaborators working at the same time on different aspects of a larger project to make better decisions. Such a tool would have many applications, such as a cognitive design studio, a cognitive boardroom, a cognitive medical diagnosis room, or a cognitive classroom.

Collectively, these digital tools and technologies are so powerful that they have applications in almost every field of human endeavor and an important role to play in answering almost every question. Allow me to offer a few examples. Over and over, in different parts of the world in recent years, we have seen the rapid rise of new global security risks in non-state actors, as well as inspiring pro-democracy movements. How can we identify such movements in their infancy? How can we diffuse dangerous networks? How can we recognize when popular opinion is being swayed for positive ends?

Thanks to the digitization of so many communications between and among people—and the treasure trove of opinion, sentiment, gossip, and persuasion available on Twitter, Facebook, and Tumblr—a data-driven revolution is underway in fields such as sociology and psychology. This revolution is analogous to the transformation of the life sciences with the rise of genomics.

At Rensselaer, we host the Social Cognitive Networks Academic Research Center, or SCNARC. Directed by Dr. Boleslaw Szymanski, our Claire and Roland Schmitt Distinguished Professor of Computer Science, this is a collaboration among the U.S. Army Research Laboratory, IBM, Rensselaer, and a number of other universities. The Center seeks to understand, using the data available on social networks, how ideas and movements form, spread, influence, and create societies. It also examines cultural and linguistic nuance on such networks. This fascinating endeavor includes computer scientists, sociologists, psychologists, historians, political scientists, and linguists.

For example, Dr. Heng Ji, our Edward P. Hamilton Development Chair in Computer Science, is a theoretical linguist as well as a computer scientist. In her work with the Center, she is automating the recognition of hidden networks that use coded language in societies in which it is dangerous to express oneself openly.

One of the early discoveries of SCNARC is the significance of commitment—and the fact that when 10 percent of a population truly is committed to an idea or cause, a tipping point can be reached—and the minority opinion is likely to be adopted rapidly by the majority. I am certain that there are many people in this audience who have dedicated their lives to societal concerns or who will dedicate their lives to them. I hope you take courage from this finding that your convictions do have the power to change the world.

At Rensselaer, we also are using advanced digital tools to answer another key question: How can we become much more intelligent stewards of the environment?

With our partners IBM and The Fund for Lake George, we are using the fresh water ecology of Lake George, at the southeastern end of the Adirondack Park here in New York State, to model an answer to that question. We have named the undertaking The Jefferson Project in honor of Thomas Jefferson, who declared Lake George to be "the most beautiful water [he] ever saw." We intend to make sure that human encroachment does not cloud this famously clear water.

Lake George is best thought of as a system of systems, which include:

- Weather;
- Hydrology—in other words, runoff and the nutrients, sediments, and contaminants it introduces into the lake;
- Lake circulation; and
- The food web, including invasive species.

In such a system of systems, easy correlations may not represent causation. To understand and mitigate stresses to the environment, scientific inquiry is required: careful observations over time using advanced technologies, models that help us to integrate the data streams they create and to make predictions, and experiments that allow us to test our hypotheses.

So with our partners, we are turning Lake George into the "smartest" lake in the world. We have placed advanced sensors throughout the lake, including weather stations, tributary sensors, and vertical profilers that measure a panoply of factors influencing the lake. And we have established a new data visualization laboratory at our Darrin Fresh Water Institute in Bolton Landing on Lake George, which features advanced computation and graphics systems to help us to integrate that data with high-resolution bathymetric and topographic lake surveys—and to develop a full picture of the systems and interactions that make up Lake George and its watershed.

In our quest really to "see" Lake George, the Rensselaer Office of Research has given seed funding to a project that includes people particularly adept at seeing: namely, visual artists. Professor Kathleen Ruiz, a new media artist whose work encompasses games and simulations, and Professor Kathy High, who produces videos and installations, are part of a project that includes Rensselaer biologists and computer scientists. Together, they are developing new technology, including a novel sensor to capture, analyze, and model the distribution of plankton in the lake. Plankton are both a foundation of the food web and include invasive species, so they offer essential information about the health of the lake.

Professor Ruiz and Professor High will present the wonders of this research to a large audience by creating an immersive 3-D virtual environment artwork from it, using a team of student artists, sound designers, game developers, and programmers. The artists already have inspired our biologists to look at things differently by asking them, "What do plankton look like in three dimensions?" This is quite different from considering these creatures in two dimensions, the way they might look mounted on microscope slides, and a small example of the serendipity that arises when one brings the arts and the humanities into scientific inquiry.

In the end, The Jefferson Project will inform and undergird public policy about watershed issues, fresh water systems, and overall environmental stewardship—where science, technology, ethics, regulation, and policy formulation all come together. This is precisely where and why interdisciplinary and multi-disciplinary approaches are critical.

Another key question we are addressing under The New Polytechnic is: How do we best educate young people for this new era of interconnected challenges and great tools of connection? Helping to transform the academic experience at Rensselaer are teaching tools arising out of Rensselaer research into mixed and immersive realities, multi-player games, web science, artificial intelligence, cognitive science, computer vision, information technology management, and other fields. These tools allow us to explore exciting new ways of communicating knowledge and of collaborating.

For example, a multi-player mixed-reality game we call The Mandarin Project helps Rensselaer students to learn the Chinese language in the most effective ways, through gamification, conversation, and cultural immersion in mixed reality environments. With an engaging narrative that spans an academic semester, The Mandarin Project allows our students to use and expand their language skills in virtual environments that include the Beijing airport and a Chinese tea house. We already have found that this approach accelerates student learning. And when our students go abroad, they will have developed, through direct and virtual experiences, cultural nuance that they otherwise would not have. Very soon we will have students interacting within these scenes with artificially intelligent digital characters that link to the cognitive computing systems I talked about earlier.

Another example of pedagogical innovation at Rensselaer has been developed by Dr. Tarek Abdoun, the Thomas Iovino Professor of Civil and Environmental Engineering and associate dean for research and graduate programs. Professor Abdoun led the physical modeling research team that clarified the failure mechanisms of the New Orleans levees during Hurricane Katrina and contributed to better levee designs. Now he and his colleagues are developing a game called Geo Explorer—a mixed reality and mobile game that is the cornerstone of an innovative hybrid course module combining theoretical flood protection system design, the virtual planning and inspection of flood protection systems, actual laboratory testing, and virtual field testing. Geo Explorer is intended to help address one of the great challenges in engineering education: the fact that students are not—

and cannot be—out in the field under extreme conditions, experiencing the practical consequences of engineering decisions. With Geo Explorer, however, they can experience those conditions and consequences virtually—and become better engineers for it.

At Rensselaer, we bring a scientific and technological perspective to all we do. But we make sure that that perspective is informed by ethics and societal concerns and that the humanities and social sciences bring these issues to the fore for our students.

To drive home what the true interdisciplinarity is, we have Art_X@ Rensselaer—a new initiative designed to expose all of our students to the science in art, and the art in science, so that they can recognize the underlying patterns of thought that are common across the disciplines and be inspired to embrace creative crossover. Art_X@Rensselaer is not about art appreciation classes. Instead, we are promoting an awareness of beauty and creativity throughout the Rensselaer curriculum—through the many opportunities we offer our students for collaborative research across art, science, engineering, the social sciences, and management and through work on projects and productions, such as the immersive plankton experience I mentioned a few moments ago.

Clearly, it is crucial for institutions of higher education, such as Rensselaer, to put into place the mechanisms for multi-disciplinary learning and research, such as the Science, Technology, & Society program that is hosting me today. However, we make an equally important contribution simply by serving as a physical crossroads where scientists, engineers, artists, and scholars from diverse disciplines meet, talk, and spark the innovations and discoveries that can improve lives around the world. This both undergirds and validates the residential collegiate model. I would urge every student in the audience today to take full advantage of the delightful intellectual bazaar in which you find yourselves—and to seek out people in majors far removed from your own—just for a conversation.

Before I end today, I would like to consider another thought from Judge Newman in explaining her own journey from one discipline into another, where she made an indelible mark. I quote her: "The law seemed to summon the same parts of my mind that had attracted me to the sciences years before." I have spoken today about summoning our collective intelligence to address great challenges, as well as about encouraging both students and faculty to develop a more holistic intelligence by learning from people in other disciplines.

Of course, there is no single settled definition of intelligence, any more than there is a full understanding of the remarkable human brain that generates intelligence. However, the brilliant people around us remind us that there are many ways to accomplish great things and that we may summon analytic abilities to define problems and solutions, creativity to imagine new paths, organizational ability to help make a project real, and wisdom to guide us—all arising from our experience of life and our sense of goodwill toward the world at large.

While each of us has all of these capabilities in some measure, very few of us have developed all of them in equal measure. It is when we join forces that we truly cancel out our weaknesses and compound our strengths. To solve great problems, we must connect.

I hope that I have convinced you that with the new tools and technologies we have, what they enable and the conjoining of multidisciplinary perspectives they allow, we are educating our students within a modern definition of the liberal arts: The New Polytechnic. The intent is to engender in our students intellectual agility, multicultural sophistication, and a global view—characteristics they must have if they are to lead in a changing world, indeed, lead in changing the world.

How Are Universities Adapting to Globalization?

Nicholas Dirks
Chancellor, University of California, Berkeley

In recent years, globalization has led to unprecedented levels of change in areas from the economy to the environment, from the way we do business to the way we interact with media.

With the pace of globalization accelerating and its impact expanding, universities have begun to change as well, seeing increasing numbers of students flow from beyond national borders, coordinating, if not standardizing, degrees and calendars, and collaborating both in research and in teaching.

Despite these efforts, there is still no consensus about what globalization will ultimately mean for how universities educate students, interact with peers, collaborate with governmental and private partners, and define their fundamental missions.

The leading American universities all have substantial numbers of foreign students, offer a growing number of courses in a wide range of international subjects, support a broad spectrum of study-abroad programs, and collaborate in an expanding array of research with foreign partners. But we have only started to come to terms with the volume and velocity of global connections, and we have not gone nearly far enough in altering our content and methods to support students in a deeply interdependent world.

When planet-wide problems do not recognize either national borders or the boundaries that have traditionally separated academic disciplines, universities must adapt.

No single university can address these challenges on its own. Significant progress depends on the formation of a new, global alliance of academic and private sector partners that have the collective means to conduct the necessary multidisciplinary research; the desire to develop new ways to quickly translate discovery into beneficial goods and services; and the capability to educate, train and employ a new generation of leaders, thinkers and scientists. It will also require intellectual collaboration on a new scale.

A New Model for Universities

This is why we've decided to upend the global engagement model used by American universities. Instead of establishing an international campus overseas, Berkeley is going to build a Berkeley Global Campus (BGC) at home, less than ten miles from the main campus. At BGC, some of the world's leading universities and high-tech companies will work side by side in a campus setting.

Along with its research mission, the BGC will have a strong educational component, centered on a Global College for Advanced Study. The Global College curriculum will provide international and domestic graduate students with the tools to tackle global challenges through a curriculum centered on global governance, ethics, political economy, and cultural and international relations.

A global campus situated here in the Bay Area has significant advantages compared to the overseas campus model. Not only can we provide a safe harbor by supporting academic freedom, transparency, different forms of advocacy and political engagement, and protection of intellectual property, we can globalize in a context that will provide immediate local impact as well. As we develop new teaching curricula, research questions and protocols for collaboration, we will be able to see how these innovations can unsettle and shift some of the basic structures of our own university that have proved highly resistant to change.

BGC is more than just a new campus: It will also serve as a physical hub for an emergent "star alliance" of top-tier global universities. The idea that we must build a new global system of universities is, at one level, a basic response to the recognition that the salient challenges and opportunities humanity faces are now global in scale. Ultimately, our global interdependence is not just a contingent outcome of new forms of transportation and communication, but also an opportunity to attain new levels of mutual understanding, recognition and insight. Successfully confronting global challenges requires collaboration that reaches beyond the governmental level to institutions of higher education that can marshal innovative intellectual resources for developing solutions and strategies.

Yet there is far more to it than this: Universities are at once among our most trusted institutions and our most cosmopolitan, making them ideal vehicles for developing and sharing global ideas, values, projects and products. If we make these aspirations central to our collaborations, we can, in turn, work with governments, corporations, societies and special interests, and we can learn to trust and depend on one another. This would also give us hope for a future in which knowledge can be rendered progressive rather than dangerous, as fundamental to openness, progress, peace and a better global society, rather than as the weapon of the powerful and the dominant. In this way, a global consortium of tightly interwoven universities can serve as a model for governments, industry and societies on to trust and collaborate.

Universities Working for the Public Good

The stakes could not be higher: If the challenges we face are global in scale and transcend both national borders and traditional academic boundaries, then we must adapt our research and teaching accordingly. I am convinced that we have the institutional commitment to provide our students with the intellectual tools and moral grounding necessary to think and act beyond the narrow parameters of self-interest or beliefs about the good that are restricted to private domains. And while the public ethos at the heart of great American public universities was, for many years, primarily directed at domestic concerns and interests, we must develop the will and capability to translate and broaden our conception of the public good for our new global age.

This new institutional model is infused with a strongly held commitment to the public good and a sense that the public is global. In recent months, the political battles in California about funding for public higher education have heated up as the state's disinvestment continues, threatening to undermine the preeminence and societal contributions of America's leading system of public higher education. For us, these debates have made it clear that the future of universities, and their role in advancing the greater good, will depend on a wider range and altered composition of partnerships. The time has come for the private sector to step up and provide support for public higher education in a manner commensurate with the benefits it enjoys through the research we conduct and the future leaders we educate.

The University and Urban Revival: Out of the Ivory Tower and into the Streets

Judith Rodin
President, Rockefeller Foundation and
former President, University of Pennsylvania

Thank you, Egbert [Perry], for that generous introduction. It brings me back to those heady, challenging days when we, at Penn, didn't know how our efforts in Philadelphia were going to turn out. But thanks to your leadership—on both the Board of Trustees [of the University of Pennsylvania] and the Neighborhood Initiative Committee—we, like so many in the audience, were able to make a difference in our community.

I've been asked to reflect on Penn's experience—not because it's unique, but because it's a case study from which we can generalize. I want to thank all my colleagues at the Institute for Urban Research—which was, in fact, an outgrowth of our efforts to revitalize West Philadelphia—for your sharp focus on the role anchor institutions ought to play in similar endeavors in urban areas around the world.

We're seeing an extraordinary demographic shift today. For the first time in history, half of the world's population lives in urban areas. So understanding cities, the role of cities, and the role of institutions in their cities is never going to be more important.

Globalization is accelerating these trends. It is deindustrializing many western cities and countries and is stretching industrial sprawl across the developing world. As these forces press themselves powerfully upon cities around the planet, our discussion about the role of anchor institutions is especially relevant. This conference has demonstrated outstanding examples of the deep learning, tremendous work, and formidable expertise that have emerged over the last few years—across myriad sectors. It has also provided the perfect venue for a certain former university president to try and hock some books.

But seriously, this conference represents a clarion call for those of us who have worked and studied in the field to share our experience and expertise and to shape an intellectual architecture that can help more institutions do more good in their neighborhoods, communities, and cities.

As the Penn Institute for Urban Research and this remarkable gathering illustrate, we have a superb community gathered around these issues: policymakers, developers, planners, city leaders, scholars and activists to take up the cause. I think we're all better educated and more energized by the deep thinking and vibrant creativity that's enhancing our understanding of how single anchor institutions operate, how a variety of institutions within a city come together, and the requisite connectivity among anchor institutions, city governments, and private developers.

Over the last decade, a whole host of anchor institutions have breathed new life into neighborhoods, communities, and cities by engaging and investing in real partnerships. Universities and medical centers, in particular, have taken on this role—viewing it both as an obligation and an opportunity. It's an obligation because urban universities are a special kind of urban citizen—and good citizenship means taking responsibility, not just taking advantage of tax privileges. It's an obligation because these same institutions often helped to destroy poor neighborhoods in their drive to grow and expand.

It's an opportunity for "eds and meds" to serve a greater social good at the same time as they do well for their students, faculty, and mission. It's an opportunity to model active civic engagement for our students. If we want to teach them to lead in solving the most difficult problems of the day—issues of race and class, blight and poverty—then how we confront these issues as institutions represents a major lesson.

And it's an opportunity to be engines of economic development, because "eds and meds" are strategically positioned to drive community revitalization. They are poised with their resources and deep knowledge base to address poverty, unemployment, crime, and affordable housing. The days when industry, financial institutions, and public utilities were the largest employers in most cities are gone. As manufacturing jobs left town, and as banks and public utilities consolidated, "eds and meds" became the largest employers—the economic lifeblood—of many regions. In America's twenty largest cities, institutions of higher learning or academic medical centers are among the top ten private employers. Thirty-five percent of the people who work for private employers in those cities are employed by universities and their medical centers. In four cities—Washington, San Diego, Baltimore, and Philadelphia—institutions of higher learning and medical facilities account for more than half the jobs available.

So it is clear that "eds and meds" can drive local and regional economy—as producers, employers, and enormous consumers of goods and services—and unlike industry, they cannot be easily sold, acquired, or moved thousands of miles away. They're capable of generating an enormous impact through their purchasing power, investment strategies, real estate holdings, training and technical capacity, and employment practices.

Just think of the scale we're talking about. America's higher education sector makes up almost 4 percent of our national economy. If it were a country, the sector would have a GDP of more than $350 billion, greater than half the GDP of Mexico. In 1996, for example, more than 1,900 urban universities spent $136 billion on salaries, goods, and services—nine times greater than federal spending on urban business and job development in the same year. These same institutions accounted for 2 million American jobs and held more than $100 billion in real estate.

For these reasons and more, the efforts of "eds and meds" to serve as anchor institutions really heated up in the mid-1990s. Many university leaders, mayors, think-tanks, and organizations like CEOs for Cities saw this extraordinary opportunity and obligation. All over the United States, colleges and universities began to ask themselves hard questions about what they could and should do in their communities, and many were moved to action. Penn was among them.

By 1996, University City was a disquieting place, not only for its many problems, but for its neglected possibilities. Those of us associated with the university and city had watched Penn grow as an institution, while its relationship with the neighborhood waxed and waned over decades. In truth, the waning years far outnumbered the waxing ones. By the time I had the great privilege of leading the University of Pennsylvania, it was abundantly clear that since the future of the neighborhood and that of the university were inextricably intertwined, they were equally endangered. The blight of the neighborhood became the plight of the university—it hurt us academically, institutionally, and in terms of our reputation. Students felt less safe and parents felt less comfortable sending them here. Crime soared. One in five residents lived below the poverty level. Shops and businesses closed. Families abandoned their houses. The streets filled with trash.

Pedestrian traffic vanished. Middle class families moved out, and drug dealers moved in.

We knew by then that we could not have a future as a truly great university in a disintegrating community—even if we were foolish enough to want such a thing. Either the neighborhood would improve—becoming a safe place to live, work, study, play, and raise and educate children—or the university would deteriorate. We needed to become a force for strengthening our community and building its efficacy, rather than just acquiring its land and displacing its citizens to raise more buildings.

We learned together that we couldn't just renew the neighborhood; we had to play a part in the neighborhood's self-renewal. We needed to be a partner. We needed other partners to join with us. And in the process, we demonstrated just what a powerful impact a university can make when it accepts that its destiny is entwined with that of its neighbors—not just an impact in the community, but in the consciousness of its students, who, because of our engagement, entered their post-Penn lives better prepared, as Gandhi said, "to become the change they wish to see in the world."

We worked together on safety and security, housing and commercial development, public education and employment, on building a vibrant community. Along the way, many of us—me included—had to give up a little, struggle a little, defer a little, and trust a little. But the outcome was a much stronger, more vital community—physically and economically, but also psychologically. Hope had returned to West Philadelphia. Penn found that, like all anchor institutions, it had a crucial leadership role to play—but sometimes we played the preacher, other times we stepped back into the choir.

We also learned that it's relatively easy to discover great ideas in this work, but extraordinarily hard to implement them. Action, implementation, and execution, after all, are what matter. Of course, whenever I hear the word execution, I'm reminded of the famous quip by the late John McKay, who went from coaching national championship football teams at Southern Cal to coaching the NFL expansion Tampa Bay Buccaneers, which lost its first 26 games. During that losing streak, which stretched over two seasons, a reporter asked McKay what he thought of his team's execution. Without missing a beat, McKay replied, "I'm in favor of it."

Now, I can tell you that when Penn first proposed to devote substantial resources toward redeveloping University City, many members of the academic community were not much kinder. Although they did not call for the execution of Penn's leaders, they did wonder—often aloud—what we were smoking. This is not work for the faint of heart. But start we did, pledging to transform the neighborhood—slowly—grounded in a commitment to continuous, extensive community consultation. We also—actively and overtly—made several promises about what we would not do.

We would never expand our campus to the west or north into residential neighborhoods. We would only expand east into an area made up entirely of abandoned buildings and commercial real estate. And, by the way, that exciting new work linking Penn to Center City on the east at the Schuylkill River is being undertaken today.

We would not act unilaterally. Instead, we would candidly discuss what we could do with the community. And we wouldn't be pushed to promise what we couldn't deliver. Instead, we would limit long-term commitments to promises we could keep and leverage our resources, stimulating major investments by the private sector. We didn't set ourselves up to disappoint the community but made sure that the people who stood to gain and lose the most from our actions had a voice in shaping them.

We started by taking a holistic perspective—and this is important to stress. We worked on initiatives simultaneously rather than chronologically. We saw ourselves as an economic engine that could power renewal. We put our own skin in the game. Specifically, we focused on five interconnected initiatives—not piecemeal, but comprehensively, simultaneously and aggressively.

We systematized and integrated our intervention, looking over and over again for leverage:

- First, we would restore clean, safe, well-lit, and green streets and neighborhoods;

- Second, we would work to provide high-quality, diverse housing choices, both homeownership and rental, across a spectrum of price points;

- Third, we would revive commercial activity and accelerate overall economic development that would spill back into the community to expand growth and opportunity;

- Fourth, we would improve the local public schools; and

- Fifth, we would collaborate with the city to expand the role of an anchor institution in leading and helping Philadelphia to realize its own aspirations.

We knew that economic development, retail construction, public education, home ownership, affordable housing, and safe, attractive streets all leverage one another, creating a dynamic multiplier effect.

To make the neighborhood safer, cleaner, and lighter, we beefed up our Division of Public Safety by hiring more police officers, including bicycle units and detectives, and investing in cutting-edge technology. We opened a new police station further west beyond campus, co-locating it with the

Philadelphia police precinct substation. And we created a special services district, which employs safety ambassadors who patrol the streets of University City, and public space maintenance workers, who supplement city units and help remove graffiti and litter. Many of these people were welfare-to-work participants, thus contributing to another social action goal.

We also partnered with neighborhood residents, the electrician's union, and the local electric company to install fixtures to uniformly light the sidewalks of 1,200 neighborhood properties. Not only did these efforts create a brighter and cleaner neighborhood, which attracted increased foot traffic, but by requiring whole blocks, rather than individual homeowners, to commit, we encouraged a revival of community associations, block by block. And this led to greening projects, like planting 450 trees and 10,000 spring bulbs and creating four public and three children's gardens—all of which set the stage for a dramatic transformation of Clark Park from a dangerous, drug-infested space into a thriving recreational site for children and a weekly farmer's market.

The results of these efforts are reflected in crime statistics, streetscape improvements, and neighborhood perception and awards. Crime reports dropped 40 percent between 1996 and 2002 and another 14 percent between 2002 and 2003. I've just seen the 2007 report card, and all these gains are holding. In annual surveys, at least 70 percent of respondents indicate that the neighborhood's atmosphere has improved dramatically, and over 70 percent indicate that they feel very safe in University City. And Penn's Division of Public Safety earned recognition from all corners—including the prestigious Clery Award from Security on Campus, a national nonprofit organization.

But this was just the beginning, and along with making University City cleaner and safer, Penn also sought to expand the availability of affordable housing—both for rental and home ownership. Unless a neighborhood's declining and deteriorating housing market can be stabilized, a community cannot thrive. We believed that Penn had the resources, energy, and creative talent to help turn the housing market around. We began by acquiring twenty abandoned properties in strategic spots, rehabbing them, and then selling them to the public at a loss to the university. Penn wasn't looking to make a profit on these homes. We were looking to make West Philadelphia a more attractive place to live and work—and demonstrating with tangible actions that we believed in the residential viability of the neighborhood.

Here, too, we used a number of approaches to achieve a mix of housing options and prices. And we generated strong outcomes: Properties in University City appreciated 154 percent in value between 1994 and 2004, substantially outpacing Philadelphia and the rest of the country. Average sale prices of single-family houses rose from $78,500 in 1995 to $175,000 in 2003. To stem gentrification, Penn and its partners improved more than 200 units of low-income, rental housing—transforming them into attractive, well managed, and, most importantly, fully occupied neighborhood assets.

Private developers built and renovated apartments and condominiums as well—often on university properties with 40- to 90-year ground leases with reversionary clauses back to the university. We learned, here, that universities can also use their own policies to stimulate the housing development process. By initiating a welcoming, academically energizing, residential college house program, Penn was able to attract more undergraduates back to campus housing and away from West Philadelphia's rundown, student group houses, which could now be renovated.

But to make the neighborhood more vibrant still, we needed to provide retail and cultural amenities and to engineer radical improvements in the public schools. We resolved to undertake two large-scale, mixed-use retail development projects in hopes that they would anchor other shops, restaurants, theatres, and private development. And then we resolved to plan and build a public school.

Let me talk first about our effort to revive the retail and commercial economy and accelerate economic growth. Along one largely deserted stretch of Walnut Street, we built a 300,000-square-foot project that included the luxury hotel where we are meeting today, the beautiful new Penn bookstore, public plazas, and a raft of stores and restaurants. At the periphery of the campus at 40th and Walnut, we developed a 75,000-square-foot project that would create stronger ties between town and gown: a new movie theater and new supermarket and scores of small neighborhood-friendly stores and restaurants, artist studios, and meeting places—all to reanimate a dying commercial corridor that had divided Penn from its community.

Penn had inked a deal with Robert Redford and Sundance Cinemas in 1998 to build the movie theater. It would show independent and experimental films and feature an art gallery and café, a video library, community meeting spaces, and perhaps a jazz club. Across the street would be a multi-story parking garage atop an innovative new supermarket, Freshgrocer. Construction was proceeding apace two years later when the parent company, General Cinema, filed for bankruptcy and pulled the plug on the Sundance Theatre project. Just like that, a critical project stalled, and my lunches with Robert Redford came to a sad end.

Predictably, some admonished Penn for biting off more than we could chew, urging us to suspend the search for another partner. True, it was not easy convincing the trustees to spend more money to seal the deal we eventually struck with National Amusements. But at the end of the day, and less than two years after the Sundance project collapsed, the Bridge Cinema de Lux—a sensational state-of-the-art movie theatre complex—opened to rave reviews. The Bridge attracts a half-million patrons a year—and if you were to visit the Freshgrocer tonight at 10:00 p.m. or 2:00 a.m., you would see throngs of students and neighborhood residents shopping, noshing, and schmoozing.

Welcoming large crowds on the streets has made the neighborhood safer and more diverse. It's been a shot in the arm for the local economy. And it's made University City attractive to outside developers. But we learned first hand—and painfully—that this is risky work and needs real stakeholders and believers, as well as deep experts, because things will go wrong.

And this wasn't just about building and attracting amenities. This was also about infusing robust, sustainable economic vitality back into the neighborhood—providing new jobs and new opportunities for local businesses to thrive. We developed a detailed, inclusive approach to contracting, procurement, construction, and employment—and deployed our purchasing power more strategically. We required that our construction projects, both on and off campus, create substantial access for women and minorities to the trades that would do the actual building. We redirected 10 percent of our annual purchasing toward local vendors by 2003, injecting more than $70 million into West Philadelphia's economy. And we invested in small businesses that created opportunities for other members of a community that had been left behind by the global economic transformations of the 1980s.

We created many mentoring programs—one of which helped several small businesses acquire e-commerce capability, not just enabling them to serve us more effectively, but making them more viable and competitive in the open market. Of the $550 million that Penn spent on construction programs over a seven-year period, $134 million, nearly a quarter, was committed to minority- and women-owned businesses, mostly in the neighborhood. Penn now directly employs more than 3,000 West Philadelphia residents. In sum, all these interventions have proven remarkably effective in revitalizing University City.

But while all of this restored safety, life, and economic capacity into the neighborhood, it still wasn't enough. If we wanted to make the neighborhood a more viable place for families to live, we had to improve public education. Penn students and faculty had served this community over a number of years. They were committed in their efforts and made a measurable and meaningful impact in the lives of many Philadelphia children. But to create bold, transformational change—to give families in the neighborhood greater faith in our efforts and hope for the future—we needed to think bigger.

So we reached out to the public, the Philadelphia Federation of Teachers, the city, and the school district with an idea: that we build, together, a neighborhood public school. Nothing like this had ever been tried before, at least in Philadelphia. It took a year of thinking, persuasion, and compromise among myriad stakeholders to reach an agreement that we should move forward. It took another year of painstaking, thoughtful collaboration with educators and community representatives to design and plan the school. Then it took still another year to address the fears and legitimate concerns of residents, some of whom were suspicious of our motives, and others of whom didn't want to be left out in the cold.

Ultimately, it led to the creation of the Penn Alexander School in 2001—a pre-K-through-8 neighborhood public school near Penn's campus. You can only attend the school if you live in the neighborhood. The results were just as we hoped. The 700 faces in the student body look like the faces in the community—60 percent African American, 20 percent Caucasian, 18 percent Asian, 6 percent Latino, and 25 percent international. Class size is substantially lower than the citywide average. After its first two years, 80 percent of primary-grade students demonstrated proficiency in reading. Children are winning citywide awards in math and science. But we did not want to create one school of "haves" and leave the rest of the system for "have nots," so Penn has become more deeply involved in all the public schools in West Philadelphia as well—emphasizing technology, teacher education, and curriculum development.

As many of you have found in your communities, there is no doubt that Penn has been transformed by our engagement in our community. We overcame decades of hostile and dysfunctional relations with our neighbors. We widened the circle of opportunity so everybody would benefit. And, lest we forget, the West Philadelphia Initiatives played a crucial role in revitalizing Penn—its rankings, faculty awards, student applications, selectivity, growth in endowment—just as Penn played a crucial role in revitalizing West Philadelphia.

We had to encourage key faculty members to understand and support deployment of fungible resources on non-academic expenditures. We had to embrace local officials as partners. It was challenging work, but by reorienting the way we worked as an institution, with whom we worked, and what we were willing to commit, we found a way to help make the neighborhood and the university prosper together. Sure, many voices that used to rail against Penn are still screaming. But now that they have a seat at the table, they do not shout quite as much or quite as loud.

What have we and other engaged anchor institutions learned? While each of us had different experiences, I would venture that each of us would argue that the necessity of replacing inaction with action, isolation with partnership, is universally applicable. Skeptical bystanders can become engaged stakeholders.

From our experience in West Philadelphia, I would propose six valuable lessons about strategies and practices that can help anchor institutions and transform urban neighborhoods.

- First, any successful urban strategy must be just that: strategic. It must be bold, yet based on a realistic and full assessment of social, economic, and political forces at work—and it must have a clear roadmap toward implementation.

- Second, it must be holistic. This is the only way to capitalize on resources effectively, leverage the impact of individual interventions, and promote greater sustainability. Economic development, high quality public schools, diverse housing choices and safe neighborhoods are all essential elements of a diverse, healthy community. And the only way to heal a social ill is to mount an integrated attack on the conditions at its root.

- Third, collaboration and transparency are critical. You cannot do this work in secret. We learned in West Philadelphia that there is never a unanimously shared perspective and only rarely a shared definition of community. Individual, family, and institutional needs can vary widely just from one street to the next. Effective community development, then, requires engagement with many different elements and interests—citizens and neighborhoods, schools and churches, sometimes block by block and group by group. Since each city block has its own perspective, each block also ought to have a voice in the needs assessment. But not everyone has an equal say in making the decisions. So leadership at the top really matters.

- Fourth, be careful about raising expectations. You must be willing to say what you can and cannot do, identify and act on a few highly visible, targeted initiatives, define measurable goals, and make mid-course corrections when necessary.

- Fifth, your campus plan and on-campus building need to be integrated with your community development goals. You cannot plan your campus over here, plan your community development over there, and hope to have an impact if you do not link the two.

- Sixth, while time is of the essence, patience is essential. Community revitalization and civic leadership is a journey, not a destination. We all want it to happen in an instant, to show Polaroids of the before and after. But the truth is that change is tedious and phased. It comes in fits and starts, and the first step is just making sure you're headed in the right direction. Things don't always work out as planned. And no agenda for change—however well conceived or well received—wins unanimous support. When alliances are formed with relevant stakeholders, however, more and more allies can be recruited over term.

What did we at Penn learn? We learned that a university can—and should—play a lead role in urban transformation by changing its perspective and altering its patterns of interaction. This is not something you can do to the neighborhood, or even for the neighborhood. You must do this with the neighborhood. Revitalization must be undertaken in concert with the community: its residents and activists, its community associations and city officials, its university administrators, students, and faculty.

I believe fervently that this ties in with our most fundamental mission as educators. It is especially incumbent upon universities to engage in their communities, because it is the best way to prepare students to engage actively in the world. It is not enough to produce brilliant doctors, lawyers, writers, artists, scientists, and scholars. We must produce good citizens—we must teach people how to think and to act, to do good and to do well, and to commit to the heavy lifting of building community. In this way, Penn's engagement with its neighbors has had as profound a regenerating effect on the university as it has had on the neighborhood. I'm sure you have found the same in your endeavors.

Faculty became energized in their search for new ways to bring knowledge and experience to bear on local problems and beyond. Our mathematics chair at the time, Dennis DeTurk, told me that if anyone had told him ten years earlier that he would be writing a National Science Foundation proposal for funding to test the new math curriculum he was to implement in our local K-12 schools, he would surely have thought them crazy. Throughout the university, in all its departments and schools, many faculty members became substantively, deeply engaged. This was no longer scholarship about the community—Philadelphia was not a convenient laboratory on our doorstep—this was scholarship with the community, directly engaging its needs and its potential.

These efforts didn't just challenge and capture the scholarly imagination of the faculty; they became magnets for students who were excited by the ideas and passion this commitment represented. We educated through action, building on the powerful notion that talented students would contribute more to society when they left Penn if we offered them an institutional example of active civic engagement while they were here. Because we, as an institution, participated in the conversations of democracy, our students learned first-hand—along with us—the challenges and abiding value of participatory process.

And in the end, by breathing new life into a decaying, dying neighborhood, the very life we saved may have been our own.

In medieval times, universities were conceived apart from, not a part of, the outside world. They confined themselves inside walls and laid the bricks and mortar of a tradition that barricaded learning from acting, barricaded theory from practice, and barricaded gown from town.

It wasn't long ago that many American universities built higher walls still, behaving like they were back in the 14th century. They installed gates. They built skywalks so students never had to set foot on city streets. They may have bought themselves greater safety—or at least the illusion of safety—but through their actions, they hastened the deterioration outside their gates.

In our way at Penn, and in the wide range of endeavors others are undertaking around the county, we are tearing down the inheritance of these walls. And we are building, in their place, new opportunities: opportunities for universities to model civic engagement for their students by breaking down the curricular barriers between analyzing and assessing the world and by actively shaping it; opportunities for universities to do well for themselves by doing good in their communities.

No Country Can Be an Island

Foreign Policy Association Medal Acceptance Remarks

John L. Hennessy
President, Stanford University

Ican't help mentioning, on this beautiful day, as I took a walk through Central Park and down through the Ramble, that New York City and Stanford share one thing in particular. The same architect designed Central Park and the Stanford University campus. Frederick Law Olmsted gave us both wonderful places.

We are privileged in this country to have something that the rest of the world would like to have: the best higher education system in the world. Indeed, if you ever want to feel like a rock star, become a university president. And then go to China, India, South America, or Eastern Europe, and you will realize what a remarkable asset we have in our higher education system.

When you come back home, you have to remember you're no longer abroad. And I like to remind people of this with a little analogy. You see, a university president is like a caretaker at a cemetery. There are lots of people under him, but nobody is listening.

It reminds us all that the great work in universities is done by the faculty and the students. Increasingly, whether that work is in research or teaching, it is implicitly and very much international in perspective. It may be in the work that Secretary William Perry and Secretary George Schultz are doing on trying to make nuclear weapons a thought which we no longer have to worry about. That obviously has an international dimension.

It happens in the work that my colleagues are doing in the Center for Democracy and Development to try to figure out how we move from an authoritarian style of government to a democracy: certainly a problem that we've learned is much harder than we anticipated in Iraq and Afghanistan.

It happens in our education as well, when we bring a young person from around the world to get an education at Stanford. The very first student from Mongolia graduated about eight years ago. When the young woman appeared on our campus, I thought she was 22. It turned out she was 30, and her 15-year-old son was with her: She had a 15-year-old son at the age of 30. She completed a Master's degree in international policy studies and is now back leading the democracy movement in Mongolia. We send students abroad to try to help them understand what it means to be a global citizen. We send them around the world: to Asia, Africa, South America and Europe.

I will close with what I think is the most interesting encounter I've ever had with a student. On the day of my inauguration, we were having a reception in the main quadrangle. Up walked a young man dressed in a Maasai warrior outfit. He handed me a leadership staff. It had been made by the elder of his village, and he was now giving it to me, as he said, because "You are now the elder of my new village."

This young man continued his work at Stanford in 2000. The next fall he was headed back to Kenya for a short visit home before the school year began. He decided to stop in New York City to visit another Kenyan student he happened to know. He was with her on 9/11. Obviously, his trip was interrupted. After about two weeks, he managed to go home. He went back to his village and told people of the great tragedy that had happened in New York City. The villagers took up a collection of the most valuable asset the Maasai have, their cows, and donated them to the City of New York. You may have remembered that headline in *The New York Times*: "Fourteen Cows for the City of New York."

They took a simple view: This country was giving their young men a great education, and they had to give back in this moment of tragedy. The story reached its conclusion recently when he graduated. We brought the elder from his village over. The elder sat down with me, and with the help of Kamelli, our student, he said, "I want you to know that those cows are still there, and they're all American cows, and so are the calves." This encounter is a reminder that in this century, no country can be an island. The more we interact and mix with people around the world, the better we will make the world.

I have had the tremendous privilege as president of Stanford to travel around the world, representing Stanford and higher education. I have loved doing that. I have also had the great privilege of having a wonderful person supporting me and helping me as a co-ambassador, my wife of more than 35 years, Andrea. And I would like to say thank you to the Foreign Policy Association for this award.

ADAPTING TO A CHANGING WORLD: COLUMBIA'S APPROACH TO INTERNATIONALIZATION

FOREIGN POLICY ASSOCIATION MEDAL ACCEPTANCE REMARKS

Lee Bollinger
President, Columbia University

I am honored to receive the Foreign Policy Association Medal. I want to thank Peter Scaturro and, of course, Noel Lateef. I will talk a bit now about a global university. My basic thesis is somewhat complicated, but I want to tell you in some depth about how we at Columbia University are thinking about a global university. Columbia is a magnificent institution, as you all know, and incredibly international. We have a distinguished faculty, including Gary Sick, a member of our political science faculty at the School of International and Public Affairs and a member of the Foreign Policy Association; John Coatsworth, the provost and formerly dean of SIPA;

and Merit Janow, currently the dean of SIPA and an eminent scholar of international trade and policy. Gary, John, and Merit, who are here this evening, are among our faculty members who have specialized in areas of international issues.

Point one: Every university has to have some sort of alignment with the outside world. We can't be too close, because then we would just follow issues of the moment. Our job, after all, is to reflect on things, to think about them for a long period of time, do research, write, and be objective and scholarly. Reason and truth: Those are our values. But we have to have some alignment: We can't be so far from the outside world that we are not speaking to people and performing our role of helping people understand the world. Obviously the degrees of alignment vary. If you are in mathematics, that's a very pure field and removed for the most part. But if you are in political science or law or international affairs or economics, your role is to try to have some sort of alignment with the outside world.

Point two: What happened in America and American universities in the 1950s and 1960s, with Columbia leading the way, was a drive to understand the world. In the post–World War II era, regional institutes were set up for studies of parts of the world, and we implemented requirements for languages. A major national mission was positive intervention by the federal government to help fund science. I saw this drive in the law school world: I went to law school in the late 1960s and became a law professor in 1973. During the 1960s, law schools fundamentally changed the subject matter that they taught. If you took constitutional law in 1960, it was one course. By the time I became an expert on the First Amendment, there were fifteen people on a faculty of fifty who were teaching some branch of American constitutional law. The reason was very simple: Every single issue in the country was refracted through the American Constitution, and we needed to break it up, study it, and develop expertise.

My third point is that the world has changed during the last decade in ways that are just as significant as the changes that happened in World War II and in the post–World War II era. And we all know the causes: the growth of commerce and the global market economy, as well as the incredible communications revolution. Every time a major new communications technology is invented, the world changes. There are now 2.7 billion people who are connected to the Internet, and that number is growing massively. It's extraordinary when you couple that with global commerce and then, of course, factor in the intermixing of people. Now a billion people every year are engaging in international travel. These are major changes. But the main drivers of world change are the new issues. We can no longer leave climate change simply to one nation to solve, and the same is true of global economic governance and other issues you can name.

I read major scholars all the time who say, even in a field as broad as international law, that the game has changed. "We can no longer approach international law," one major international lawyer has written, "on the basis of nation-states, because now there is global activity that transcends nations, and we have to rethink the Treaty-of-Westphalia kind of approach that we've had for the past several hundred years."

That kind of rethinking has to take place in field after field. I see it in my own area of specialty, freedom of speech. I can be an expert in American free speech and be very happy in my field, but now if I say something in the United States, it can go global: I can be sued in any place and can be subject to criminal sanctions abroad. So I need to know what other people are thinking in other parts of the world. We have to create international norms concerning freedom of speech across the world. We created such norms here in the last century; now we have to do it on a global basis. It is a very big deal.

What do you do if you're a university? There are three theories, I think, for what universities are doing to adapt. Number one is just to continue what we've been doing but to do more of it, and that includes developing relationships with other universities, memorandums of understanding (MOUs) with other institutions, exchange of students, exchange of faculty. Maybe you try to fund some projects abroad, but basically you just try to amp up the things that you're doing: more international students and more study abroad. I don't think that is adequate. If we are rethinking discipline after discipline and field after field, expanding our scope, that's not going to do it. Provost John Coatsworth and I, in the provost's and president's offices, can go through files and not even know how many MOUs we have with other universities. They never add up to much: A few student exchanges and faculty exchanges is not going to do it.

The second approach is to set up branch campuses, and that has happened in Qatar with Education City. It is happening in Abu Dhabi with New York University, and it is happening in Singapore with Yale. This is an approach that many universities are following. It's a very interesting approach, and I want to give it a lot of credit as an effort to try to expand the reach of the American university.

But we are not doing that, and there are several reasons why we are not doing it. One reason is that it is actually very expensive to run a university: We are experts at losing money, at not making money. It takes a lot of effort to set up a foreign campus, and when you do it, you are likely to go to places that have a lot of money to give you, like Abu Dhabi, Dubai, Qatar, Singapore, and the like. And I think that at the end of the day, that is not enough for globalization. Another reason is that branch campuses are built on the idea that we will bring our expertise to the world. That is a very good idea, and we have some expertise to share, but the fundamental point here is that the world has changed. We don't know enough about it. We are ignorant, and we need to correct this situation. We are not going to correct it with branch campuses. With branch campuses, typically, the faculty and the student body are somewhat separate from the surroundings, despite all the efforts to overcome the separation.

What we have done is to create eight Global Centers. That's how we've started out. They are in Paris, Istanbul, Amman, Nairobi, Mumbai, Beijing, Santiago, and Rio de Janeiro. They function as a network—not as a single place to go, but as a network that tries to help our faculty and our students to work around the world on real problems.

One of the things that you realize when you have a change in the world is that you have to rebuild the experience base of knowledge for the people that you are educating and for your own faculty. So much of what we know is actually based on having some kind of life experience from which we can then build theories and greater knowledge and expertise. We need to get people out into the world so that they can understand it better, and the Global Centers help in that. We also need an elevation in the general knowledge that people have. Nobody would ever think of hiring a faculty member who doesn't have a basic understanding of how the American political system works. How many people really have a basic understanding of how the Chinese political systems works, or the Indian political system works, or the Turkish political system works? This kind of understanding is something that has to happen more broadly. We have great experts such as Gary Sick and John Coatsworth and Merit Janow and so on, but we need more people who are just better educated about the world, and the Global Centers will help in that.

We have two dozen projects in which we help faculty devise interdisciplinary efforts and work on this or that with local partners, utilizing the Global Centers, and we send students abroad to work in the Global Centers. Study abroad is not adequate, because you take junior students, and when you ask where they are going to go for a semester, nine times out of ten, they will say Paris or London. They are risk-averse. We really need to get them to all parts of the world.

That's the approach, and that's basically the reasoning. What we're hoping to do over time is to grow this, with other universities as well. We are not selfish about this. What I'm saying about Columbia, I believe, is true about other universities. The School of International and Public Affairs is our lead international school and has the ability to bring together non-traditional kinds of faculty, which I think is critically important in this kind of world. We want to bring all of this together with the Global Policy Institute, the Earth Institute, and various projects we have, putting it all in a Global Center building in Manhattanville. That is one of our ambitions.

The last ambition that I will describe is this: We are not really very organized as universities. We have a wonderfully disorganized system. Faculty members do what they want, they hire two research assistants, and they write a book. And that is fantastic. That has been great for many decades, but we have greater problems that need to be addressed by more organized faculty and policy people working on them. The Surin Project for physics is what I think should happen for lots of other issues that we face politically, economically, and socially. The Surin Project is massive numbers of physicists working through incredible machinery to understand things that they could not understand otherwise. They have to be organized to do it. For climate change, global economic governance, movements of people, global freedom of expression and speech—for these issues we need these kinds of solutions and, hopefully, Columbia can be the home for that broader effort. A lot depends on this approach, because I think that universities—not nongovernmental organizations, not the government, not private enterprises, but universities—are the one institution that we have to depend on. All those others have a role to play, but the role of universities is to address significant issues in the unique way that we do.

Acknowledgments

This undertaking would not have been possible without the encouragement and support of many. I owe a great debt of gratitude to the Foreign Policy Association family, including Louis Bacon, Kevin F. Barnard, Nani Beccalli-Falco, Norton Belknap, Walter A. Bell, John H. Biggs, Judith L. Biggs, Roger A. Blissett, Julia Chang Bloch, Douglas L. Braunstein, Gary W. Brown, Hilary Cecil-Jordan, Terrence J. Checki, Michael H. Coles, David A. Coulter, Edward F. Cox, Alan A. D'Ambrosio, Gonzalo de Las Heras, David B.H. Denoon, Brendan P. Dougher, John Duncan Edwards, Jonathan Feigelson, Henry A. Fernandez, Joseph R. Ficalora, Peter A. Flaherty, Maurice R. Greenberg, Patrick W. Gross, Mary R. "Nina" Henderson, John D. Hofmeister, J. Michael Hopkins, Elbrun Kimmelman, Peter F. Krogh, Michael Kumin, Richard S. Lannamann, A. Alex Lari, Nadia Malik, Donna Dillon Manning, Thomas B. Michaud, Robert C. Miller, Lester S. Morse, Jr., Richard A. Navarre, Jeanne C. Olivier, Douglas L. Paul, Reed Phillips III, Ponchitta A. Pierce, Irene D. Pritzker, W. Michael Reisman, William R. Rhodes, Hugh R. Roome III, Theodore Roosevelt IV, Edward B. Rust, Jr., Sana Sabbagh, Michael Sabia, Francis A. Sevilla-Sacasa, Dame Jillian Sackler, Peter K. Scaturro, Boon Sim, Paul H. Simpson, Wolfgang A. Schmidt, Daisy Soros, Keith Stock, Daniel F. Sullivan, Marco Tronchetti Provera and Enzo Viscusi.

I am grateful to the contributors to this book. I would single out John Sexton for fitting us into his daunting schedule and delivering a riveting keynote address at the Globalization and Higher Education Conference in Istanbul in the fall of 2014. I am likewise beholden to Sunder Ramaswamy for traveling from Monterey, California to deliver his cutting-edge keynote address in Istanbul. Sunder is a dynamic university leader; I have had the privilege of seeing him perform up close while serving on his advisory board. Nina Henderson, a trustee of Drexel University and a director of the Foreign Policy Association, Jerry M. Hultin, former president of the Polytechnic Institute of New York University, and Colonel Cindy R. Jebb, deputy head of the Social Sciences Department at the United States Military Academy at West Point, made seminal contributions while participating on the Conference panel on globalization and higher education. I would like to thank our joint-venture partner, Gülay Barbarosoğlu, rector of Boğaziçi University in Istanbul, for hosting the Conference. Originally known as

Robert College, Boğaziçi is the oldest American-founded institution of higher learning outside the United States. The Conference contributed to celebrations marking the 150th anniversary of the University's founding. Special thanks to Asu Kirdar for her meticulous preparatory work for the Conference.

I am grateful to Richard Levin for the insightful remarks he delivered before the Foreign Policy Association's membership while president of Yale University. I am likewise grateful to Lee C. Bollinger, John J. DeGioia, John L. Hennessy, and Ruth J. Simmons for gracing the Foreign Policy Association's forum and sharing their views on how their institutions are adapting to the new global realities.

Many of the narratives brought together here capture a transformative moment when leaders of U.S. higher education fully embraced the international dimension of their institutions' missions. I am indebted to several remarkable scholars who were prescient in their appraisal of the phenomena of globalization.

I think of the late John W. Ryan, chancellor of the State University of New York (SUNY) and a Foreign Policy Association director. Early in his tenure as chancellor, Jack convened presidents from dozens of SUNY campuses for a presentation I was privileged to make in Albany on the Foreign Policy Association's Great Decisions outreach program.

I think of long-time Foreign Policy Association director Carol Baumann whose annual lecture on globalization at the University of Wisconsin I was honored to deliver.

I think of W. Michael Reisman whom I have long admired for his erudition and for his extraordinary academic and public service contributions. Michael has added enormous luster to many global initiatives of the Foreign Policy Association.

I think of Peter F. Krogh who, notwithstanding his onerous responsibilities as dean of the School of Foreign Service at Georgetown University, made time to moderate the Foreign Policy Association's Great Decisions Television Series from 1981 to 2005. Peter has my sincere gratitude.

I think of David B.H. Denoon, who chairs the Great Decisions Editorial Advisory Board. The Board includes Barbara Crossette, Michael Doyle, Christine E. Lucas, Ponchitta A. Pierce, Lawrence G. Potter, Karen M. Rohan and Thomas G. Weiss. They render an invaluable public service for which I am most grateful.

I think of the keen awareness of H. Fenwick Huss, dean of the Zicklin School of Business at Baruch College, of the importance of preparing his students for leadership positions in a global economy and the outstanding Honors Program overseen by Gloria P. Thomas that includes the Great Decisions Seminar I have been privileged to conduct.

And I think of the pioneering work of David A. Hamburg on conflict prevention—so critical to peace and stability in the Age of Globalization. David has identified the root causes of conflict and, with his wife Betty, addressed these challenges frontally in their classic work, *Learning to Live Together: Preventing Hatred and Violence in Child and Adolescent Development*, as well as in his remarkable books, *Preventing Genocide: Practical Steps Toward Early Detection and Effective Action* and (with Eric Hamburg) *Give Peace a Chance: Preventing Mass Violence.*

I wish to acknowledge the extraordinary service rendered by directors of the Foreign Policy Association who are no longer with us. They include Mary L. Belknap, Leonard H. Marks, John Temple Swing, Spiros Voutsinas and John C. Whitehead. They are missed and their vision will never cease to inspire me.

I am grateful to our World Affairs Councils leadership across the country, including Dixie Anderson, Carol Engebretson Byrne, Bill Clifford, James N. Falk, Schuyler Foerster, Mimi Gregory, Anna Lambertson, A. Alex Lari, Roman Popadiuk, Barbara A. Propes, Jane M. Wales and Maria Wulff.

Foreign Policy Association Fellows have played a key role in the life of the Association, and I would like to express my gratitude to Mahnoush Arsanjani, James Barclay, Philippe Bourgoing, Stephen J. Di Cioccio, Patrick Hyndman, Üner Kirdar, Jean-Claude Lauzon, Jacques P. Merab, Kathleen A. Murray, Susan Perkins, Elizabeth Jacks Scott and Jill G. Spalding. I am beholden to Karen Hsu for being such a supportive and caring friend.

This undertaking benefited from the careful preparation of the logistics for many presentations included herein for which I am grateful to Karen Faulkner, Kristen Glaude and Adam Camiolo. This project benefited enormously from the dedication of Tonya Leigh, Rosemary Scott, Nelda Lateef, Ned Lateef, Karen M. Rohan, Loïc Burton, Peter Scaturro, Jr., and Satyen Gupta. I cannot thank them enough for their perseverance. I am beholden to Emilie Trautmann, an editor's editor. For her tireless efforts at my side, for seventeen years, I am grateful to Marion Foster.

I am grateful to my family members—Nadia, Nelda, Nora, Ned, Sage, Harris, Casey and Lauren—for their unstinting support. For an abiding interest in the world of higher education, I am indebted to my father. I recall from a young age joining him on excursions he led to universities across the United States and around the globe. My father revered higher education—a reverence that can be traced to his childhood in Cambridge, Massachusetts. He frequently invoked his family doctor who, when asked the secret to success in life, was credited with saying: "Read! Read! Read!"

My father read throughout his life and he instilled a passion for reading in his children and in his grandchildren. It is with admiration and gratitude that I dedicate this book to Victor Lateef, a member of the Greatest Generation, who served his country selflessly as soldier and diplomat.

Noel V. Lateef is President and CEO of the Foreign Policy Association, America's oldest nonpartisan, not-for-profit organization devoted to citizen education in international affairs. In New York City, FPA sponsors an active meetings program with world leaders and experts on foreign policy. FPA publications and television programs reach a national audience. Before joining FPA, President Lateef was Chairman of The Bowery Savings Bank, a venerable New York-based financial institution founded in 1834. He received his BA degree *magna cum laude* from Princeton University, where he majored in international relations at the Woodrow Wilson School of Public and International Affairs. He received his JD degree from Yale Law School, where he was elected Executive Editor of the *Yale Journal of International Law* and Editor of the *Yale Law Journal*.